The Anthropology of Language

AN INTRODUCTION TO
LINGUISTIC ANTHROPOLOGY

HARRIET JOSEPH OTTENHEIMER
KANSAS STATE UNIVERSITY

THOMSON
™
WADSWORTH

Australia • Canada • Mexico • Singapore • Spain • United Kingdom • United States

The Anthropology of Language
An Introduction to Linguistic Anthropology
Harriet Joseph Ottenheimer
Kansas State University

Publisher: Eve Howard
Senior Acquisitions Editor: Lin Marshall
Assistant Editor: Nicole Root
Editorial Assistant: Kelly McMahon
Technology Project Manager: Dee Dee
  Zobian
Advertising Project Manager: Linda Yip
Project Manager, Editorial Production:
  Katy German

Art Director: Maria Epes
Print Buyer: Lisa Claudeanos
Permissions Editor: Chelsea Junget
Production Service: G & S Book Services
Text Designer: Diane Beasley
Copy Editor: Julie Nemer
Cover Designer: Laurie Anderson
Printer: Transcontinental Printing/
  Louiseville

For more information about our products,
contact us at:
**Thomson Learning Academic Resource
Center
1-800-423-0563**
For permission to use material from this
text or product, submit a request online at
http://www.thomsonrights.com.
Any additional questions about permissions can be submitted by email to
thomsonrights@thomson.com.

Library of Congress Control Number:
2005920352

ISBN 0-534-59436-0

**Thomson Higher Education
10 Davis Drive
Belmont, CA 94002-3098
USA**

Asia (including India)
Thomson Learning
5 Shenton Way
#01-01 UIC Building
Singapore 068808

Australia/New Zealand
Thomson Learning Australia
102 Dodds Street
Southbank, Victoria 3006
Australia

Canada
Thomson Nelson
1120 Birchmount Road
Toronto, Ontario M1K 5G4
Canada

UK/Europe/Middle East/Africa
Thomson Learning
High Holborn House
50–51 Bedford Row
London WC1R 4LR
United Kingdom

Latin America
Thomson Learning
Seneca, 53
Colonia Polanco
11560 Mexico
D.F. Mexico

Spain (including Portugal)
Thomson Paraninfo
Calle Magallanes, 25
28015 Madrid, Spain

In memory of my father, William Joseph,
who taught me the joys of dictionaries,
encouraged me to explore ideas,
and nurtured my love of languages.
And to my mother, Belle Joseph,
who taught me how to read,
encouraged me to explore the world,
and nurtured my love of anthropology.

BRIEF CONTENTS

DETAILED CONTENTS

Chapter 1

LINGUISTIC ANTHROPOLOGY   1

Chapter 2

LANGUAGE AND CULTURE   14

Chapter 3

THE SOUNDS OF LANGUAGE 33

Chapter 4

WORDS AND SENTENCES 59

Chapter 5

LANGUAGE IN ACTION 89

Chapter 6

NONVERBAL COMMUNICATION — 120

Chapter 7

WRITING AND LITERACY   146

Chapter 8

HOW AND WHEN IS LANGUAGE POSSIBLE? 172

Chapter 9

CHANGE AND CHOICE   205

Chapter 10

DOING LINGUISTIC ANTHROPOLOGY 248

TABLES, FIGURES, AND BOXES

✳ TABLES

✳ FIGURES

✳ BOXES

Cross-Language Miscommunication

Doing Linguistic Anthropology

PREFACE

✳ PURPOSE OF THE BOOK

The Anthropology of Language is a unique package consisting of a text, a workbook/reader, a set of applied projects, and a companion website designed to make the intersection of linguistics and anthropology accessible and interesting to undergraduate students. It is an entry-level introduction to the field of linguistic anthropology that should appeal to students from a wide variety of fields and at a wide variety of levels, from freshmen to seniors. The package is based on my thirty-plus years of experience teaching an introductory course in linguistic anthropology at Kansas State University. The textbook is designed to introduce basic concepts as succinctly as possible. The workbook/reader and the various guided projects challenge students to think critically about basic concepts and guide them to practical ways of applying their new knowledge to everyday situations. Projects and exercises are doable, enjoyable, and sufficiently challenging to keep student interest high. The idea is to get students to actively apply the concepts to their everyday lives as effectively, and as early, as possible. The companion website provides links to additional articles and sites of interest, as well as to study guides and review questions for students. The entire package provides a comprehensive user-friendly introduction to linguistic anthropology for undergraduates.

Organization of the Package

All of the components of the package (text, workbook/reader, guided projects, and companion website) are carefully linked together. The text points to the workbook/reader and vice versa. Both point to the companion website, where students can find additional exercises and readings, links to relevant additional websites, study questions, instructions for the guided projects, and key words to guide them in searching through the readings in the InfoTrac collection of articles.

Organization of the Text

The text serves as the primary jumping-off point for the entire package. The text provides a brief, readable introduction to linguistic anthropology, stressing the kinds of questions that anthropologists ask about language and the kinds of questions that students find interesting with regard to language. It covers all four fields of anthropology: physical anthropology, archaeology, cultural anthropology, and linguistic anthropology and includes the applied dimension of anthropology as well. It teaches basic descriptive/structural and transformational/generative approaches to describing and analyzing languages and shows how to apply these approaches to everyday situations. Each chapter points students to additional exercises and readings, both in the workbook/reader and on the companion website.

Phonology, Morphology, Syntax, and Semantics

The chapters and sections on phonology, morphology, syntax, and semantics have been written so that they may be taken in any order. I know that some instructors prefer to begin with syntax and work "down," whereas others (myself included) prefer to begin with phonology and work "up." Some instructors like to preface all the technical material with semantics; others prefer to conclude with semantics. When I first learned linguistic anthropology, we started in the middle with morphology, then progressed to semantics, then phonology, and finally finished with syntax. Each approach has its advantages and disadvantages, and each is probably more "intuitive" for some students and less so for others. In my own classes, I begin with semantics and then progress to phonology, morphology, and syntax, primarily because the language-creation project works best this way but also because semantics seems to be the most accessible and interesting to students, particularly when it is introduced in the context of language and culture. Instructors should feel free to take the chapters in any order. Each has been written as an independent unit.

Gender, Ethnicity, and Power

Special care has been taken to include issues of gender, ethnicity, and power throughout the text. In addition, several chapters address these issues directly, making them the focus of the discussion. I find that infusing gender, ethnicity, and power into the materials throughout the semester helps students to appreciate the importance of staying aware of these issues. Still, it is also important to focus on each area separately in order to explore it fully, so I have done both. This is true as well for issues of identity, colonialism, language prejudice, and so on. Each of these issues is addressed in its place in the book, but each is infused throughout the book as well. This enables instructors to keep all these issues continually relevant to the study of linguistic anthropology rather than compartmentalizing them into discrete sections and then abandoning them for the rest of the semester.

Sign Language

Special care has been taken to include discussions of sign language in many different locations in the book. In addition, a special section in the chapter on nonverbal communication presents current research into sign language and underlines the importance of understanding sign language as *language,* and not as a secondary phenomenon. Again, the idea is to keep reminding students that sign language is indeed language in its own right and not an adjunct to spoken language.

Language Play, Language Origins, and Language Acquisition/Learning

Grouping these three subjects together helps students to appreciate the complex connections between them. Many reviewers feel that this is a significant strength of the book. This helps students to think more constructively about the various sides of the debate over whether language is innately programmed or learned in speech communities. The key question of exactly how and when language began still cannot be answered with any certainty, but the chapter brings much of the latest research to bear in helping students to think about the possibilities. This is one of the areas in which information from all four subfields of anthropology can contribute significantly, and it is one of the chapters that most engages students with a primary focus on archaeology or physical anthropology.

Variation, Change, and Choice

Most texts treat each of these subjects separately, with the result that students get a disconnected sense of the important questions hidden in these three areas. In fact, the three are very complexly intertwined and at an introductory level it seems more important to help students to see the interconnections than to separate the three into three separate chapters. This is another area that reviewers of this book have supported strongly. Chapter 9, although longer than most of the others, takes care to continually interweave the various themes of language change and language choice, of standards and dialects, and of power, prejudice, and language loyalty so that students come away from the chapter with an enhanced understanding of the value of language and the importance of expressing identity through language. The question of language endangerment is also introduced in this chapter, but it gets special focus in the concluding chapter, where specific examples are provided. The chapter should be spread out over two weeks, if possible. This means that, although it can be scheduled as if it were two chapters, it will be easier to keep the concepts and their connections alive for the students.

Special Features of the Book

"In The Field" Chapter Openers

Each chapter opens with a vignette from the author's field experiences. Some chapter sections also open with these vignettes. Designed to capture the attention of the reader, the vignettes introduce the chapter or section in an engaging way, piquing student curiosity and setting the stage for the material to come. Personal stories help the students to relate to linguistic anthropologists as "real" people. Chapters and sections refer back to the material in the vignettes to show how they can be better understood by using the tools presented in the chapter. The idea is to make it clear to students that real-life experiences can be used to understand and explore linguistic anthropological issues and that it is possible even for novices to tackle such explorations on a beginning level and to learn from such explorations.

"Cross-Language Miscommunication" and "Doing Linguistic Anthropology" Boxes

The boxes provide additional insights into the subject matter covered in each chapter. They are real stories, taken from real people. Some derive from stories told to me by students. Others are from incidents that have happened to me or to colleagues of mine. Some are written by colleagues. In a few cases, students contributed directly to the boxes. There are two kinds of boxes: those that describe real cases of cross-language miscommunication and those that describe situations in which someone has applied linguistic anthropology to solving a real problem. Throughout the text, the idea is to show students that the skills and understandings that they gain from linguistic anthropology can be applied to their own lives. The boxes help to establish the fact that it is indeed possible to recognize and repair a rich point or to "do linguistic anthropology" in their own lives.

Chapter Summaries, Key Terms, and Suggested Readings

Each chapter ends with a concise summary of the key points introduced in the chapter, followed by a list of key terms introduced in the chapter. These summaries and key term lists help students to review the subject matter and to study the important concepts. A complete glossary of key terms and definitions is provided at the end of the book. A list of suggested readings helps to guide students to further research and study should they wish to read more. The readings have been selected primarily for their currency and their readability, although a few classic readings are included. They have also been selected for their ability to engage students in thinking about the issues in question. The suggested readings are grouped by subject category, and a brief description is provided for each one.

Student Activities: Guided Projects

The guided projects are designed to help the students to apply their knowledge to specific situations. Students find these to be engaging and fun, perhaps even more so than reading the text or doing the workbook exercises! Each project has a set of specific assignments that the students complete as they work through the relevant chapters. The exercises and guidelines for these projects are housed in the instructor's resource section of the companion website so that the individual exercises can be assigned as the relevant concepts are introduced. Instructors can choose one or more projects, depending on their resources and time limitations. I generally try to do at least two projects in a semester, but it takes careful coordination. Students comment favorably on how much the projects have helped them to grasp the basic concepts and to understand the applications of linguistic anthropology to everyday life. There are two guided projects: the language-creation project and the conversation-partner project.

> **The language-creation project:** The language-creation project guides students in the process of creating a "real" language in a group setting. There are ten units in this collection (sound charts, allophones, words and affixes, sentence construction, transformations, dialectical differences, greetings/taboos/euphemisms, social differences in languages, gestures and teasing, borrowing, and orthography). It is best to use as many of these as possible during the course of the semester. I use them all. At the end of the semester, I have each group present a short skit using their invented language and I ask them to briefly discuss their language for the rest of the class. A general debriefing rounds out the experience. Students think that this project is "Really cool!" or "Lots of fun," and often comment on how the experience helps them to understand how languages work. One of the key benefits of the experience is the way that it helps students to understand how phonemes and allophones work!
>
> **The conversation-partner project:** The conversation-partner project pairs English-speaking students in the class with international students on their campus. I ask students in my classes whose first language is not English to pair up with an English-speaking student in the class. The point is to have students paired up with someone whose first language is different from their own. There are currently six exercises in the collection (comparative phonology, language and culture, nonverbal communication, cross-cultural communication, language families, and dialects). Each is designed to get students talking with their conversation partners about how their languages are similar and different. I generally select three or four exercises to assign in a given semester. I find that if the language and culture exercise is done early it helps to break the ice between the students and their conversation partners. I generally always include the comparative phonology exercise, which asks students to draw up phonetic charts showing their own and their conversation

partners' consonant inventories, because it helps them to learn a little bit about how phonetic charts really work. This leaves room for one or two other exercises, depending on the time you have available and what you want to stress. Some recent comments from students are "It was hard at first to start talking but once we started it was hard to stop. The entire subject of the CP is really interesting," and "The conversation partner is a great idea! The CP assignments were good because they made you think about and apply knowledge." I often find that students keep in touch with their conversation partners long after the class has ended.

The Workbook/Reader

The workbook/reader provides classic and contemporary exercises and readings. These have been chosen because of the way they illuminate or expand on the basic concepts introduced in the textbook, and they range from beginning to intermediate in skill level. Each reading or set of exercises is introduced by a brief paragraph explaining its relationship to the textbook. The readings provide additional background or insight into the subject introduced in the textbook. For example, where Chapter 9 of the textbook introduces linguistic nationalism and the pressures toward linguistic assimilation in the United States, the workbook/reader provides a reading on English Only laws passed in 1921 in Nebraska. Students from Kansas, Nebraska, and Missouri can be asked to discuss or write about the ways that these kinds of laws have impacted their own families; other students can reflect on whether forcing people to give up their language has led to increased national unity. The exercises are keyed to specific sections of the textbook as well. For example, the exercises for working with phonetic charts go with the discussion of phonetics in Chapter 3 of the textbook and the exercises for reconstructing protolanguages go with the section in Chapter 9 on language change and development. A series of workbook exercises drawn from a single language (KiSwahili) shows students the interconnectedness of different levels of analysis.

The Companion Website

The companion website designed for the package provides guidelines for the projects and exercises, study questions for the readings, and links to other useful and interesting websites. It also features a pointer to Info-Trac, a database of journals where students can find additional articles of interest and relevance along with suggested key words to help them to search the InfoTrac collection. Students may explore the website on their own, or instructors can assign specific readings or project segments from the website as they fit into the general flow of the course.

A separate instructor's resource area on the website (password protected) provides additional advice and suggestions for using the exercises, readings, and guided projects. There are sample syllabi, solutions to workbook exercises, suggestions for good audiovisual materials to use in class, and specific guidelines for implementing the applied projects and for integrating them into the syllabus.

Throughout, the textbook, workbook/reader, and companion website are designed to provide an engaging, enjoyable introduction to linguistic anthropology and to encourage students to explore further on their own and to try their hand at applying what they have learned to their everyday lives.

✳ ACKNOWLEDGMENTS

Many people have contributed to the development of this book, both directly and indirectly. I owe, first of all, a debt to those creative people under whom I studied language, literature, and linguistic anthropology: Ben Bellit, Kenneth Burke, and Stanley Edgar Hyman at Bennington College; and Marshall Durbin, Mridula Adenwala Durbin, and John Fischer at Tulane University. They have all influenced my thinking and my writing in important and indescribable ways. I also owe much to my students at Kansas State University, who put up with my experiments and provided feedback over the years and who suffered through the early drafts of the book. Countless students commented on readability issues, identified sections that needed clarification, contributed anecdotes in class, and even gave me lists of typos or attempted to write chapter summaries (for which I gave them extra credit as just one way of thanking them). Particularly helpful in this process were Lynda Colston, Isaac Dennis, Connie Emig, Janet Jackson, Kyle Klipowicz, Jocelyn Mattoon, Chris Toms, and Marie Wilson. I owe a special debt to my teaching assistants over the years: Leo Walsh, Kathiellen Gilligan, Ilija Hardage, Loubnat Affane, Anne Halvorsen, Lucas Bessire, Janet Jackson, Lynda Colston, and Nick Endicott. Each of these young people has contributed something important to the gradual development of my teaching and writing ideas, whether it be new ideas for exercises for the workbook or obscure but fascinating articles that added to students' understandings of the issues. In addition, my anthropology colleagues at Kansas State University have provided support and encouragement over the years, acknowledging the importance of developing a curriculum in linguistic anthropology and maintaining a strong four-field approach to the teaching of undergraduate anthropology. They include Laura Bathurst, Janet Benson,

Michael Finnegan, Pat O'Brien, Martin Ottenheimer, Harald Prins, Lauren Ritterbush, Robert Taylor, and Michael Wesch.

Although some of the individuals who contributed ideas and materials wish to remain nameless, many others can be publicly thanked, including Loubnat Affane, Nounou Affane, Soifaoui Affane, Jun Akiyama, Barbara Babcock, Laura Bathurst, Ritu Bhatnagar, Renuka Bhatnagar, Laada Bilaniuk, Bill Bright, Jill Brody, Margie Buckner, Martin Cohen, Lelah Dushkin, Begona Echeverria, James Flanagan, P. Kerim Friedman, David Givens, Dinha Gorgis, Ilija Hardage, Wendi Haugh, Jane Hill, Barbara Hoffman, Pamela Innes, Alexandra Jaffe, Alan Joseph, Ron Kephart, Bernard Kripkee, Roger Lass, Linda Light, Mike Maxwell, Rob MacLaury, Bunny McBride, Emily McEwan-Fujita, Leila Monaghan, Matt Moore, Afan Ottenheimer, Davi Ottenheimer, Martin Ottenheimer, Carsten Otto, Isaku Oweda, Bill Palmer, Jeremy Peak, Judy Pine, Harald Prins, Jana Rybková, Jan Šabach, Jaroslav Skupnik, Ann Stirland, Jess Tauber, František Vrhel, and Brian Wygal.

Thanks are also due to individual reviewers who made suggestions for strengthening the text: Laura Bathurst, University of California–Berkeley; Jill Brody, Louisiana State University; Martin Cohen, California State University–Northridge and Los Angeles City College; Barbara Dilly, Creighton University; James Flanagan, University of Southern Mississippi; Laura Greathouse, California State University–Fullerton; Joan Gross, Oregon State University; James Hamill, Miami University; Andy Hofling, Southern Illinois University–Carbondale; Pamela Innes, University of Wyoming; Shepherd Jenks, Albuquerque TVI Community College; Martha Macri, University of California–Davis; Nancy McKee, Washington State University; Judy Pine, Shoreline Community College and University of Washington; Cindi Sturtz Sreetharan, California State University–Sacramento; John Stolle-McAllister, University of Maryland; Isabel Terry, North Carolina State University; and Hervé Varenne, Columbia University. I appreciate the time they took to provide comments and suggestions and, in some cases, additional examples for inclusion in the text.

Anita de Laguna Haviland deserves a special mention for encouraging me to think of writing a textbook, as does Lin Marshall, editor at Thomson Wadsworth Press for cajoling me into taking on such a project. It is in large part thanks to her careful critiques and her principled challenges that the book has taken on the form that it has. I will always cherish the friendship that developed between us in the process. I also want to thank Eve Howard, publisher; Analie Barnett, Kelly McMahon, Nicole Root, and Amanda Santana, assistant editors; Sarah Harkrader, permissions editor; Maria Epes, art director; and Katy German, production manager, and everyone else who worked on this project at Wadsworth. Special kudos to Leah McAleer, production coordinator at G&S Book Services and her able team, including Carolyn Brown, project editor, and Julie Nemer, copyeditor, for their supremely competent attention to detail. It was a pleasure working with them.

The greatest debt of course is to my family—my parents, to whom this book is dedicated; my husband and colleague Martin; my children Afan, Davi, and Loubnat; and my daughter-in-law Ritu—all of whom put up with my whining and complaining on slow writing days. Their patience was enduring and gracious. It is impossible to thank them enough. Special thanks go to my granddaughter, Raia, who cheerfully provided all sorts of examples for me while I was writing the chapter on how children learn language!

ABOUT THE AUTHOR

Harriet Joseph Ottenheimer, professor of anthropology at Kansas State University, received a B.A. from Bennington College and a Ph.D. from Tulane University. Her research interests include music, language, and other creative and performative expressions, particularly in African American and African cultures. In addition to extended periods of field research in New Orleans and in the Comoro Islands, she has traveled and lectured widely throughout many other parts of the world. She has special interests in blues, autobiography, transcription, dictionary construction, fieldwork ethics, and ethnicity. Among her publications are *Cousin Joe: Blues from New Orleans* (with Pleasant "Cousin Joe" Joseph), a blues singer's autobiography; *The Historical Dictionary of the Comoro Islands* (with Martin Ottenheimer), an encyclopedia; "Music of the Comoro Islands: Domoni" (also with Martin Ottenheimer), in vinyl, cassette, and CD formats; *The Quorum* (with Maurice M. Martinez), a documentary film; and the *Shinzwani-English/English-Shinzwani Dictionary,* a bilingual, bidirectional dictionary data set. She has taught at the University of New Orleans, Charles University in Prague (on a visiting Fulbright appointment), and Kansas State University. At Kansas State University, she was the founding director of the interdisciplinary American Ethnic Studies Program, teaching introductory and advanced courses in that program as well as in cultural and linguistic anthropology. She has received the Kansas State University President's Award for Distinguished Service to Minority Education and the Charles Irby Award for Distinguished Service to the National Association for Ethnic Studies. She has served as president of the National Association for Ethnic Studies and the Central States Anthropological Association. She can get by (sometimes just barely) in five languages—English, Spanish, French, Russian, and Shinzwani—and she is currently attempting to learn to speak and read Czech.

STUDENT PREFACE

Dear Students: User-friendly is a term that I believe was first used to describe computers, but that is exactly what I intend for this book to be, a user-friendly introduction to linguistic anthropology. It is also intended to be brief! It will give you an idea of how language works and how people use it. It will also give you some basic analytical skills and show you some ways to apply those skills to real-life situations. We will cover all four fields of anthropology: physical anthropology, archaeology, cultural anthropology, and linguistic anthropology. So, for example, you will read about the origins and evolution of language, the fossil record and archaeological evidence for language beginnings, dating and tracing language change, and reconstructing ancient languages. You will read about language diversification, issues surrounding dialects and standards, bilingualism and the English Only movement in the United States, and endangered languages and language revitalization programs. You will read about sociolinguistics and the ethnography of communication, nonverbal communication, writing systems, and the role of play in language. You will learn basic descriptive/structural and transformational/generative approaches to describing and analyzing languages, and you will learn how to apply these approaches to everyday situations. A special feature of the book is its stress on contemporary issues and the applied dimensions of linguistic anthropology. At the end of each chapter, you will find pointers to additional exercises and readings, both in the workbook/reader and on the companion website. On the companion website, you will find study questions, links to other sites, information for several applied projects that you can do, and access to InfoTrac, a collection of journal articles that you can search for additional interesting readings.

This textbook is designed to be brief and basic—a simple and straightforward jumping-off point. The workbook/reader will provide you with additional depth, expand on specific themes, and give you practice with the technical aspects of linguistic anthropology. The guided projects will take you even further, providing you with practical applications of the ideas you are reading about. The companion website will point you in still more relevant directions for exploration and practice. Your instructor will be your guide. Follow carefully, and be sure to ask lots of questions.

CHAPTER 1

Linguistic Anthropology

"Table," we had said. "We'll need a table. For writing. For eating."

We figured one table could do for both tasks, much as kitchen tables serve both purposes in the United States.

"Okay," our young translator had said, "the landlord says he will provide a table."

But now here we were, exploring our new apartment, and we couldn't find the table. We searched the two rooms thoroughly and explored the outdoor kitchen and bathroom areas as well, but there was no table. Just a large flat metal tray, leaning up against the wall.

"Table," we said when our translator stopped by to see how we were doing. "You said the landlord would provide a table."

The translator looked around the apartment. "Here it is," he said brightly, picking up the metal tray.

"Ah," we said, "but we meant a table with legs, so we can use it as a writing desk."

"Okay," he said, "I'll explain it to the landlord and we'll see if we can find a desk for you."

The next day our monolingual landlord brought us a wooden table with legs. We smiled and tried to remember how to say "Thank you," and felt like our fieldwork was finally beginning. We also knew that in order to fit into this new culture and do good anthropology we were going to have to learn the language. We were going to need linguistic anthropology.

HJO

W hat is linguistic anthropology, and why do anthropologists need it? Linguistic anthropology draws from a remarkable combination of disciplines. Taking its clue from the even broader discipline of anthropology, of which it is a part, linguistic anthropology reaches out in every direction to make sense of language in every sense of the word. **Linguistic anthropology** goes beyond analyzing the structure and patterning of language (a central focus of linguistics) to examine the contexts and situations in which language is used. It looks at how language might have begun; how it is learned; how it changes; and how it is written down, read, and played with. And it wonders whether speaking different languages causes humans to view the world differently from one another. In this book, we will explore some of these directions and provide a basic understanding of the general field of linguistic anthropology, particularly within the context of anthropology.

✳ ANTHROPOLOGY

Because linguistic anthropology is a part of anthropology, it is important to take a moment to describe anthropology more generally and to show where linguistic anthropology fits in. **Anthropology** can be briefly defined as the study of all people, at all times, and in all places. Broadly conceived and comparative in nature, anthropology seeks to understand differences and to discover similarities in human behavior. It is holistic, it is comparative, and it is fieldwork-based.

Anthropology Is Holistic

Anthropology can be said to be **holistic** because it is concerned with seeing the whole picture, with finding all the parts of the human puzzle and putting them together in a way that makes sense. In the United States, in particular, this quest for holism has resulted in what many of us refer to as the **four-field tradition,** in which anthropology is thought of as incorporating four general branches (commonly called subfields): physical (or biological) anthropology, archaeology, cultural anthropology, and linguistic anthropology. Anthropologists trained in the United States are expected to have a thorough understanding of the basics of all four branches of anthropology, together with an in-depth specialization in one branch. Anthropology has always had an *applied* dimension as well, and in recent years some have argued that applied anthropology should be considered a fifth branch. This is not the place to review the pros and cons of this idea; suffice it to say that all four traditional branches of anthropology have always had—and probably will always continue to have—an applied dimension.

Why do we insist on this breadth of knowledge in anthropology? Why not just focus on the areas that interest us the most? Most anthropology students ask these questions at one time or another. Why know about stone tools, for example, if you are going to be a linguistic or cultural anthropologist? Or why learn the fine points of phonemes (sounds) and morphemes (meanings) if you are going to be an archaeologist or physical anthropologist? The answers reveal a lot about the holistic nature of anthropology and the rich interconnections between its branches: To explore the beginnings of human language you need to understand the biological possibilities, interpret the archaeological record, and assess the complex relationship between the development of language and the development of culture; you need to be able to interpret skeletal remains, tool collections, and settlement patterns just to be able to begin to pinpoint when human language might have been possible. Or you might be able to figure out exactly where specific populations might have lived in archaic times, just by knowing how to reconstruct the language they might have spoken, particularly if that archaic language includes words for certain plants and animals and not for others.

I must admit to having had similar reservations about learning all four branches of anthropology when I was a student. I didn't quite see the point of studying archaeology, for example, when I was interested in linguistic anthropology. But I will never forget the thrill of recognizing a roughly hewn stone tool lying along a riverbank in the Comoro Islands and the subsequent thrill of learning, from an archaeologist with expertise in the area, that it might be an example of a long-sought-for Proto-Polynesian hand ax. Had I been more narrowly trained, focusing only on linguistic anthropology, I am sure I would never have "seen" that stone tool, nor would I have bothered to show it to an archaeologist. Instead, I can feel as though I have contributed in some small way to the archaeology of the Indian Ocean region, to the study of ancient migrations in the region, and perhaps even to anthropology as a whole.

The four-field holistic approach in anthropology implies that for a full and complete understanding of human beings it is necessary to understand biological origins, prehistory, cultural traditions, and language use. Each of these overlaps with the others in significant ways, and the anthropologist who ignores any one of the subfields runs the risk of missing out on significant insights for his or her own area of focus. In other words, anthropology is holistic because it is the only way to really understand human behavior and beliefs at all times and in all places.

Anthropology Is Comparative

The **comparative** nature of anthropology refers to its goal of gathering and comparing information from many cultures, times, and places. The more examples we can draw from and compare to other examples, the more complete a picture we can get of how and why humans behave as they do. Collecting and analyzing information about human beings from many different places in the world makes it possible to gain an understanding of the full range of what it means to be human. It even makes it possible to extend our understanding of this range as we encounter examples from additional locations. We learn from this enterprise that the color of our skin or hair or eyes or the way we make tools or clothing or choose our marriage partners or cook our meals or talk to one another is not the only way to be or the only way to do things. We learn that other possibilities exist and that they work as well (or as badly) for other people as our ways work for us. Anthropologists have a term for this understanding. We call it "cultural relativity."

Cultural relativity is the idea that differences exist among cultural systems, that different cultural systems can make as much sense as our own, and that we can learn to understand these different systems. "Ethnocentrism," another term developed by anthropology, is almost the opposite of cultural relativity. It is sometimes defined as judging others by one's own terms but it is really more subtle than this. **Ethnocentrism** means *not* understanding different systems on their own terms. There are two aspects to this: The first involves using your own system to interpret what others are doing; the second involves insisting that your own system is the only one that makes any sense. An example of the first is traveling to another country where the monetary system is different and wondering how much things cost in "real" money (meaning your own money from back home). An example of the second is deciding that there is no functioning economic system in the country to which you have traveled because you don't recognize what they are using as money at all! It is this second kind of ethnocentrism that anthropologists generally are referring to when they caution you to "avoid ethnocentrism."

The first kind of ethnocentrism is fairly easy to identify and to overcome. Generally all it takes is shifting our frames of reference enough to comprehend how the other system works. **Frames of reference** are the ways we see, and interpret, and understand the world. Think of the frames on eyeglasses; not only do they hold the lenses, but they define what will be in focus and what will not, what we will notice and what we will ignore. Contrary to popular opinion, learning other frames of reference does not require us to abandon our own. The fear of losing one's own frames of reference is what seems to cause the second kind of ethnocentrism and also what makes it more difficult to identify and overcome. If you truly believe that the way in which you view the world is the only true way to view it and that all other points of view are dangerous and might cause you to lose your footing in your own world or cause changes in your own world that you are not prepared to accept, then you will have difficulty—in fact you will probably be afraid of—truly understanding another culture or language.

Perhaps the idea that language and culture are intimately connected to one another helps to fuel these fears. And perhaps the idea, held by many monolingual Americans, that it is only possible to really know one language or culture completely fluently adds fuel to the fire. Although these are real fears, all of the data available to us suggests that language and culture, although related in intriguing ways, are not really the same thing and that it is possible to speak two, three, or even more languages competently without losing one's sense of culture or self. We will address these issues more fully in the chapters to come. For the moment, it is sufficient to note that not only is it possible to learn new languages without losing competence in your own, it is also possible to understand other cultural systems in their own terms without losing confidence in your own. In fact, learning about other languages and cultures can help you to better understand your own language and culture and to also understand how they work and how they influence you. Anthropology, and especially linguistic anthropology, provides the framework and methodology, the tools and the techniques, for doing this. You will learn many of these skills in this book.

Anthropology is also comparative in another sense. In addition to seeking diversity in our understanding, we attempt to compare and analyze differences in order to discover possible underlying similarities. We may find, for example, that there is a wide variety of kinship systems around the world or that there are some dramatically different ways of talking about time and place, but underneath it all we find that all humans classify kinfolk as opposed to nonkin and that all languages have verbs and nouns. It is just as important for us to understand our similarities as our differences if we are going to make sense of what it means to be human.

Anthropology Is Fieldwork-Based

I said earlier that anthropology provides us with the means to understand other cultural systems on their own terms. It is fieldwork that makes this possible. Spending time in another cultural system is not only the best way, it is probably the only way to truly gain an insider's understanding of that system. Although there is some kind of fieldwork in all four branches of anthropology, it is **fieldwork** in cultural and linguistic anthropology that takes you into another living human culture where you are expected to adapt and adjust your frames of reference until you can understand and operate successfully within that cultural or linguistic system. Once you have successfully adjusted your frames of reference, you are better equipped to translate across cultures, to interpret contrasting concepts, and to explain divergent views. And it is here, perhaps more than in any other part of anthropology, that there is significant potential for the application of anthropology in everyday life.

One good example of how different views of the same information can be expressed in different languages and can have an impact on everyday life is the ways in which English and Czech talk about the passage of time. In English, the phrase *half-past ten* expresses the clock time 10:30. In Czech, the same clock time is expressed by a phrase that translates as

---

Cross-Language Misunderstanding 1.1

GLASSES OF SHERRY

One evening, in a bar, my son observed a German couple attempting to order sherry. "Two glasses of sherry, please," said the German gentleman to the bartender. "Dry sherry?" the bartender asked. "No, *two* sherry," replied the German man. "Yes, but do you want *dry* sherry?" repeated the bartender. "No," repeated the German man, some exasperation creeping into his voice, "we want only *two* sherry!" "Perhaps I can help," said my son. "The bartender wants to know if you would like your sherry *troken* ['dry'] or not." "Yes, *troken* would be fine," replied the German man, a bit relieved to find someone who could help translate for him. So the German couple got their sherry and my son got to practice his German.

What had gone wrong? The English word *dry* sounds just like the German word *drei* 'three,' so to the German man it sounded like the bartender was asking him if he wanted three sherries, not two. Sometimes it's something as simple as a word that creates cross-language difficulties. Sometimes it's something more complicated, like the way a word fits into a sentence or the tone of voice or general style of speaking that someone is using. Whenever people from different language communities try to communicate, there is always room for misunderstandings.

HJO

'half of eleven.' We could speculate on the difference of perspective that this seems to imply, but we should also note that if you do not pay close enough attention to the way the time is expressed in spoken form, you could miss your appointment.

Not only is fieldwork essential in cultural and linguistic anthropology, but, to gain a true understanding of people and culture, the fieldwork should be conducted in the language spoken by the people among whom you are going to be living and learning. The fieldwork story from the Comoro Islands (at the beginning of this chapter), which illustrates the different meanings of the word *table,* shows why it is never sufficient to rely on dictionaries or interpreters to communicate effectively. If your goal is to learn a different worldview, to understand different frames of reference, then learning and using the language in the field is essential.

The strong emphasis on fieldwork in American anthropology traces its origins to the teachings of Franz Boas (1858–1942), the first professor of anthropology in the United States. When Boas first came to America from Germany in the late 1800s, many scholars in the United States were working to document and describe Native American languages and cultures. They were analyzing texts, word lists, and other linguistic data looking for clues about how the different native languages could be classified into family groupings. This was an extension of the kind of linguistic work that was already being done in Europe; the kind of work that led to the classification of French, Spanish, Italian, and Portuguese—all of which had "descended" from Latin—into a single language family. It reflected the kind of evolutionary thinking that was dominant at the time. Many scholars of the day assumed that by classifying languages into groups they would also be classifying the people who spoke those languages into related groups, or cultures. Different cultures were thought to represent different levels of complexity from ancient beginnings to modern times, from early groups of hunters and gatherers to contemporary civilizations. It was even thought that cultures representing "earlier" levels were closer to nature and therefore closer to an ideal state that modern humans had drifted (or evolved) away from.

Boas, however, wasn't sure that it was correct to classify cultures in terms of language. He also worried that the kinds of evolutionary theories and romantic writings that supported such classification were likely to lead to racist and nationalist thinking. So when he published his *Handbook of American Indian Languages* in 1911, he wrote in the introduction about how difficult it was to find significant one-to-one correlations between race and culture, between language and culture, and between language and race. These early statements about the separability of language, race, and culture made an important contribution to early anthropology in the United States, taking the strong stance that it did against the growing racist and nationalist sentiments of the time.

Boas did link language and culture in more subtle ways, however. Arguing that language played an important role in culture, he suggested that the study of language was an important part of cultural anthropology. He wrote that, because cultural anthropology (he called it "ethnology") focused on people's "mental life" (or worldview) and human language was "one of the most important manifestations of mental life," then the study of human language belonged "naturally to the field of work of ethnology" (Boas 1911, 63). And he therefore taught his students that learning the language was an important part of learning a culture.

Boas also insisted that his students do extended fieldwork. Although much interesting data had been collected about other cultures by European and American missionaries, travelers, explorers, and in some cases even colonial administrators by the turn of the twentieth century, most of the information was gathered during short visits or collected by individuals who lived somewhat apart from the people they were writing about and who made extensive use of interpreters and translators. As a result, much of the information that had been gathered was limited, faulty, or just plain shallow, interpreted through the lens of the collector's or interpreter's culture, and as such was not reliable enough to use for anthropological analysis. Boas argued that in order to fully understand another people and their cultural system it was necessary to live with them for an extended period of time, on their own terms, and using their language. His position was that you could go into the field, live with other people, and observe their daily activities, but that you could not really gain a sense of how they viewed the world around them unless you could speak with them directly and not through an interpreter.

Once Boas and his students began collecting data through fieldwork in the language of the people they were studying, the quality of understanding of different cultural and linguistic systems improved dramatically. Because Boas was instrumental in founding the study of anthropology in the United States, fieldwork conducted in the language of the people has been considered an essential part of American anthropology and every cultural and linguistic anthropologist trained in the United States is expected to spend at least one full year in the field.

Part of Boas's legacy is linguistic anthropology's continued reliance on fieldwork as a primary source of data. Although it is possible to learn the fundamentals of a language in a classroom or from a tutor or from a book, none of these approaches provides a full picture of the way that language is actually used. You can pick the words you need out of a dictionary and string them together in accordance with the appropriate grammatical rules, but unless you learn to speak among actual speakers of a language you will never be able to know when *bad* really means 'good' or whether *bogus* means 'false' or 'fantastic!' The fact that words can have specific meanings in specific situations and can shift their meanings depending on the situation and on who is saying what to whom and why means that to get a full understanding of a language you must study it in its cultural context. This means fieldwork.

Fieldwork is often discussed, but it is little understood. In some cases, it is highly romanticized; in some cases, it is diminished to meaning nothing more than a brief trip to an unusual (for the traveler) destination. In fact, what it means, especially for linguistic and cultural anthropologists, is living in another place among people who are different from you, on their own terms, learning and speaking their language, and gaining, insofar as possible, a sense of how the world appears through their eyes, how to speak about the world as they might. Because we are guests of the people whose language and culture we wish to learn, anthropologists have adopted a code of ethics that guides behavior, both in the field and when writing about the field and the data collected there. First articulated formally in the 1940s and refined and annotated over the years, the American Anthropological Association's Statement on Ethics can be read at the association's website.

 WEBLINK   To read the AAA statement on ethics, go to http://anthropology.wadsworth.com/ottenheimer_language.

Doing Linguistic Anthropology 1.1

ETHICS IN LINGUISTIC ANTHROPOLOGY

Because our research involves the collection and analysis of cultural property (language), linguistic anthropologists must adhere to a code of ethics. We frequently collect information that is of great interest to the people who speak the language we are studying and may cover some sensitive topics. We also work closely with elders and other respected members of society whose trust and confidences must be retained through ethical conduct.

In order to maintain the trust of the speakers of Muskogee, a language spoken by the Muskogee/Creek and Seminole people of Oklahoma, I have provided copies of our interviews to those people with whom I have worked. Through this means, the consultants get to keep a record of everything we have discussed. In many cases, these tapes have been copied for members of the consultants' families and/or others in the community. Thus, my consultants not only have a means of verifying what they have told me, but also are able to keep the information and knowledge they have available for other community members to know.

Ethics also has stimulated my practice of allowing consultants to read through drafts of written work about their language. Consultants' comments on the material produced from our work often point out things I have missed in my own analysis or alternate readings of what I had analyzed. Their feedback allows for an accurate portrayal of the emic perspective on linguistic issues. This practice also allows consultants to decide whether information they have shared with me should be made public. In some cases, I have been told things that I had not considered to be confidential, only to find out that my consultant did not want their views or knowledge to be shared with a larger audience!

Pamela J. Innes, University of Wyoming

The essential core of the statement is often summed up in the phrase "do no harm," but it is more complex than that. As professionals, anthropologists are expected to be particularly attentive to ways in which their presence, or their writings, might cause dangers to the people who are hosting them, from revealing sensitive political or religious information to introducing damaging changes. Of course, just the presence of an outsider in another culture will introduce some changes, but the idea is to be aware of one's potential impact on one's hosts and to be as respectful as possible of their concerns.

For the successful linguistic anthropologist, data collection can take place on at least two levels: the level of carefully collecting, cataloging, analyzing, and writing about the language; and the level of total immersion in the language, to the point that you can speak it naturally and competently. Only in this way is it possible to compare and contrast worldviews as they are encapsulated within languages and address the larger issues of comparison on a holistic basis.

✳ THEORETICAL LINGUISTICS

If anthropology is holistic, comparative, and fieldwork-based; contemporary **theoretical linguistics,** by contrast, can be described as focused, specific, and intuitive. It is "focused" in that its primary goal is to describe the underlying structure of a language, apart from the social and cultural contexts in which that language is used. It is "specific" in that it seeks language universals in the underlying structures of single languages. And it is "intuitive" in that its primary data-gathering method is introspection, in which the linguist thinks deeply about his or her own language or works with a single native speaker of a language, assessing whether various possible constructions "feel" grammatically correct or not. As a result, theoretical linguists can fall into a trap in which they incorrectly generalize that languages "like English," in which objects follow verbs, as in *to see the cat*, always use prepositions, for example, *to see the cat in the tree* (Pinker 1994, 204). One problem with this, however, is that it is easy for linguistic anthropologists to think of such languages as Shinzwani (a language spoken in the Comoro Islands), where objects follow verbs just like in English, as in *huona mpaha* 'to see the cat,' but where postpositions are used rather than prepositions, for example, *huona mpaha mwirijuu* 'to see the cat tree-**in**.'

Another problem with theoretical linguistics is that because it focuses primarily on language form and structure, rather than on the social contexts in which language is used, it is unable to explain phenomena such as The Great English Vowel Shift (a major shift in the way vowels were pronounced in English, which occurred in the fifteenth century). When students in linguistics classes ask why the vowels changed pronunciation as they did, they are generally told that such changes in language are arbitrary and cannot be accounted for, that they can only be described. Linguistic anthropologists, on the other hand, who have observed similar kinds of changes in contemporary language use, understand and can explain the role that language change plays in defining differences between populations. For example, my own "New Yawk" pronunciations mark an older style of speech that was losing favor while I was growing up. Not only do my New York vowels mark me as a New Yorker, but they mark me as a person of a certain age and class as fewer and fewer New

Yorkers sound like me. Understanding language and language use from a holistic, comparative, and fieldwork-based perspective is what sets linguistic anthropology clearly apart from theoretical linguistics. We will have more to say about these kinds of understandings in the chapters that follow.

SUMMARY

Linguistic anthropology seeks to make sense of language. It is a subfield within the field of anthropology, which itself is a holistic, comparative, and fieldwork-based discipline. In addition to linguistic anthropology, there are three other subfields of anthropology: physical (biological) anthropology, archaeology (historical anthropology), and cultural anthropology. The interconnections among the four subfields make it possible to develop a full and complete understanding of human beings.

Because anthropology is holistic it views the whole picture. Because it is comparative, it has the goal of gathering and comparing information from many cultures, times, and places. As a fieldwork-based discipline, it explores other cultures, requiring the explorers to not only adjust their frames of reference but also to learn the languages of the people among whom they are living.

Through anthropology we can get beyond our sense of ethnocentrism and learn to understand different systems on their own terms. To do this we need to shift our frames of reference so that we can see, interpret, and understand the world in different ways. Through comparing different frames of reference, we can discover underlying similarities between different cultures.

Fieldwork was a firm emphasis of Franz Boas. Boas taught that there was no intrinsic one-to-one connection among language, race, and culture; yet he believed that language and culture might be linked in subtle ways. As a result, he insisted that learning a language was an important part of fully learning a culture. Collecting data in the language of the people you are studying improves the quality of your understanding of their cultural and linguistic system. Learning about other languages and cultures also helps you to better understand our own language and culture.

In contrast to linguistic anthropology, theoretical linguistics can be described as focused, specific, and intuitive. The primary focus is on form and structure, with little or no attention to the social contexts in which language is used, and generalizations about universal patterns in language may be made from limited data. This book takes the position that understanding human language is best approached from the perspective of a holistic, comparative, and fieldwork-based discipline such as linguistic anthropology.

KEY TERMS

anthropology
comparative
cultural relativity
ethnocentrism
fieldwork
four-field tradition
frames of reference
holistic
linguistic anthropology
theoretical linguistics

FURTHER READING

About Linguistic Anthropology

Duranti, Alessandro. 2001. Linguistic anthropology: History, ideas, and issues. In *Linguistic anthropology: A reader,* ed. Alessandro Duranti, 1–38. Oxford: Blackwell. This is a good summary of the development of the field of linguistic anthropology.

About Theoretical Linguistics

Pinker, Steven. 1994. *The language instinct: How the mind creates language.* New York: Harper Collins. This is an introduction to language from the perspective of theoretical linguistics.

About Fieldwork

Bohannan, Laura. 1966. Shakespeare in the bush. *Natural History* 75 (August/September): 28–33. This essay explores the idea of universal themes and cultural relativity.

Lee, Richard. 1969. Eating Christmas in the Kalahari. *Natural History* 78 (December): 14, 16, 18, 21–22, 60–63. This essay explores coming to terms with teasing in a fieldwork situation.

Mitchell, William E. 1988. A goy in the ghetto: Gentile-Jewish communication in fieldwork research. In *Between two worlds: Ethnographic essays on American Jewry,* ed. Jack Kugelmass, 225–39. New York: Cornell University Press. This is an account of doing fieldwork in the United States and learning to negotiate differences in communicative style.

STUDENT ACTIVITIES

Readings

The workbook/reader for this book has readings that can help you to further explore and understand the issues introduced in this chapter.

Exercises

Exercises in the workbook/reader will assist you in understanding the issues introduced in this chapter and in further exploring the intersection between language and other areas of study.

Web Exercises

The companion website for this book has a series of links designed to help you explore anthropological fieldwork in greater depth and to better understand the ethical issues raised by anthropological fieldwork. The companion website also contains study questions to help you to review important concepts.

Guided Projects

There are two guided projects that are designed to work with this book. In one, you will create a new language; in the other, you will learn to work with someone whose first language is different from your own. Both are semester-long projects. Your instructor will be your guide for these projects.

CHAPTER 2

Language and Culture

In the Field, Somewhere over Oklahoma, December, 2001

"Remind me again, who is it that we are going to see first?" asked Loubnat, as we sipped our drinks and ate our peanuts on the airplane. We were halfway to Arizona, where my mother's sister lived and where we were going to spend the night before traveling on to visit my husband's relatives in New Mexico. Loubnat was a Comorian student at Kansas State University, and I had promised her father that I would look after her and help her to adjust to American life. She was, in a way, my daughter.

"My mother," I said, deciding to use Shinzwani kinship terminology, even though we were speaking English. I was curious to see what would happen.

There was a pause as Loubnat absorbed my response. She knew full well that my mother, my biological mother, my "real" mother in English kinship terminology, lived in New York, yet here we were en route to Arizona and New Mexico. What was going on?

Loubnat is a sharp cookie, and she figured me out almost immediately. "Your mother *how?*" she asked, joining the game with a smile.

"My mother's sister," I responded, smiling back.

"OK," she said, "I get it." And we both had a private laugh together.

We had just successfully created, and played, a unique kind of cross-cultural game. It was a game in which we were both using Shinzwani cultural frames of reference, but speaking English. It was only possible because both of us knew both cultures and both languages, and the similarities and differences between them. The game was especially fun because of the way that it highlighted the complex interrelationship between language and culture for each of us.

HJO

HOW LANGUAGE REFLECTS CULTURE

Anthropologists have always been fascinated by the complex interrelationship between language and culture. Different languages appear to encapsulate different worldviews, as anyone who has tried to translate between languages will agree. Some languages have words for things that others do not, and most languages divide up and name the world differently from one another. Franz Boas, widely acknowledged as the founder of American anthropology, must have encountered such differences in immigrating from Germany to the United States. It is probably one reason why he argued that ethnographers should learn and use the language of the people they were working with rather than trying to do their research through interpreters.

Working among Yupik (Inuit) speakers of central Canada, in the 1880s, Boas noted the relatively large number of distinct words for such things as snow, ice, and seals. Words for seals, for example, distinguished between male and female, older and younger, and even specific location (e.g., basking in the sun, floating on ice). In American English, where these distinctions are not part of the everyday culture, there is just one basic word for seals of all sorts and qualifying words and phrases are added to make further distinctions (e.g., bull seal, cow seal, circus seal, seal in the zoo).

Some Inuit Words for 'Seal' and for 'Snow'

natchiq	seal (or hair seal)	aniu	packed snow
kiieaaq	male seal in mating season	mixik	very soft snow
tiggafniq	strong smelling bull seal	natibvik	snowdrift
qaibutlik	ringed seal	mavsa	snowdrift overhang, ready to fall
ugruk	bearded seal	nutabaq	fresh snow, powder snow
		pukak	sugar snow
		sitxiq	hard crusty snow

Source: www.alaskool.org

WEBLINK To locate sources for Inuit words for seal and snow, go to http://anthropology.wadsworth.com/ottenheimer_language.

Boas's study is occasionally misquoted or misunderstood; some writers mistakenly suggest that Inuit have hundreds of words for snow, for example, when in fact there are perhaps only a few dozen different words. Still Boas's study remains a classic example of one way in which language seems to reflect culture.

Cultural Emphasis

The complete vocabulary of a language may indeed be looked upon as a complex inventory of all the ideas, interests, and occupations that take up the attention of the community.
EDWARD SAPIR

The idea that language reflects the culture of its speakers suggests also that areas of linguistic emphasis, such as those in the Inuit example, reflect areas of **cultural emphasis.** In other words, if there are lots of different words for snow in a language, then snow is probably an important aspect of the culture of the speakers of that language; an area of cultural emphasis.

For American anthropologists, the idea that vocabulary reflects cultural emphasis has become an accepted axiom, and anthropologists in the field make a point of learning how different cultures divide up and name the world. Examples of how different cultures name body parts, kin, and colors are standard fare in anthropology textbooks, and such terminological differences are linked to differences in cultural emphasis. For example, the fact that Russian has a single word, *ruka,* for a part of the body that English divides into two words, *hand* and *arm,* suggests that the speakers of Russian and English attach different degrees of importance to naming these body parts (see Figure 2.1). Would it surprise you to learn that Russian also uses a single word for foot and leg?

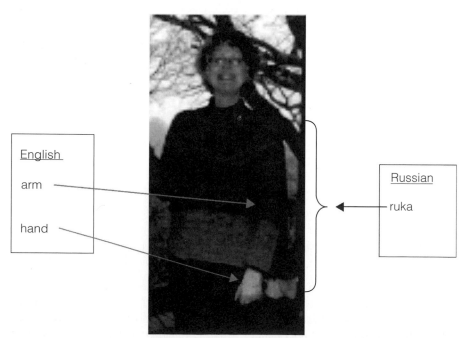

FIGURE 2.1   Comparison of word ranges for English *hand* and *arm* versus Russian *ruka*

Here's another example. In Shinzwani (spoken in the Comoro Islands, in the western Indian Ocean) there is a single word, *mama,* for kin that in English are divided into two categories, *mother* and *aunt.* In this case, the kinship terminology reflects a difference in the way in which people interact with these relatives; speakers of Shinzwani expect to relate to their aunts in the same way that they relate to their mothers and can be disciplined by either relative in pretty much the same way. English speakers, in contrast, interact quite differently with their aunts and mothers, reserving the phrase "she's just like a mother to me" for special aunts who are closer. In contrast, English speakers use a single term, *cousin,* while in many languages male and female cousins are distinguished by different terms: *cousin* and *cousine* in French, for example, or *bratranec* and *sestřenice* in Czech. It should be clear from these examples how different languages can reflect differences in cultural emphasis.

Different Kin Term Systems for 'Mother,' 'Aunt,' and 'Cousin'

Czech	English	French	Shinzwani
matka	mother	mère	mama
teta	aunt	tante	mama
bratranec	cousin	cousin	mshemwananya
sestřenice	cousin	cousine	mshemwananya

The linguistic reflection of cultural emphasis can even be seen in different varieties of a single language. Growing up in New York City, for example, I learned a complex vocabulary for negotiating my way around the city in subways and buses, distinguishing verbally between locals and expresses, IRTs and BMTs, D trains and A trains, and more. After I moved to Kansas, I found that I no longer needed this level of specificity and could just refer to subways or buses in my conversations about transportation. When I learned to sail, however, I found that the word *sailboat* was no longer sufficient for conversations with sailors; I needed a new set of words to distinguish different kinds of sailboats such as *yacht, yawl, ketch, catboat, catamaran, dinghy,* and so on. Different cultural emphases, different vocabularies. There's a good chance that people who ski have more words for kinds of snow than the Inuit do.

From Cultural Emphasis to Ethnosemantics

We learn much of a culture when we learn the system of meanings for which its linguistic forms stand. Much descriptive ethnography is inescapably an exercise in descriptive semantics.   WARD GOODENOUGH

If we agree that different cultural emphases are reflected in different degrees of specificity of vocabulary, then the next step is to note the fact that different vocabularies might reflect something deeper than differences of cultural emphasis. Different degrees of specificity might actually reflect something about the ways that speakers carve up their worlds. If that were so, then perhaps we could use languages to gain insight into how their speakers perceive and categorize the world around them. In the 1950s and 60s anthropologists began exploring these questions in earnest, trying to see how the words that people used for describing specific areas of experience revealed underlying systems of meaning and perception. This new approach to ethnographic research was variously termed **cognitive anthropology, ethnoscience,** or **ethnosemantics.** The idea was to explore, as thoroughly as possible, the way a specific area of cultural emphasis (or **semantic domain**) was divided up and named. The assumption was made that a complete and detailed representation of all of the words for a particular subject (such as fish, or colors, or diseases, or plants) would constitute an accurate picture of the categorization system of the speakers of a language. It was further argued that the **categorization system** encapsulated in the language, or the way a language categorizes items, was an actual **model,** or image, of the mental map that speakers had of that particular part of the world. So a depiction of all of the words for plants, for example, including the way each word related to each other word, could be assumed to be an **ethnoscientific model,** or a **mental map,** or, in other words, an indigenous scientific categorization system of plants for the culture in question. If, for example, both you and I identify and name dandelions, but in your culture dandelions are a kind of lettuce and can be put into salad and in my culture dandelions are a kind of weed and must be dug out of lawns and gardens and thrown away, then we can be said to have two very different ethnoscientific views of dandelions and two very different mental maps of the world of plants (see Figure 2.2).

Ethnosemantics as a Field Method Although there are questions about whether one is really getting at mental maps or whether one is just building elegant models from sets of words, the value of ethnosemantics for learning about cultures, as well as languages, is clear. Ethnosemantics can help you to learn precise, culturally informed meanings for sets of words and is therefore a great way to get off to a rapid start in learning and understanding the nuances of a new language and culture. It is also an excellent way to learn how to communicate effectively in a new lan-

FIGURE 2.2 Two mental maps for dandelions

Doing Linguistic Anthropology 2.1

SPEAKING "COMPUTER"

Although I had begun keeping a dictionary of Shinzwani in the 1960s, I realized, in the 1980s, that the project had become too large to maintain by hand any longer. It was time to transfer the materials onto a computer. I found a set of computer programs called LEXWARE that promised to not only keep track of all of the words but also to sort them in as many ways as I wanted. The programs were installed on my university's mainframe computer and I began learning the "job-control language" I needed to use. Note that this was before PCs and PC programs were widespread; large jobs were done on mainframe computers, and instructions for each job had to be written for the mainframe using punch cards or "dumb terminals." My guide was patient, but I was hopeless. Even my questions made no sense. The language seemed impenetrable. It sounded frustratingly like English but it was different. Familiar words had different meanings and were used in ways that made no sense to me.

Finally, in desperation, I decided to try an ethnosemantic analysis. Instead of asking for definitions of words, I decided to try to build a taxonomy of the entire semantic domain of job-control language. Every time my guide used a new (to me) word, I stopped him and asked what it was a "kind of," and if there were any other words that fit into that same category. Gradually I got a better sense of the overall picture and of how to string appropriate sets of words together into sentences. I was delighted (and so was my guide) when I finally was able to form a question that "made sense," and I almost thought I understood the answer. After several weeks of ethnosemantic fieldwork, I was finally ready to run my data on the mainframe computer!

HJO

guage and culture, helping you to learn how to put words into the right order and place in a sentence and how to construct appropriate sentences. For example, once I know that dandelions are a kind of lettuce in your language, I am less likely to offer to weed the dandelions out of your garden. In addition to feeling as though we are using each other's language correctly, we will also have a sense of understanding one another's categorization systems more completely. This has been called getting an "emic" or insider view of the world, in contrast to an "etic" or outsider view of the world. Chapter 3 explains etics and emics more fully.

To the anthropologists of the 1960s and 70s, it made good sense to use ethnosemantics in their fieldwork. Not only did it help them to learn a language and culture, but it gave them deeper insights into the way that the language seemed to map out the underlying categorization systems in the culture. The new linguistic-based field method that they developed was called the **new ethnography.** An **ethnography** is a study of a culture, and in most cases an anthropologist researching a culture and writing an ethnography about it needs to learn the language spoken by the members of that culture. In most older ethnographies, language learning was seen as necessary to converse with speakers rather than as a key focus of the research. In the new ethnography, language became a key focus of the research. Language was seen, in the new ethnography, as a way to discover how members of a culture viewed and organized the world around them. It was regarded as a key to the underlying structure of the culture itself.

Although a brief description of the new ethnography is provided here, to give a sense of how it works, the workbook/reader accompanying this book gives a more detailed discussion and suggests a project to try. To analyze a language using the methodology of the new ethnography, you need to first identify a specific **semantic domain,** or area of meaning (plants, for example). Next you collect as many words as possible from that semantic domain (all the different plant words that people can think of, for example). Then, you try to build a **taxonomy** for those words, or a chart showing how the words are related to one another (*lettuce* and *weeds* are kinds of *plants*, for example, and the word *plants* includes both *lettuce* and *weeds* in its meaning). Finally, a **componential analysis** (also called a **feature analysis** or a **contrast analysis**) reveals the culturally important features by which speakers of the language distinguish different words in the domain (being edible, for example, is an important feature by which plants might be distinguished from one another). This is an interesting way to learn a language, as well as to gain insight into the culture of its speakers, and anthropologists who have pursued this approach have written some very interesting and insightful ethnographies, especially of American subcultures. It is not as mechanical as it sounds, and often it takes many months of research before you learn all the words you need and all the pieces fall into place. Ethnographies of this sort, analyzing specific semantic domains, have opened up windows into the worlds of long-haul truckers, cocktail waitresses, and alcoholics, resulting in better understandings of these different American ways of life. Although limited in focus, and a bit mechanical in style, the new ethnography can give excellent insight into another culture or subculture and can help in learning another language or culture. Today, it is still a valuable approach to learning another language and the worldview that it reflects.

Linguistic Relativity

Different languages vary in the semantic domains that they identify, in the taxonomies that they identify, in the number and range of levels in each taxonomy, and in the distinctions made between them. Body parts,

Doing Linguistic Anthropology 2.2

LANGUAGE ON THE JOB

A student in the linguistic anthropology class at Kansas State University decided to explore the underlying categorization system at the heavy industrial company for which she worked. She interviewed one of the workers at the company, collecting terms for equipment and tools; then she collated the terms into a taxonomy and analyzed the semantic relationships among the terms. She decided to present her findings to the company, with the suggestion that job safety could be improved if the categorization system that the workers had developed were adopted as part of the training manual for new workers. The management reviewed its training program, incorporated the workers' system into the manual, and found that on-the-job-injuries were indeed reduced as a result. The student got a promotion and a bonus (and an A on her project). (Because this student wishes to remain anonymous, no further detail can be given here about this project.)

HJO

foods, diseases, kinfolk, colors, animals, and many more semantic domains are grouped and named differently in different languages. Further, each system of dividing the world and naming it appears to be arbitrary, in the sense that there does not seem to be any clear connection between the physical world being named and the way in which it is divided up and named. Different systems are just different, and it is more efficient and productive to learn the differences than to try to figure out why the categories named by the language you are learning are not identical to those of the languages you already know. This idea, that languages are different, that they are arbitrary systems, and that knowing one language does not allow you to predict how another language will categorize and name the world, is referred to as **linguistic relativity.**

A classic example of linguistic relativity is the way different languages divide and name the rainbow of colors that appears when light is refracted through a prism. In American English, six colors are commonly identified and named: *red, orange, yellow, green, blue,* and *purple* (in earlier times, the last color was called *violet*). If you learned the old "ROY G. BIV" mnemonic for the names of the colors you might now be asking what happened to *indigo* (which used to be located between *blue* and *violet*). In fact, although the word *indigo* exists in English (much like *aqua* and *bluegreen*), it may never have been a common part of the basic English color-naming system. The use of *indigo* as a color to be named in the spectrum was suggested by Sir Isaac Newton (1642–1727) and modeled after the Western system of musical notation in which a scale contains seven notes. If there are seven notes, he argued, then there should also be seven colors. Although many of us are taught these seven color names in school, the mental maps of English speakers appear to contain only six basic colors. In fact, some English speakers classify colors into just three primary colors (*blue, yellow,* and *red*) and consider the colors called *green, orange,* and *purple* as secondary—made by combining the primary colors!

Linguistic Relativity and Cultural Emphasis   The ways in which different languages divide the world of color, and name colors, are dramatically different. Some languages combine 'blue' and 'green' under a single term (linguists have coined the English word *grue* to describe this larger color range). Others divide up this range into even finer distinctions and more terms. Not surprisingly, in a study of Hanunóo (Philippines) color terms Harold Conklin (1955) indicated a close link between primary color terms and cultural emphasis (341). The Hanunóo primary terms are as follows:

ma-bi:ru	'black, very dark colors (including dark blue)'
ma-lagti?	'white, very pale colors'
ma-latuy	'green, freshness, succulence'
ma-rara?	'red, dryness, desiccation'

These four terms provide a framework, or model, in which it is clear that the important contrastive features are lightness/darkness and freshness/dryness. Note that Hanunóo can refer to colors using more descriptive phrases (e.g., ashy gray), but these four terms are primary. It should come as no surprise that plants and their condition form a cultural focus for the horticultural Hanunóo culture. The different terminological system for colors reflects a different view of the world.

Although the world of color seems to be a natural domain, and most humans appear to see the same spectrum of colors, the fact that the domain is carved up and named differently by different cultures indicates that the domain of color is not experienced exactly alike by all humans and that different cultures do in fact identify different ranges of color as significant within their unique cultural systems and name them accordingly. Different cultures divide and categorize the world around them differently. These different emphases are reflected in language. Learning to speak another language well requires learning these different categorizations and emphases.

Challenging Cultural Relativity: The Search for Universals   The idea of cultural relativity is occasionally challenged, as anthropologists wonder whether there are universal patterns underneath the cultural differences that they study. One such study, which focused on linguistic relativity, and on color-naming systems in particular, was conducted in 1969 by

Brent Berlin and Paul Kay. Berlin and Kay thought that there might be some underlying universal pattern to the way that people experienced and named colors. They wondered if different color-naming systems were really as different as they seemed. To study this question, they first asked speakers of different languages to name the words for primary or basic colors in their own languages and then to identify the focal points (and boundaries) of each of those basic color terms on a standard color chart.

 WEBLINK   To review the Hale color chart and color naming in different languages, go to http://anthropology.wadsworth.com/ottenheimer_language.

Comparing the focal points of color terms across a sample of different languages (the reddest red in each system, the bluest blue, and so on), Berlin and Kay suggested that all languages had a common underlying system for identifying and naming colors. They also suggested that systems with more terms for colors were evolutionarily more "advanced" than those with fewer terms for colors. Here is the sequence by which terms for colors were thought to emerge.

Stage 1. Languages with two color terms (black and white)
Stage 2. Languages with three color terms (black, white, and red)
Stage 3. Languages with four color terms (black, white, red, and green *or* yellow)
Stage 4. Languages with five color terms (black, white, red, green, and yellow)
Stage 5. Languages with six color terms (black, white, red, green, yellow, and blue)
Stage 6. Languages with seven color terms (the above plus brown)
Stage 7. Languages with eight or more color terms (stage 6 colors plus purple, pink, orange, and/or gray)

Berlin and Kay noted that many of the stage 1, 2, and 3 color systems are found in languages spoken by technologically "simple" societies, while stage 7 systems are found only in modern industrialized societies (Berlin and Kay 1969). The study was later revised to make some of the stages more flexible, to acknowledge that some colors appeared in different orders in different stages and to account for languages with a single term for 'blue' and 'green,' using the term *grue* to describe this color range.

A continuing problem with Berlin and Kay's approach to analyzing color-naming systems is the uneven way in which they apply their definition of basic color terms. For example, according to Berlin and Kay, a basic color term should not also be the name of an object of the same color. If this is so, however, then they should not have included the English words, *orange* (an orange is a kind of fruit) and *pink* (a pink is a kind of flower) in the list of basic color terms of English. They also said that basic color terms should not be borrowed words, but this means that the English words *brown, gray, purple,* and *blue* (all borrowed from French) should not be counted in the set of basic color terms for English. If the rules were applied to English in this way, then English would end up with five basic color terms and would be classified as a stage 4 language rather than at the top of the scale, as Berlin and Kay had it.

A greater difficulty with the research on color-naming systems is the fact that there really *is* some physical variation in color perception that the research did not allow for. Cataracts, for example, have an effect on color perception. The more developed the cataract, the yellower things become, so that a person with well-developed cataracts will see blue-green as mostly green, while a person with no cataracts will see blue-green as blue-green. As long as there is no universally accepted standard marking the focal points and boundaries of various colors on a spectrum in terms of some absolute measure (much like there is a system of standards for linear measures, which is kept in a vault and used as a template against which you can measure your own yardstick for accuracy, or agreement with the standard), there is no way to really measure color perception and how it varies among individuals and cultures. As a result, the study, as well as similar searches for linguistic universals, remains controversial and perhaps fundamentally unprovable.

✳ THE INFLUENCE OF LANGUAGE ON CULTURE

The worlds in which different societies live are distinct worlds, not merely the same world with different labels attached.   EDWARD SAPIR

Recall that the relationship between language and culture is complex. It is relatively easy to talk about how different languages carve up and name the world differently (**linguistic relativity**). It is far more difficult to know whether this is because people of different cultures perceive the world differently and talk about it accordingly, or because the languages that people speak actually *cause* them to perceive the world around them differently. This second view, that your language affects, even determines, your ability to perceive and think about things, as well as to talk about them, is referred to as **linguistic determinism.**

Many scholars have wrestled with the concept of linguistic determinism, including philosophers, psychologists, and anthropologists. However, two individuals remain primary in terms of influencing the way anthropologists (and others) think about the subject. These are Edward Sapir (1884–1939) and Benjamin Lee Whorf (1897–1941). Both men worked primarily with Native American languages. Edward Sapir was a student of Franz Boas, and Benjamin Lee Whorf was a student of Edward Sapir.

Recall that Boas was an early proponent of linguistic relativity, arguing that each language had to be studied on its own terms. Sapir took this concept further, suggesting that although words and categories might be initially based on experience, once they had become a part of a linguistic system they would then be more likely to be "imposed on it because of the tyrannical hold that linguistic form has upon our orientation in the world" (Sapir 1931, 578). In other words, our language can determine our experience of the world.

Sapir's thinking and teaching had a profound impact on Benjamin Lee Whorf. Whorf was a fire insurance inspector, working for an insurance agency in Connecticut. His interest in linguistics was sparked by his observations on the job. During investigations, he discovered that workers were scrupulously careful around full gasoline drums, but fairly careless around empty ones. If you throw a lighted match into a drum full of gasoline, however, the gasoline will simply burn. Empty gasoline drums are another matter entirely; they are actually full of gasoline vapors. Throwing a lighted match into an "empty" gasoline drum will cause the vapors in the drum to explode! Whorf interpreted the workers' behavior around gasoline drums as conditioned by the words they used to describe them. In particular, he thought, the word *empty* was signaling that something was not dangerous, that it was in fact innocuous. (The explosion in the air of a TWA airplane in the late 1990s may be attributed to exactly the same linguistic effect; electrical wires passing through "empty" fuel chambers appear to have shorted out, sparking and causing the explosion!)

Whorf began taking Sapir's classes in linguistic anthropology at Yale University in the fall of 1931 and was fascinated by what he found. Studying Native American languages, in particular Hopi, Nootka, and Shawnee, he concentrated on attempting to describe the relationship between language, thought, and perception. Developing what he called his **principle of linguistic relativity,** he suggested that "users of markedly different grammars are pointed by their grammars toward different types of observations and different evaluations of externally similar acts of observation, and hence are not equivalent as observers but must arrive at somewhat different views of the world" (Whorf 1940/1956, 221). In other words, if different languages possessed different grammatical categories, then those categories should *oblige* speakers to think along certain lines, as laid out by the categories, and make it more difficult (perhaps even impossible?) for them to think in ways not provided by those categories.

For example, the Hopi verb system creates verbs of repeated or prolonged action by making a simple addition to single-action verbs:

Hopi Single-Action and Repeated- or Prolonged-Action Verbs

Single-action verb		Repeated/prolonged-action verb	
róya	'it makes a turn'	royáyata	'it is rotating'
tíri	'he gives a start'	tirírita	'he is trembling'
wíwa	'he stumbles'	wiwáwata	'he is hobbling along'

Single-action verb		Repeated/prolonged-action verb	
kʷíla	'he takes a step forward'	kʷilálata	'he walks forward'
rípi	'it flashes'	ripípita	'it is sparkling'
ʔími	'it makes a bang'	ʔimímita	'it is thundering'
ngáro	'his teeth strike something hard'	ngarórota	'he is chewing on something hard'

Data from Trask (1995, 62)

English speakers, Whorf would argue, perceive such actions as *stumbling* and *hobbling along* as two different activities because they use two different and unrelated verbs, while Hopi speakers perceive them as related aspects of a single activity, much as English speakers might sense *he stumbles* and *he stumbled* as related aspects of a single activity. The result is that Hopi and English speakers would need to be doubly careful about how they were describing such motions to one another or they might make mistakes in communicating.

Although never formulated as a hypothesis by either man, the concept of linguistic determinism became variously known as the **Sapir-Whorf Hypothesis,** the **Whorf-Sapir Hypothesis,** or even just the **Whorfian Hypothesis.** There are two basic forms by which the idea has come down to us: "Strong Whorf" and "Weaker Whorf." Anthropologist Michael Agar suggests that **Strong Whorf** might be compared to the idea that language is a prison, providing no escape, while **Weaker Whorf** might be compared to the idea that language is a room, which provides you with specific ways of seeing but you can leave the room, enter other rooms, and return to your original room, shifting perspectives as you go (Agar 1994).

Testing Linguistic Determinism

Of course the Strong Whorf form of linguistic determinism is impossible to test. If your language forces you to think and perceive in only certain ways, then there is no way you can get outside of your linguistic system to test whether it is in fact determining your perceptions. The fact that we can and do translate fairly successfully between different languages and that we coin new words and modify our grammatical patterns over time suggests that the strong form of linguistic determinism cannot be accurate. The Weaker Whorf form of linguistic determinism, however, appears to be more amenable to testing, and there have been several attempts to do so over the years.

One of these attempts that is especially interesting is John Lucy's comparison of Yucatec and English speakers with regard to shape and material. In Yucatec, a single word *che'* can be used to create additional words for objects such as trees, sticks, and planks, all of which are made out of wood but are of different shapes. In contrast, in English, objects made of the same material are generally given unrelated labels. Objects made of wood, for example, in English are labeled *tree, stick, plank, table, chair, shelf, desk,* and so on. (Another example of this tendency in English, noted by Boas, is the way that English labels different shapes of water differently using words such as *lake, river, stream, creek, ocean,* and so on.) Focusing on this difference, Lucy hypothesized that *"English speakers should attend relatively more to the shape of objects."* He also hypothesized that *"Yucatec speakers should attend relatively more to the material composition of objects* in other cognitive activities" (1992a, 89, emphasis in the original). When Yucatec and English speakers were asked to recognize and remember pictures of items, the results showed that they did indeed group objects differently: Yucatec speakers grouped items in terms of common *material,* while English speakers grouped items in terms of common *shape.* As Lucy concluded, "These patterns suggest strongly that the underlying lexical structures . . . in the two languages have an influence on the nonverbal interpretation of objects" (1992a, 144).

Experiencing Linguistic Determinism

What is important to recognize, even more than the idea that you might think or perceive the world differently depending on the language that you speak, is that before you can really use a new language comfortably, without thinking about what you are saying, you need to wrap your mind around the new concepts that the new language is presenting to you. For example, in order to use Shinzwani fluently, and to talk about something being *meza juu* 'at/on the table,' I need to actually comprehend that it doesn't matter whether something is at the table or on the table, I can just go ahead and use the phrase *meza juu* to say 'I am sitting **at the table**' (*nikukentsi **meza juu***) and 'the plate is **on the table**' (*shisahani sha **meza juu***). Note that *meza juu* is the same in each expression. Also note that *meza* means 'table' (it was borrowed from Portuguese) and that *juu* means 'at/on.' This is probably easier when you move in the direction in which things that you usually keep separate are combined. It is probably more difficult when you are moving in the direction in which things that you normally combine need to be separated in the new language. In learning Shinzwani, for example, I needed to learn to distinguish *masinza* 'eating bananas' (i.e., bananas for eating ripe) from *ntrovi* 'cooking bananas' (i.e., bananas for cooking green) and to remember when to use which word, even though most bananas looked the same to me.

Here's another example. While Standard English separates *lend* and *borrow,* Shinzwani uses one word, *-kopa,* for both actions. English speaking learners of Shinzwani need only adjust to speaking about a generalized concept of transfer, regardless of the direction. Shinzwani speakers learning English, however, have the more difficult challenge of separating this general concept into two different actions, based on the direction in which the transfer will be made. If the item is being given to someone, then the owner *lends* it. For example, *You lend* (give) *a book to me* and *I lend* (give) *a book to you.* Conversely, if the item is being taken from the owner, then someone *borrows* it. *I borrow* (take) *a book from you* and *You borrow* (take) *a book from me.*

One more example, which brings us back to the question of time that Whorf explored. When I am speaking English, I say that 9:15 is *a quarter past nine,* 9:30 is *half-past nine,* and 9:45 is *a quarter of (or a quarter to) ten.* When I began learning Czech, I found that 9:15 is a phrase that translates as 'a quarter of ten,' 9:30 is 'half of ten,' and 9:45 is 'three-quarters of ten.' This puzzled me for a while, and I had to double-check every appointment I made. Once I figured out the underlying difference between the two systems, however, I found myself thinking about time differently depending on whether I was using English or Czech. In English, I think about the hour that has just sounded on the clock (a quarter past nine, half-past nine, at least for the first half of the hour) and in Czech I think about the hour that is coming up next (one quarter of the way to ten, half of the way to ten, three-quarters of the way to ten). I'm not sure if this indicates that Czechs are more future oriented than Americans or that Americans are always thinking about the past rather than the future, but it certainly does suggest a difference, and if one is not careful one could confuse times and miss appointments. The interesting thing is that even as a beginner I found myself thinking differently when I used these two different languages.

Different Ways of Talking about Clock Time in Czech and in English

Time	Czech	English
9:15	čtvrt na deset 'a quarter of ten'	a quarter-past nine
9:30	půl desáté 'a half of ten'	half-past nine
9:45	tři čtvrtě na deset 'three-quarters of ten'	a quarter to (of) ten

People who speak only one language think that it is confusing to speak different languages and think in different ways. Research, as well as experience, suggests that this is not so. In fact, some individuals, such as professional interpreters and translators, have developed the art of language-switching to a high art. Of course, it can be confusing if you are stuck in one language and worldview while everyone else is using another one. That would be something like constantly wondering how much something weighs in kilos when everyone else is talking in terms of pounds (or vice versa). Although it might seem obvious, it is really simpler to use the categories of whatever language you are speaking and not worry about how they translate into any of the other languages that you might know. It also saves a lot of energy.

SUMMARY

What does all this mean? Do people who speak different languages really see the world differently or do they just talk about it differently? Is ethnosemantics "God's truth"? Or is it "hocus pocus," as some critics have suggested (Burling 1964)? Certainly ethnosemantics provides an important and useful technique for learning another language and culture through its system of categorizations. Certainly members of different cultures and speakers of different languages divide and talk about the world in terms of what is most important to them. Perhaps their view of the world is also influenced by the languages that they have learned to speak.

Linguistic relativity is a fairly well accepted concept by now. Most people accept the idea that learning another language is not just learning new labels for the same things. Instead, it is all about learning a different set of cultural assumptions and about what things are considered worth labeling in that culture. It means learning something of the world that that language makes sense of. It also is about learning the complex and intriguing systems by which the items labeled are classified and organized and related to one another. Learning another language takes you into the less easily charted territory of learning a new set of grammatical principles: new tenses, new ways to think about time and the physical world, new ways to organize words into sentences, and new idioms and expressions. Finally, learning a new language gives you a unique opportunity to reflect back on and to gain new insight into your own language and world, and to recognize the similarities and differences between the two (or more) languages and cultures that you now have access to.

Linguistic determinism, on the other hand, has been a controversial issue for as long as it has been around. It is controversial because it is still unclear, after years of theorizing and experimenting, whether language really does organize the world for us or whether it just expresses how our culture has taught us to organize the world. It is also challenging because those of us who have lived and worked in more than one language are sure that there is *something* going on, but have difficulty articulating it clearly enough that it can be identified, tested, and proven (or disproven). In fact, it is quite probable that language both organizes the world *and* expresses a culture's organization of the world. This complex interrelationship between language and culture makes the subject of primary importance to anthropologists.

KEY TERMS

categorization system
cognitive anthropology
componential analysis
contrast analysis
cultural emphasis
ethnography
ethnoscience
ethnoscientific model
ethnosemantics
feature analysis
linguistic determinism
linguistic relativity
mental map
new ethnography
principle of linguistic relativity
Sapir-Whorf Hypothesis
semantic domain
Strong Whorf
taxonomy
Weaker Whorf
Whorfian Hypothesis
Whorf-Sapir Hypothesis

FURTHER READING

About Language and Culture

Gentner, Dedre, and Susan Goldin-Meadow, eds. 2003. *Language in mind: Advances in the study of language and thought.* Cambridge, MA: MIT Press. This is a collection of essays on the ways in which language may or may not influence culture.

Lakoff, George, and Mark Johnson. 1980. *Metaphors we live by.* Chicago: University of Chicago Press. This is an intriguing study of another way that language affects culture.

Some Classic Examples of The New Ethnography

Agar, Michael H. 1986. *Independents declared: The dilemmas of independent trucking.* Washington, DC: Smithsonian Institute Press. This ethnography uses ethnographic semantics to explore the world of independent truckers.

Spradley, James P., and Brenda J. Mann. 1975. *The cocktail waitress: Woman's work in a man's world.* New York: McGraw Hill. This ethnography uses ethnographic semantics to explore the world of cocktail waitresses—one of the first of its kind.

About Whorf and Linguistic Relativity

Lucy, John. 1992. *Language, diversity, and cognitive development: A reformulation of the linguistic relativity hypothesis.* Cambridge: Cambridge University Press. This overview presents linguistic relativity from Boas, through Sapir and Whorf, and beyond.

Carroll, J. B. 1956. *Language, thought and reality: Selected writings of Benjamin Lee Whorf.* New York: Wiley; Cambridge, MA: MIT Press. Whorf's style is quite readable for beginners, even though a bit dated.

About Universals in Color Terms

Berlin, Brent, and Paul Kay. 1969. *Basic color terms: Their universality and evolution.* Berkeley: University of California Press. This is the original study on universality in color terms.

 # STUDENT ACTIVITIES

Readings

The workbook/reader for this book has readings that can help you to further explore and understand the issues introduced in this chapter.

Exercises

Exercises in the workbook/reader will assist you in understanding the issues introduced in this chapter and in further exploring the complex relationship between language and culture.

Selected exercises in the workbook/reader will help you to explore the relationship between language and culture in specific languages, to try your hand at ethnosemantic research, and to compare words for colors in various languages.

Web Exercises

The companion website for this book has a series of links designed to help you explore the interrelationship between language and culture in greater depth. The companion website also contains study questions that will help you review important concepts.

Guided Projects

If you are creating a new language, you will need to develop a cultural emphasis for your language. If you are working with a conversation partner, your instructor may ask you to explore similarities and differences in the ways that language categorizes experience in your two languages. Your instructor will be your guide.

CHAPTER 3

The Sounds of Language

"You mustn't to say the r*," said Nounou, patiently.*

He was correcting, yet again, my miserable attempts to produce a sound that seemed—at least to me—to be somewhere between the *t* of *train* and the *ch* of *chain.* Try as I might, I couldn't locate the proper place for my tongue. Nor could I find the exact right mechanism for pushing the air over my tongue to get the right sound.

Nounou was a Lycee (high school) student who was learning English. He was helping us with our Shinzwani for a few hours each week, and we were helping him with his English. We had already taught him that *enough* was pronounced [enuf] and not [cnugu].

Today we were working on sounds that were difficult for each of us. We had shown him how to hear and pronounce the *th* in *thanks* so that he could differentiate English words like *both* and *boat.* Now he was trying to get us to hear and pronounce *tr,* so that we could differentiate Shinzwani words like *ntru* 'hermit crab' and *ntu* 'arrow' or *hutrona* 'to put on makeup' and *hutona* 'to skin an animal.'

It was important to learn this new *tr* sound, otherwise we could easily end up talking about putting makeup on goats. But there was nothing like *tr* in English, and both of us—my anthropologist husband and I—kept inserting an *r* in our attempts to say *tr.*

"You mustn't to say the *r,*" Nounou repeated. And I wondered if I would ever get this right. Just trying hundreds of times was going to be slow and would test the limits of Nounou's (and my) patience.

I decided to get technical and to draw on my linguistic anthropology training.

"Where are you putting your tongue?" I asked.

"Here," he said, sticking his finger into his mouth and pointing upward.

"Can I look?" I asked.

"Sure," he said, setting his tongue in place and opening his mouth wide.

"Aha," I said, "it looks like a retroflex. So *that's* what they sound like!" And setting my tongue in the correct spot for a retroflex, I produced a perfect *tr.*

"Exactly," he said. "That's great."

"*Ntru,*" I said. "*Ntru, ntu, ntru, ntu,*" I alternated. "Can you hear the difference?"

"Yes," he said, "you've got it!"

HJO

✳ SOUNDS

No linguistics course can ever teach you to hear and pronounce every sound used in every language. Nor should it. There are so many different languages and so many different possible sounds and sound combinations that it would take you a very long time to learn them all. And you might miss some that had not been "discovered" yet. My linguistic anthropology professor could not have known that I would encounter retroflex sounds in the field. In fact, he could not have known which sounds *any* of us in the class would encounter, either in the field or in everyday life. So he taught us something more important and more useful; he taught us the basics of sound production—the rules for producing any sound that is humanly possible to produce and use in a language.

Knowing the basics of sound production is a fabulously useful skill. It can help you to speak a language—or just pronounce a few important words—with minimal accent. It can help you to communicate clearly in another language, especially if there are sounds that make a difference in what you communicate, like the difference I describe at the beginning of this chapter. Learning another language—whether for school, business, or tourism—means learning to hear and pronounce language sounds that are different from those you grew up with. It means learning the basics of sound production, which means learning a little phonology.

✳ PHONOLOGY

Phonology is the study of language sounds. The first time you hear another language, whether in the classroom or in everyday life, the fact that it *sounds* different is probably the first thing you notice about it. Some of this difference stems from the fact that every language actually uses a different collection of sounds. And some of it can be attributed to the fact that every language arranges the sounds in different ways.

Phonology deals with these two kinds of differences by splitting the study of language sounds into "phonetics" and "phonemics." **Phonetics** identifies and describes language sounds, and **phonemics** analyzes the way sounds are arranged in languages. Put another way, phonetics pays attention to the tiniest details in the way language sounds are produced and tries to catalog each and every variation in sound that the speakers of a language use. Phonemics pays attention to the ways that those variations are grouped together or separated and, if so, which ones are grouped with which others, and where in a word each sound can occur, and what kind of difference that might make. You might think about it this way: Phonetics helped me to identify (and pronounce) the Comorian *tr* sound, but phonemics made it clear to me that the difference between the sounds of *tr* and *t* was important in that language.

Here's a good example of the difference between phonetics and phonemics in English. If you pay very close attention to the way English speakers pronounce words like *pill* and *spill,* you can hear a tiny difference between the way the *p* sound is produced in those two words. You can hear (or feel, if you place your hand in front of your mouth) an extra puff of air following the *p* in *pill* but no such puff following the *p* in *spill*. A "phonetic description" of English gives detailed information about these differences, so that speakers of other languages have the information they need to produce both kinds of *p* successfully.

English speakers do not generally notice that they are producing two different kinds of *p* unless you point it out to them. They tend to group the two sounds together and treat them as one single sound. They also don't generally notice that the two sounds are used in different, and predictable, locations (the puffy one at the beginnings of words and the other one—the nonpuffy one—following *s* sounds). Because of the way that English speakers group the different variations of *p* into a single sound, they tend to treat that single sound as a unique, or distinctive, sound of their language. They hear it as different from other sounds of their language, and they use it to differentiate words such as *pill, till,* and *kill* from one another. A "phonemic description" of English describes this entire arrangement so that speakers of other languages know where in a word to use each kind of *p* and know that they need to be careful to use *p* rather than *t* or *k* in English words (just like I needed to use *tr* rather than *t* in Shinzwani).

To take this just a bit further, a **phonetic chart,** a chart that shows *all* of the sounds of a language, would show both kinds of *p* for English. Such a chart would use different symbols for the two different sounds so it would be clear which is which. It would use [pʰ] for the puffy version and [p] for the other one. (Note that we are using square brackets here.) The sounds on a phonetic chart are called **phones.**

A **phonemic chart,** a chart that shows just the distinctive sounds of a language, would use just one symbol /p/ for the whole group of *p* sounds. (Note that we are using slanted brackets here.) The sounds on a phonemic chart are called **phonemes.** Most language dictionaries provide you with a list of phonemes, often calling these "the sounds" of the language. This can be very misleading, especially if some phonemes represent groups of phones, like the two kinds of *p* in English. Dictionaries or grammars prepared by linguists and linguistic anthropologists generally provide more information than this, giving phonemic charts as well as full discussions of the phonetic variations in sounds, along with any rules for how each phonetic variant is used in the spoken language.

You can think of the relationship between phonetics and phonemics this way:

Kind of Analysis	Units of Analysis
Phonetics	Phones
Phonemics	Phonemes

The difference between phonetics and phonemics sometimes drives beginning students crazy. One way to think about the two is to use the image that the noted field linguist Kenneth Pike developed. Phonetics, Pike suggested, "gathers raw data"; phonemics "cooks" it. By the time you have finished reading this chapter and solving the puzzles in the workbook/reader, the differences—and the complex relationships—between phonetics and phonemics should be clear. You should also know how to do basic phonetic and phonemic analyses.

Most people use the phonological system(s) of the language(s) they grew up with, no matter how many additional languages they learn. If you grew up speaking (or even just hearing) more than one language you probably know (and can use) the phonological systems of each of those languages. Using the phonological system of one language to speak another one will generally give you a "foreign-sounding" accent. If you want to get rid of your "accent," try paying more attention to the phonological system of the language in question. Learn its phonemic groupings and its phonetic intricacies. Do the analyses yourself if you have to, working with books and with individuals who speak the language.

Phonetics

There are actually three kinds of phonetics. **Acoustic phonetics** studies the physical properties of sounds and the nature of the sound waves that they produce. It uses complex laboratory equipment to produce spectrograms of sounds and can be useful in making "voice prints" that can be used to identify specific individuals. **Auditory phonetics** studies how sounds are perceived. It uses laboratory experiments in which speech sounds are played under various conditions and in various configurations (sounds interrupted by coughs, for example) to determine how individuals receive and interpret the sounds of speech. **Articulatory phonetics** studies how speech sounds are produced. It uses fieldwork to develop an understanding of how sounds in various languages are articulated, and it attempts to collect and catalog all of the sounds that humans can and do make and use in language. Articulatory phonetics is the kind of phonetics we introduced in the beginning of this chapter. It is sometimes also called **descriptive phonetics** because it describes language sounds in detail. Although all three kinds of phonetics are of interest to linguistic anthropologists, it is articulatory phonetics that is the most useful for field research and for research concerning the world's languages. It is also the most useful for learning and teaching new languages.

Articulatory phonetics is what you need to learn if you want to know how to pronounce sounds in other languages or to explain the sounds of your own language to others. Learning the basics of articulatory phonetics is a little bit like learning the basics of cooking or carpentry, except that articulatory phonetics helps you to pronounce (or articulate) speech sounds, while cooking and carpentry help you to produce meals and furniture. In each case, you need to learn how to understand and follow specific kinds of directions.

The directions for how to identify and produce speech sounds assume that you know something about human anatomy; Figure 3.1 is a diagram showing the main areas involved in speech production. Pay special attention to the **lungs** (which force air out), the **larynx** (where the vocal cords modify the air, creating sound waves), and the area *above* the vocal cords where the sound waves take on distinctive shapes and become recognizable speech sounds (this area is sometimes called the "supralaryngeal vocal tract").

The Larynx: Voicing   As air moves through the larynx, it passes through the **vocal cords** (sometimes called the **vocal folds**). At this point the vo-

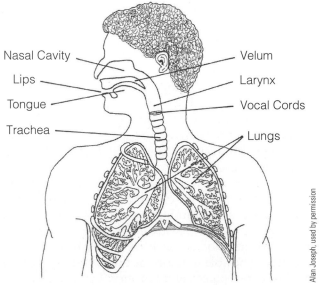

FIGURE 3.1   Diagram of the speech organs

Nasal Cavity
Lips
Tongue
Trachea

Velum
Larynx
Vocal Cords
Lungs

Alan Joseph, used by permission

cal cords can either be open and relaxed or they can be close together and vibrating. If the vocal cords are open and relaxed, the sound produced is called **voiceless.** If the vocal cords are close together and vibrating, the sound produced is called **voiced.** You can feel the difference between voiced and voiceless sounds by putting your hand on your throat and comparing the sounds of *z* and *s.* You can feel the vocal cords vibrating when you say *z.* Switch to saying *s,* and you will feel the vocal cords stop vibrating.

The difference between voiced and voiceless sounds is an important one to learn. Nearly every language in the world makes use of it in some way. In English, for example, the difference in meaning between the words *kill* and *gill* is signaled by how the first sound in those two words is produced: voiced or voiceless.

Articulation above the Larynx After passing through the vocal cords, air reaches the mouth and nose areas (the supralaryngeal vocal tract) where there are a lot of ways that it can be **articulated,** or modified. One important way that the air can be modified is by constriction in the mouth, or oral cavity. The tongue, in particular, can be moved around in the mouth to affect the quality of the air moving through the mouth and nose areas. In addition, the velum can open and close the passage into the nasal cavity, and the lips can be opened or closed, so the direction through which the air finally escapes can be either through the nose or the mouth. All of these details of articulation will affect the outcome of a sound.

The articulation of speech sounds is described in terms of **place** (*where* the air is being modified) and **manner** (*how* the air is being modified). If you want to identify a speech sound and pronounce it accurately, then you need to know something about the place and manner in which it is modified. You also need to know about whether it is voiced or voiceless. A phonetic chart will give you these three pieces of information about the sounds you are interested in. In addition, it can provide you with a convenient grid for cataloging the sounds of any language you are learning. Table 3.1 is a scaled-down phonetic chart showing the sounds we have talked about so far in this chapter. Notice that information about place of articulation is placed across the top of the chart and information about manner is placed along the left side of the chart. Voicing is included as a subcategory under each place.

Notice that there is a special symbol used for the retroflex [ʈ] that we mentioned at the beginning of the chapter. The value of a phonetic chart is that it presents a clear and unambiguous way to represent every speech sound, providing the essential basics for producing the sounds of any language. Once you learn about the different places and manners of articulation, you should be able to figure out how to pronounce the sounds being described by those places and manners.

TABLE 3.1 Scaled-down version of a phonetic chart for consonants

		PLACE							
		bilabial		alveolar		retroflex		velar	
		voiceless	*voiced*	*voiceless*	*voiced*	*voiceless*	*voiced*	*voiceless*	*voiced*
MANNER	stop	p	b			ʈ		k	g
	aspirated stop	p^h							
	fricative			s	z				

Phonetic Charts and Symbols

A phonetic chart is important because relying on a language's spelling system can be misleading. For example the letter <c> in English represents both a [k] sound, as in *cat* and an [s] sound, as in *ceiling*. Conversely, the English sound [k] can be spelled <c> as in *cat,* <k> as in *kit,* or <ck> as in *tack*. In addition, different languages often spell the same sounds differently. English <sh> and French <ch> represent different spellings of the same sound, for example. And different languages use the same symbol for different sounds. The letter <c> is pronounced one way for the English word *cat,* a different way for the French word *ciel* 'sky,' and yet a different way for the Czech word *cizí* 'foreign.' A phonetic chart cuts through this complexity and assigns a single symbol to each sound used in a language. On a phonetic chart, both the English <sh> and the French <ch> are written [ʃ], the <c> of *cat* is [k], the <c> of *ciel* is [s], and the <c> of *cizí* is [ts].

Not every phonetic chart uses the same set of terms and symbols. This can be quite disconcerting for beginning students. Some of the explanation for this variation comes from the way that phonetic charts have developed over time. At least as early as the 1800s, European linguists, collecting data on the sounds of different languages, came to the conclusion that some sort of unambiguous method of writing sounds needed to be developed. For each unique sound, they reasoned, there should be just one unique symbol. One symbol, one sound. Clear and unambiguous and easy to use. The result was the **International Phonetic Alphabet (IPA)**, a system of phonetic transcription still in use today.

WEBLINK To read about the IPA and other phonetic resources, go to http://anthropology.wadsworth.com/ottenheimer_language.

Over time, as more languages and sounds were studied, the IPA was modified. New symbols were added to describe "new" sounds, and different groupings of sounds were proposed. But many of the symbols were complex and required expensive typesetting or careful hand-lettering. In the 1940s, as typewriters were becoming more commonly used, missionary linguist Kenneth Pike developed a set of phonetic symbols, which later came to be called the **American Usage System,** that could be easily typed. He also changed some symbols, using the more English-based symbol [y], for example, instead of the more European-based IPA symbol [j] for the sound that begins the word *yellow.* Using Pike's symbols, the English <sh> and the French <ch> are written [š] instead of [ʃ], while the <c> of *cat* remains [k] and the <c> of *ciel* remains [s]. (The <c> of *cizí,* however, is written [¢] to reflect the fact that in Czech (at least) it seems to be one single sound rather than a [t] followed by an [s].)

Pike's symbols were rapidly adopted by American anthropologists. Even after computers began to replace typewriters and IPA fonts were developed for computers, many American anthropologists continued to use Pike's set of symbols. Today, some of those anthropologists are beginning to switch back to using IPA symbols, others continue to use Pike's symbols, and still others continue to use combinations specific to the languages that they work with.

Instead of memorizing lots of different phonetic charts and symbols, it makes more sense to memorize the underlying principles of phonetic charts. If you understand the concepts of voicing, place, and manner, and you can sort out how and where each of these is labeled on a phonetic chart, then you will be able to identify and produce any speech sound on any phonetic chart. You will also be able to place any sound you hear into its correct location on a chart and use an appropriate symbol for it. Stay flexible. You never know which languages you'll encounter in your studies and which set of symbols you'll need, so being familiar with the underlying principles of phonetics, and with how phonetic charts are organized, is the best way to be prepared. Just remember that each language is likely to use its own unique spelling system, but that phonetic symbols allow you to transcribe and pronounce the sounds of any language accurately and to communicate about those sounds with speakers of other languages.

There are two kinds of phonetic charts: one shows **consonants,** or sounds with more constriction in the air flow, and the other shows **vowels,** or sounds with less constriction in the air flow. The reduced phonetic chart in Table 3.1 is a chart showing consonants.

Consonants Phonetic charts for consonants show *where* a sound is articulated (place) and *how* it is articulated (manner). If you treat these details about place and manner as a set of directions, then you just need to follow those directions and, with a bit of practice, you should be able to pronounce just about any consonant. If you know the meaning of a specific place and a specific manner, then the spot in the chart where that place and manner intersect should be occupied by a sound (actually a symbol for a sound) that is produced at that place and using that manner.

Here's how to produce the kind of consonant known as a "bilabial stop" following the directions provided by the mini–phonetic chart in Table 3.1. "Bilabial stop" means that the *place* is bilabial and the *manner* is stop. Notice that place is always listed first when describing a consonant phonetically. **Bilabial** means two lips, so to produce a bilabial stop, start by putting your two lips together. **Stop** means stop the air (do this just for a moment and then release the air and let it continue). So, stopping the air with your two lips will give you either a [b] or a [p] depending on whether you let your vocal cords vibrate [b] or you keep them relaxed [p]. Information about voicing usually comes first when describing a consonant, so a [b] should be called a voiced bilabial stop and a [p] should be called a voiceless bilabial stop.

That's it. Those are the basics of identifying and pronouncing specific sounds at a phonetic level. All you need to do is learn the meanings of the different named places and manners of articulation and to apply that information to whatever sound you are interested in. That's the kind of information that I used to identify and pronounce the *tr* [ţ] sound in the Comoros and the infamous Czech ř (see Doing Linguistic Anthropology 3.1).

To help you get started, here are some brief descriptions of the places and manners of articulation that you are likely to find on a phonetic chart of consonants. The workbook/reader gives more complete details, with examples and alternative terms (remember, different charts may use different terms for some places and manners). Careful study of the charts and diagrams in the workbook/reader should help you to build your skill at recognizing the various combinations of places and manners of articulation so that you can zero in on whatever sounds you are interested in.

Places of Articulation

Glottal	In the glottis, or the space between your vocal cords
Pharyngeal	In the pharynx, above your vocal cords
Uvular	With back of tongue and **uvula** (hangs down in the back of your mouth)
Velar	With back of tongue and **velum** (in front of the uvula)
Palatal	With middle of tongue and hard palate (roof of your mouth)
Retroflex	With tip of tongue and hard palate
Alveopalatal	With tip of tongue just behind alveolar ridge (the ridge just behind your teeth)
Alveolar	With tip of tongue against alveolar ridge
Interdental	With tip of tongue between the teeth
Labiodental	With the lower lip against the upper teeth
Bilabial	With both lips

Manners of Articulation

Stop/plosive	The air stream is stopped, then released
Fricative	There is friction in the air stream (the air hisses or buzzes)

Doing Linguistic Anthropology 3.1

LEARNING THE CZECH ř

As soon as I heard the Czech ř I knew it was going to be a challenge. It was unlike anything I had ever heard before, but it seemed to be made up of elements that sounded familiar. It sounded like *r* and *h* and *s* and *sh* and *g* (as in *rouge*) all together. Our instructor tried to reassure us that we didn't need to get it "right." She said that even some Czechs don't get it "right"! But I was determined. I even felt that it was my obligation, as a linguistic anthropologist, to figure out how to get it "right." It seemed like a perfect opportunity to use my knowledge of phonetics.

So I stayed after class and asked the instructor a few more questions. Where, for example, was her tongue: Was it placed where she said *s* or was it further back on her palate where she said *sh*? Closer to *sh*, she thought, so I noted it as an alveopalatal. Next, I needed to know the manner in which it was produced. It buzzed, like the *g* of *rouge,* so it was a fricative, but it also trilled, like the *rr* in Spanish. In addition, it was voiced. So, I concluded, it was a voiced trilled alveolar fricative. Now that I had identified all the components, the trick was to practice combining them. I soon discovered that it was easier for me to add friction to an alveolar trill than to trill an alveolar fricative. I also found that it was easier to practice a voiceless version than a voiced one, so I began with that and added voicing later on. After a few weeks of practice, I was ready to try using the sound in a word. I started with short words, such as *tři* 'three' and *hořký* 'dark.' Next, I worked on longer words, such as *třicet* 'thirty' and *stříbrných* 'silver.' Eventually, with the encouragement of my Czech friends and teachers, I was even able to handle some tongue-twisters: *třista třicet tři stříbrných křepelek . . .* 'three hundred and thirty-three silver cranes. . . .' The key had been to identify the components of the sound first, using a phonetic chart for guidance, so that I could practice combining the components until I could produce the entire combination.

HJO

Affricate	The combination of a stop followed by a fricative
Tap/Trill	Like an ultra-brief stop: a tap is one touch; a trill is many fast ones
Approximant	Minimum obstruction to air flow, less than a fricative
Nasal	The velum is lowered; air resonates and escapes through the nasal cavity

Doing Linguistic Anthropology 3.2

SUN AND MOON CONSONANTS IN ARABIC

One year I decided to learn Arabic, so I enrolled in a beginning class at my university. The instructor began by teaching us the sounds of Arabic and some words to use them in. We followed an alphabet order, and every so often the instructor would note that one or another of the sounds could be doubled, or lengthened. He called these "sun" letters, and he said that some other letters were called "moon" letters. He also said that we just needed to memorize which was which; that there was no other way to learn the difference. Of course, I took this as a challenge and started making lists of sun and moon letters. The first thing that my lists revealed to me was that all the sun and moon letters were consonants; none of them were vowels. My next step was to try locating all the sun and moon letters on a phonetic consonant chart. Once I had completed my chart of sun and moon letters, the pattern literally jumped out at me, just as clear as day! All the sun letters were in the middle of the chart (alveolars and palatals), and all of the moon letters were at the edges of the chart (bilabials, labiodentals, velars, uvulars, pharyngeals, and glottals). I was gratified and passed the test on sun and moon letters with flying colors.

HJO

Vowels The difference between consonants and vowels seems to be one of degree. In general, consonants are sounds in which the air stream is modified by some sort of constriction, while vowels are sounds in which there is much less (in some cases almost no) modification of the air stream. Open vowels such as *a* are clearly vowels, and stops such as *p* are clearly consonants, but knowing exactly where to place the borderline between consonants and vowels (or where to chart sounds such as *y, w,* or *r*) is a challenge that different linguists have solved differently.

Phonetic charts that show voicing, place, and manner are useful for consonants, but they are not as much help for vowels. For vowels, it is more useful to know something about the shape of the space in which the air stream resonates, so we need a chart that can describe that space for us. There are three important ways that the air stream for vowels can be modified: by "height" of tongue, by "place" of tongue, and by "rounding" of lips. The height and the place of the tongue provide the primary axes of the vowel chart, with height (the tongue can be high, mid, or open) labeled on the left side of the chart, and place (the tongue can be front, central, or back) labeled across the top of the chart. Lip rounding can

TABLE 3.2   Scaled-down vowel chart

		PLACE					
		front		central		back	
		unrounded	*rounded*	*unrounded*	*rounded*	*unrounded*	*rounded*
H E I G H T	close-high	i	y				
	close-mid	e	ø	ə			u
	open-mid	ɛ	œ				o
	open-low			a			

be marked as a third dimension or as a second vertical column for each "place." Some charts also show "tenser" or "laxer" positions for each tongue height. Although different vowel charts may be presented or labeled differently (for example, some charts use the terms close, mid, and open to describe height), the axes of height and place are basic to every vowel chart. Table 3.2 is a scaled-down vowel chart showing the basics.

Here are some brief descriptions of the three main dimensions of vowel production (height, place, and rounding). As with consonants, more detailed charts and descriptions, and additional modifications and the terminology describing them, can be found in the workbook/reader.

"Tongue height." This really does mean how high your tongue is in your mouth. You can test this by comparing the *ee* [i] sound (as in English *beet*) with the *a* [a] sound (as in English *father*). Not only is your tongue higher in your mouth for the *ee* [i] sound but your mouth is also more closed than for the *a* [a] sound.

"Tongue place" (also called "tongue advancement"). This refers to how far forward or back your tongue is in your mouth. For example, your tongue is further forward for an *ee* [i] sound (as in English *beet*) and further back for an *oo* [u] sound (as in English *boot*).

"Rounding" (also called "lip rounding"). This refers to how you hold your lips—in a **rounded** or a flat (unrounded) position. In French, some of the front vowels are flat (such as the *i* [i] in *pire* 'worse') and some are rounded (such as the *ue* [y] in *rue* 'street'). The *eu* [ø] in French *dejeuner* 'have breakfast' and the *eu* [œ] of French *jeune* 'young' are two different front rounded vowels that are spelled the same way in French. Phonetic charts for vowels help to make the difference between the two pronunciations clear. Turkish is just one language in which back vowels can be unrounded. In English, all the back vowels are rounded and all the front vowels are unrounded. This means that English speakers generally have a difficult time rounding front vowels and un-rounding back vowels (and learning to pronounce German or French or Turkish, for example, can be a challenge) but, as with different consonants, understanding the phonetic principles can get you started more effectively than the usual hit and miss approach. After that, it is just a matter of practice.

Vowel sounds that are new to you are sometimes more difficult to reproduce than consonants. This is probably because finding the exact placement for your tongue is tougher for vowels than it is for consonants. Although individual speakers of a language might vary somewhat in exactly how they produce their consonants, they vary quite a lot in how they produce their vowels. For example, I pronounce the *o* in the English word *coffee* with a mid high back [ɔ], while most of my Kansas students pronounce it with a lower and more open [a] sound. My students find my pronunciation of *coffee* humorous, as well as just different, but in fact we all respond to such differences in our daily lives. The way we react to people is often affected by the way they speak; some accents, such as my New York accent, carry different kinds of status (more about this in Chapter 9), with the result that people may get treated differently depending on how they sound. When I pronounce *coffee* my way, I sound like a New Yorker or an "outsider" in Kansas. If I pronounce *coffee* with the more open Kansas [a] sound, I blend in better. (By the way, I pronounce the *or* sound of *York* with the same [ɔ] as in *coffee*).

Not only can it be a fun challenge to try to sound like the people around you, it can also help you to fit in a little better if that is your goal or to be more easily understood by the people you are speaking with. It's also fun (and impressive) to be able to guess what parts of the United States people come from after just listening to them speak for a little bit. My own vowels are pretty much Kansas vowels after living in that state for over thirty years, but when I visit New York I find I sometimes need to revert to my New York vowels, especially if I want to get a cup of coffee. One of my students once told me that when she moved from Kansas to New York as a young child she couldn't understand her teachers for a little while and her teachers had similar difficulty with her own speech, until she learned the new vowels. These days, with people moving around the United States (and even the world) as much as they do, it probably would be useful for teachers to know something about such linguistic differences so that they could understand and communicate with their students more quickly.

Beyond Phonetic Charts: Suprasegmentals

Phonetic charts show you the ordinary or basic sounds of a language. These basic sounds are called the **segments** of a language. But every language also makes use of some additional modifications to the basic consonants and vowels. Some examples of additional modifications include **nasalization** (letting the sound travel through the nasal cavity instead of the mouth), alteration of **pitch** (higher or lower "notes"), **lengthening,** (holding the sound for a longer period of time), and releasing air inward rather than outward. Because the basic sounds are called segments, the additional modifications are called **suprasegmentals** (*supra* means 'over' or 'above') or **suprasegmental features.** Suprasegmental features are not generally included in the phonetic charts. To do so would clutter the chart unnecessarily. Instead, these additional modifications are indicated with **diacritics,** or a special set of symbols. Diacritics are especially handy because they can be added to many different symbols. For example a tilde [˜] can be added to any vowel symbol, such as [ã] or [õ], to indicate that it is a nasal vowel. Many languages (French, Yoruba, Hindi, and Navajo, for example) include nasal vowels in their sound inventories. Or a colon [:] can be added to either a consonant, such as [d:] or [k:], or to a vowel, such as [e:] or [a:], to indicate lengthening, or holding a sound for a longer amount of time. Numbers can be added to vowels to indicate different pitches: high, low, middle, rising, falling, rising and then falling, and so on. And little arrows can be added to stops to indicate that the air is released inward, rather than outward, producing **clicks** (which are voiceless) or **implosives** (which are voiced). Different languages make use of different combinations of these suprasegmental features. Sometimes the difference between two words is just a different pitch, or different length of vowel or consonant, so you should be prepared to learn something about suprasegmentals and the diacritics that mark them for whichever language you encounter. A more detailed description of these suprasegmental features, as well as others, and a list of the diacritics used for each one are in the workbook/reader.

With a solid understanding of phonetic charts and suprasegmentals, you have the basic toolkit for learning (and teaching) languages. Whether you are trying to learn another language or dialect or to teach your own to someone else, you will find that these basics will take you a long way. Phonetics can help you figure out how to hear and pronounce any language with as little "foreign" accent as possible. After that, it's a matter of practice and dedication. The older you are, the more likely your speaking muscles are used to moving in certain ways and not others and the harder it will be to retrain them, but it is not impossible. The first step, in any case, is to map out the sound inventory of the language in question so you will understand what is involved in producing the sounds of that language.

Phonemics

Mapping out the sound inventory of a language is a beginning, but it is only a beginning. In order to really learn a language you need to know how those sounds are *used*. And you need to be able to use them the same way that speakers of the language use them. Otherwise, you will continue to sound like an outsider, speaking with an accent. Recall my experience with the Shinzwani retroflex [ʈ]. Phonetics could help me to identify it and to place it into the correct spot in a phonetic chart and to pronounce it correctly. But it couldn't tell me how the sound was actually used in Shinzwani, where it fit in the overall sound system of the language, and how it worked with other sounds to build words. For that kind of information, I needed "phonemics." Phonemics analyzes the way sounds are arranged in languages. A phonemic analysis helps you to identify which phones are "important" in a language. It helps you to sort out which sounds function to make a difference (like [ʈ] and [t] in Shinzwani) and which ones don't (like [pʰ] and [p] in English).

By showing you how sounds are actually used in a language, phonemics takes you deeper into language than phonetics can. Phonetics may give you a more objective, externally valid description of language sounds, but phonemics can give you more of an insider's view of the language. An insider's understanding of a language is essential if you are going to learn a language well. Anthropologists need this kind of understanding to truly comprehend other cultures and languages from the inside out. Doing anthropology requires living with the people you want to learn from, and living with people successfully means learning and speaking their language. Linguists also need this kind of information to analyze and compare languages and study sound systems. In fact anyone who is learning or teaching a language, or spending time in a different culture, needs an appreciation of the insider's view of language and culture. Phonemics provides a valuable approach to understanding how things work from an insider's perspective.

Phonemes　Fundamental to phonemic analysis is the identification of the phonemes of a language. A phoneme is a sound that functions to distinguish one word from another in a language, just like [ʈ] and [t] function to distinguish [nʈu] 'hermit crab' from [ntu] 'arrow' in Shinzwani, for example, or like [t] and [d] function to distinguish [tai] *tie* from [dai] *die* in English. So /ʈ/ and /t/ are phonemes in Shinzwani and /t/ and /d/ are phonemes in English, and we can now use slanted brackets / / to signify that status. Missing out on the contrasts that a language deems important can impede your understanding of, or your ability to speak, that language. If I had missed catching the contrast between [ʈ] and [t] in Shinzwani, I would have had continuing difficulty hearing (and saying) all of the different words that use this contrast. Using my own English [t] in the wrong place, I might have ended up talking about finding an arrow on the beach when I really meant to say that I'd found a hermit crab on the beach. Learning how to use phonemes correctly is an important part of learning to speak a language correctly.

Minimal Pairs   A pair of words, like [tai] and [dai] in English, or [nʈu] and [ntu] in Shinzwani, is called a "minimal pair." A **minimal pair** is a pair of words in which a difference in sound makes a difference in meaning, and it is the clearest and easiest way to identify phonemes in a language. If you are trying to learn a language in the field, then one good strategy is to keep an ear out for minimal pairs. Groups of minimal pairs, such as [nʈu] and [ntu] in Shinzwani, or [ʈona] 'put on makeup' and [tona] 'skin an animal,' make it clear that /ʈ/ and /t/ are separate phonemes in Shinzwani and that anyone learning to speak that language will have to pay attention to the difference between the two. You don't have to wait until you've collected and identified and charted every phone before looking to see which ones are phonemes in a language. In fact, phonemic contrasts such as the ones between /ʈ/ and /t/ in Shinzwani and between /t/ and /d/ in English will generally appear quite early in your encounter with a new language and will alert you to those sounds that need your immediate attention in the learning process.

This is pretty straightforward, so let's try a few more examples. Let's look at an interdental fricative [θ] and an alveolar stop [t]. English has a minimal pair (*both* and *boat*) that uses both of these phones, but Shinzwani does not. In fact, Shinzwani does not use the interdental fricative [θ] at all. It just doesn't exist in that language. This not only means that /θ/ and /t/ are phonemes in English, it also means that Shinzwani speakers need to learn to pronounce the English /θ/ if they want to speak English clearly. Other languages that do not have the English /θ/ include French and Czech. This means that French, Czech, and Shinzwani speakers who do not learn to pronounce the English /θ/ will have a difficult time communicating clearly in English, and English speakers would have to figure out whether the words [bot ʃuz], uttered by someone who hasn't learned how to say the English /θ/, is *both shoes* or *boat shoes*.

Some years ago I took an Italian student sailing (yes, we sail in Kansas). He had raced sailboats in Italy and knew all the sailing terminology in Italian but not in English. He wanted to learn the English terms so he could race with us, so we began going around the boat and naming all the parts. When we got to the ropes that control the sails I said to him, "These are the *sheets*." Now, English has several minimal pairs that distinguish the *ee* sound (as in *beets*) from the *i* sound (as in *bits*), but Italian does not. When he asked me to repeat the word a few times, and he repeated it carefully to be sure he had it right, I realized that he was well aware of these two vowel phonemes in English and didn't want to make any mistakes with this particular word.

One last example. In Hindi the word [pʰəl] means *fruit* and the word [pəl] means *minute* (ə is a mid central vowel that sounds like the *u* in the English word *rum*). If we examine this minimal pair closely, we discover that the primary difference between the two words is the aspirated [pʰ] of [pʰəl] and the unaspirated [p] of [pəl]. This means that the two kinds of *p* are separate phonemes in Hindi and can be written as /pʰ/ and /p/. It

Cross-Language Miscommunication 3.1

HOT AND BITTER CHOCOLATE

Most of the time it doesn't matter if you can't pronounce the Czech ř correctly (see Doing Linguistic Anthropology 3.1: Learning the Czech ř). If you say [tri] instead of [tři] most people will still be able to figure out that you are saying the number 'three.' You will just sound like you've got some sort of accent if you use the wrong *r*. Saying [tɾi], for example, will make you sound more Spanish, while [tɹi] or [tɻi] will make you sound more American, and [tʀi] will make you sound more French. But all of these variants will still sound like the Czech word for 'three.' That's because none of them means anything different.

Occasionally, however, it *does* make a difference how you say your *r* in Czech. And then you have to be careful. I found this out when I asked a grocery store clerk where I could find the chocolate bars. I'm not partial to milk chocolate so I took the trouble to look up the word for bitter chocolate (*hořká čokoláda*) so that I could be more specific about what I was looking for. But the Czech word for 'hot chocolate' is *horká čokoláda*. The only difference between the two is the ř or *r*. I could tell that I had used the wrong *r* when I found myself in the aisle with all the hot chocolate mixes, with no candy bars or baking chocolate in sight. It was a good lesson in minimal pairs. It also meant that my ř was going to need more practice.

HJO

---

also means that non-Hindi speakers will need to learn to hear and pronounce both sounds if they want to speak Hindi correctly.

Allophones   But wait! Earlier we said that English speakers already know how to pronounce both of these kinds of *p*. Does this mean that English speakers will have an easier time pronouncing Hindi? Not exactly. There's something different about the way that English and Hindi speakers use these sounds. Let's take a closer look.

First of all, let's see if the two sounds constitute a minimal pair in English. If you change the pronunciation of *pool* from [pʰul] to [pul] does the meaning of the word change? The answer, for most English speakers, is no. It's still the same word; it just sounds a little different. Try as we might, it's not possible to find a minimal pair in English in which [pʰ] and [p] contrast with one another. And without a minimal pair, we can't say that the two sounds are separate phonemes in English.

When we find two or more sounds that don't seem to make a difference in a language, the next step is to ask whether they might be "allophones." **Allophones** are variant forms of phonemes. They are members of a group of sounds that together form a single phoneme. Think of the fingers on your hand. Each one is a separate unit, but together they make up the larger unit of your hand. Allophones are a little bit like this. Each one is a separate phone, but together all of them make up the larger unit of a phoneme. If we think this way about the English phones [pʰ] and [p], then we can see how they are probably allophones of a single phoneme /p/ in English. Some linguists speak of this as an underlying abstract phoneme with different surface manifestations. The whole idea of phoneme is pretty abstract anyway. In any case, if two (or more) sounds don't make a difference in meaning, then they are probably allophones of one phoneme.

Interestingly, Ken Pike used to call pairs of sounds like these "suspicious pairs" (or "suspicious groups" because sometimes there were more than two sounds involved). He meant that they were so close together on a phonetic chart that he suspected that they might be allophones of a phoneme and that it was worth trying to figure out if they were.

One of the interesting things about the difference between phonemes and allophones is how well you can predict their behavior. With phonemes, you generally can't predict much of anything. There's no predictable pattern to help you to learn whether English words will start with /p/ or /t/ or /b/ or /d/. So you have to memorize every word that starts with one of these sounds. The situation is refreshingly different for allophones. Wherever you find allophones in a language, there is an excellent chance that you will also be able to find a pattern that defines how and where they are used in the language. And once you find the pattern, you can use it to help you speak the language better.

Let's take the English [pʰ] and [p], for example. Earlier we said that aspirated [pʰ] always occurs at the beginnings of words and that unaspirated [p] always occurs in the middle of words, following [s]. No matter how many English words we examine, we will find this pattern operating. Let's try it. Here are some English words using [pʰ] and [p]:

Words with [pʰ]	Words with [p]
[pʰik] peak	[spik] speak
[pʰat] pot	[spat] spot
[pʰul] pool	[spul] spool
[pʰes] pace	[spes] space
[pʰɛnd] pend	[spɛnd] spend
[pʰok] poke	[spok] spoke
[pʰən] pun	[spən] spun

From these words, and any others that you can add to the list, it's clear that [pʰ] is always used at the beginnings of English words and [p] is always used in the middle of English words, following [s]. The advantage of finding patterns like this is that once you've found them you can just memorize the patterns rather than having to memorize long lists of words. This makes it much easier to learn (or teach) a new language.

This kind of patterning is called "complementary distribution," or "conditioned variation." **Complementary distribution** means that the different variants (or allophones) are distributed between complementary (differing) word environments. **Conditioned variation** means that the variation among allophones is thought of as conditioned (affected) by the sounds around them. It's really just two ways of saying the same thing. What's especially interesting about sounds that occur in complementary distribution (or conditioned variation) in a language is that they often seem like the "same" sound to native speakers of that language. The pattern of distribution is so predictable that it is used by speakers without even thinking about it. In fact, most speakers don't even know that they are following these patterns. It's also interesting that once you discover a pattern of complementary distribution in a language and you point it out to speakers of that language, those speakers usually can confirm the pattern for you and can think of additional examples. Confirmation like this can help linguistic anthropologists to know that they are on the right track with their analyses.

So let's sum up the Hindi/English question. At the phonetic level of both languages, we have two phones, [pʰ] and [p]. At the phonemic level, however, things are different. In Hindi the two phones function as separate phonemes, /pʰ/ and /p/, while in English the two phones function as two allophones, [pʰ] and [p], grouping together to form *one* phoneme, /p/. As allophones, [pʰ] and [p] are in complementary distribution in English, with [pʰ] at the beginnings of words and [p] in the middles of words, following [s]. Representing this information graphically makes it a bit easier to see.

Hindi:

/pʰ/
/p/

English:

/p/   [pʰ] at the beginnings of words
       [p] in the middle of words, following [s]

It also makes it easier to understand why it is that although both sounds are present in both languages, it is difficult for English speakers to use the two kinds of *p* as separate phonemes, as Hindi speakers do. The patterns of complementary distribution are largely unconscious, forming habits that are not easy to change. English speakers are used to using unaspirated [p] following [s], not at the beginnings of words. But the Hindi minimal pair of /pʰəl/ 'fruit' and /pəl/ 'minute' makes it necessary for them to overcome those unconscious English allophone habits. Otherwise, they'll probably end up talking about fruit when they want to be talking about minutes. Can you imagine telling someone that you will be ready to go in just a few fruit? Using unaspirated [p] at the beginnings of words will seem strange to English speakers, at least at first. But it is not impossible. It just takes practice. And understanding phonemes, allophones, and complementary distribution can give you a head start in the process.

Hindi speakers have a somewhat different problem with English. Although English speakers are not used to hearing unaspirated [p] at the beginning of a word, they can adjust to it fairly readily. It's not a different phoneme for them, so they will just hear it as a misplaced allophone of /p/. It doesn't matter a whole lot if someone uses the wrong allophone in the wrong part of a word; the meaning of the word will still be the same and they will still get their message across, but they will have a "foreign-sounding" accent and could be more difficult to understand than if they are able to put the right allophone into the right environment. Hindi speakers, then, need to limit their use of aspirated /pʰ/ to the beginnings of English words and to try to use unaspirated /p/ only in the middle of words in English. Again, an understanding of phonemes, allophones, and complementary distribution can go a long way in helping here.

This is a good illustration of the fact that different languages can make different uses of their sound inventories. Even if two languages have the same phones, they may not group them into phonemes and allophones in the same way. A phone that serves as a phoneme in one language might be working as an allophone in another language. In other words, two languages that are identical at the phonetic level may be quite different at the phonemic level.

As you develop your phonemic analysis of a language, you can refine your phonetic chart to a phonemic chart—one that shows just the phonemes of the language. A useful exercise when you are learning or teaching a new language is to superimpose the sound charts of the two languages. Try using a different color of highlighter for each language—blue for one language and yellow for the other will give you green for sounds in both languages. Most of the time, it's enough to do this with phonemic charts rather than the more detailed phonetic charts. However, if you want to show both phonemes and allophones you can do this with slashes and square brackets on the same chart. An exercise of this sort allows you to predict and explain the kinds of accents that speakers of each language might have in speaking the other language. It can also help you to create exercises for learning or for teaching speakers of one language to pronounce the other more accurately. Note that individuals encountering a new sound will first try to approximate it using the linguistically closest sound to it from their own sound inventory. What does close mean? Think in terms of place or manner. Suppose you want to pronounce [θ] but don't have it in your own language. What's close? In terms of *place*, it might be [t] because it is the tip of your tongue that is involved in both sounds, so if you have [t] that's one good choice for a sound to use instead of [θ]. Another good choice might be a fricative. Because [θ] is a fricative, you could search among similar fricatives in your language for a good substitute. In this case, you'd be thinking in terms of *manner* rather than place. So, for example if you have [s] or [f] in your language, one of those fricatives might seem like a good choice. Every pair of languages will have different contrasts and solutions, and it is even possible that individual speakers will have their own individual variations.

Even if two different languages have the same phonemes, there is no guarantee that those phonemes will combine in the same ways in both languages. For example the *ng* sound at the end of the English word *sing* is identical to the *ng* sound at the beginning of the Shinzwani word *ngoma* 'drum,' but no English words begin with <ng> and so most English speakers have a difficult time pronouncing *ngoma* and other Shinzwani words beginning with the *ng* sound, tending instead to say something sounding like *nigoma* or *engoma*. In contrast, although Shinzwani has sounds that are identical to English *s* and *k*, these two sounds are never clustered together in Shinzwani as they are in the English word *skill*. Most Shinzwani speakers tend to separate the two sounds and say something like *sikill*. English speakers also try to separate the sounds in the Czech word *zmrzlina* 'ice cream,' saying things like *zumerzilina* (and making themselves difficult to understand at the ice cream store as a result)!

Just like learning to pronounce new sounds, it is also possible to learn to pronounce old sounds in new ways and in new combinations. If you understand phonemics, or how sounds are arranged in different languages, then you will understand how to approach the task of learning the sound combinations of a new language. An understanding of phonemics gives you an understanding of phonemes, allophones, and the principles of complementary distribution. After that, it's just a matter of practice and dedication. It takes an extra effort to get beyond the unconscious habits of pronunciation that you learned when you learned your first language(s), but the payoff in terms of accent and understandability in every new language that you approach will be impressive. The workbook/reader gives you some practice with finding minimal pairs, identifying phonemes, and analyzing the distribution and conditioning of allophones in a variety of languages. The exercises there will help you to stretch your abilities by providing different kinds of contrasts, groupings, and patternings of sounds. It will also give you ideas for additional exercises and projects that you can try with your new understanding of phonetics and phonemics.

❋ ETICS AND EMICS

So I took the word *phonemic,* crossed out the *phon-* part meaning "sound", and generalized my use of the new emic term to represent any unit of culture, at any level, of any kind, which was reacted to as a relevant unit by the native actors in that behavior. In the same way, I created the word *etic* from *phonetic.*   KENNETH L. PIKE

It should be clear from the examples so far, and from the workbook exercises, that native speakers of a language generally think about the units of their language in terms of phonemics, while outsiders/nonspeakers of a language often find themselves noticing phonetic distinctions in that language rather than phonemic ones. In fact, it takes a bit of analysis before an outsider/nonspeaker of a language can fully grasp the phonemic groupings of a language. While the specific languages in question, both of outsider and insider, can contribute to the complexity of the task, in general it is true that phonetics proceeds most easily from outside of a language and phonemics from inside a language. It is also true that a good phonemic analysis will be recognized by the speakers of a language. This kind of confirmation is truly gratifying to an anthropologist trying to learn a language in the field; it means you are on the right track with your analyses.

In the 1950s, struggling to understand the relationship between language and culture, Pike realized that there might be cultural units similar to phonetic and phonemic units. As he has written, "[C]ulture had to be viewed in relation to the people who utilized their units within that culture. What was crucial to them? What kind of "native reaction" made one item relevant and another one not noticed? These items forced us to look at the analogue of "phonemics" in anthropology, and we needed to build on our experience with phonemic analysis" (Pike 1998, 154). So, building on his experience with phonemic analysis Pike proposed the terms **etics** and **emics** to describe the levels at which outsiders and insiders might identify cultural units, variants of those units, and patterning among the variants. The terms were first published in Pike's 1954 book, *Language in Relation to a Unified Theory of the Structure of Human Behavior.* They were adopted quickly by anthropologists and have become a part of the basic toolkit of anthropology. The idea that different cultures can be organized around different perceptions of reality and described at both etic and emic levels became a central concept in contemporary anthropology, as well as an important contribution to contemporary thought. It is this etic/emic distinction that underlies our ability to understand and interpret different cultures as we do. This is why a good understanding of phonetics and phonemics is so valuable. It is easier to learn the concepts, and the analytical techniques, with sounds than with cultures, but once learned, it is not such a stretch to apply the concepts and techniques to the understanding of cultures and of cultural and linguistic relativity.

SUMMARY

Although sound and sound combinations are numerous and varied, knowing the basics of sound production is an enormously useful tool. Phonology is the study of language sounds and is divided into phonetics and phonemics. Phonetics identifies and describes language sounds; phonemics analyzes the way sounds are arranged in a language. A phonetic chart shows all of the sounds of a language, and a phonemic chart shows just the distinctive sounds of a language. There are three different types of phonetics: acoustic (physical properties of sound and sound waves), auditory (how sounds are perceived), and articulatory (how speech sounds are produced).

Phonetic charts are important because a language's spelling system is misleading; the IPA assigns every possible speech sound its own unique symbol. These symbols provide an unambiguous system of phonetic transcription. Kenneth Pike also developed a set of phonetic symbols, and this set was used by American linguistic anthropologists for many years.

Rather than memorizing phonetic charts and symbols, it is better to know the underlying principles of phonetic charts. By understanding how a chart represents the place and manner of production of a sound, you can produce any speech sound on any phonetic chart.

There are two phonetic charts: one for consonants and one for vowels. Consonant charts show where (place) and how (manner) a sound is articulated, while vowel charts show height and place of the tongue and rounding of the lips.

Phonemics not only helps you to identify which phones are vital in a language, but also takes you deeper into a language than phonetics. With phonemics, you get an insider's understanding of the language, which in turn enables you to become more aware of the culture in which that language is spoken.

A phoneme is a sound that distinguishes one word from another in a language. A minimal pair is a pair of words in which a difference in sound makes a difference in meaning. The minimal pair *tie* and *die* in English is an example that shows that /t/ and /d/ are two different phonemes of English. It is not possible to predict the distribution, or occurrence, of phonemes in a language.

An allophone is a variant form of a phoneme. Allophones can also be thought of as members of a group of two or more sounds that together form a single phoneme. The distribution of allophones in a language is frequently predictable. Close study of the different allophones of a phoneme can reveal the distribution patterns. For example, in English, aspirated [pʰ] always occurs at the beginnings of words, while unaspirated [p] always occurs in the middles of words, following [s]. Together [pʰ] and [p] form a single phoneme /p/ in English.

A good understanding of phonetics and phonemics is essential; by learning the concepts and analytical techniques, we can more readily understand cultures and languages.

KEY TERMS

acoustic phonetics
affricate
allophones

alveolar
alveopalatal
American Usage System
approximant
articulated
articulatory phonetics
auditory phonetics
bilabial
clicks
complementary distribution
conditioned variation
consonants
descriptive phonetics
diacritics
emics
etics
fricative
glottal
glottis
implosives
interdental
International Phonetic Alphabet (IPA)
labiodental
larynx
lengthening
lungs
manner
minimal pair
nasal
nasalization
palatal
pharyngeal
phonemes
phonemic chart
phonemics
phonetic chart
phonetics
phones
phonology
pitch
place
plosive
retroflex
rounded
segments

stop
supralaryngeal vocal tract
suprasegmentals
tap
trill
uvula
uvular
velar
velum
vocal cords
vocal folds
voiced
voiceless
vowels

FURTHER READING

About Phonetics

Ladefoged, Peter. 2001. *A course in phonetics*. 4th ed. Fort Worth: Harcourt College Publishers. This is a textbook with exercises.

Ladefoged, Peter. 2001. *Vowels and consonants: An introduction to the sounds of languages*. Malden, MA: Blackwell. This textbook includes acoustic as well as articulatory phonetics.

About Phonetic Alphabets

Pullum, Geoffrey, and William A. Ladusaw. 1996. *Phonetic symbol guide*. 2nd ed. Chicago: University of Chicago Press. This fascinating dictionary of symbols, both historic and current, includes the International Phonetic Alphabet, the American Usage system, and more.

International Phonetic Association. 1999. *Handbook of the International Phonetic Association: A guide to the use of the International Phonetic Alphabet*. Cambridge: Cambridge University Press. This book contains the underlying principles of the International Phonetic Alphabet, a guide to phonetic analysis, exercises, illustrations, information about computer fonts and conventions, and other resources.

About Etics and Emics

Headland, Thomas N., Kenneth L. Pike, and Marvin Harris, eds. 1990. *Emics and etics: The insider/outsider debate*. Newbury Park, CA: Sage Publications. This is an interesting book, summing up the debate between Marvin Harris and Kenneth Pike on the meanings and applications of the etic/emic distinction.

Pike, Kenneth L. 1998. A linguistic pilgrimage. In *First person singular III: Autobiographies by North American scholars in the language sciences.* ed. E. F. K. Koerner, 143–58. Studies in the History of the Language Sciences 88. Amsterdam/Philadelphia: John Benjamins. Available at: http://www.sil.org/klp/lingpilg.htm. This is an entertaining autobiographical essay, with humorous insight into the man and his work.

 ## STUDENT ACTIVITIES

Readings

The workbook/reader for this book has readings that can help you to explore phonetic and phonemic analysis in greater depth.

Exercises

A set of exercises in the workbook/reader will give you more practice with phonetic and phonemic analysis.

Web Exercises

The companion website for this book has a series of links designed to help you explore phonetics and phonemics in greater depth. The companion website also contains study questions that will help you to review important concepts.

Guided Projects

If you are creating a new language, you will need to develop a sound system for your language. If you are working with a conversation partner, your instructor may ask you to explore similarities and differences in the sound systems of your two languages. Your instructor will be your guide.

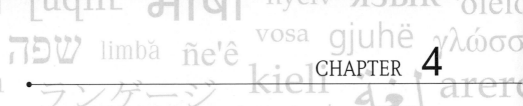

CHAPTER 4

Words and Sentences

In the Field, U Zlatého Zvonu, Praha, February 2001

"Dvě pivo, prosím," I said to the waitress, wanting to try out my Czech.

"Prosím?" she asked, instantly deflating any confidence I might have had.

  "Dvě pivo," I repeated, with a hopeful smile. According to the dictionary, *dvě* was 'two,' *pivo* was 'beer,' and *prosím* was 'please.' What was wrong?

  The waitress calmly surveyed the scene: There were two of us, my husband and I, sitting at the table. We had just rented an apartment across the street and, having finished unpacking for a four-month stay in Prague, we had decided to try the closest restaurant for a meal and a beer. There was a long silence as the waitress looked us over and thought about what to do.

  "Dvě piva!" she finally said with a note of triumph, and as she left to get our two beers I scribbled the plural form for beer into my notebook.

HJO

In the Field, U Zlatého Zvonu, Praha, April 2001

"Šest piva, prosím," I said, as we sat down at our usual table. This time we had four friends with us.

"Prosím?" she asked, and I knew something had gone wrong.
  "Šest piva," I repeated, hopefully.
  *"Šest **piv**,"* said the waitress, and I wondered what I should write in my notebook.

HJO

Whenever we set out to learn a new language we begin by trying to learn some words and some simple sentences. What's the word for X, we want to know. Or how do I say Z? And we generally turn to dictionaries and phrase books for help. My Czech-English dictionary tells me that 'beer' is *pivo*. Not *piva* or *piv* or any other of the forms of *pivo* that I actually encountered in the Czech Republic. My Czech phrase book has a quick list of words I might use in a restaurant. It reminds me that 'beer' is *pivo*, but then it goes on to suggest the mysterious phrase *"Pivo/dvě piva, prosím* (A beer/two beers, please)." It's up to me to figure out that these are actually two different sentences: *Pivo, prosím* '(one) beer, please' and *Dvě piva, prosím* 'two beers, please.' Neither dictionary nor phrase book tells me anything about the way that *piva* '[two?] beers' changes to *piv* '[more than two?] beers.'

Czech speakers in the United States aren't likely to fare much better. English-Czech dictionaries can tell you that 'pivo' is *beer*, but they don't provide any information about alternative forms that might be useful such as *beers* or *beer's*. Phrase books don't generally bother to distinguish between the subtleties of *the beers on the table* and *the beer's on the table*.

Every language has linguistic complexities of this sort. Words change, depending on how they are used. And combining words into sentences often yields unexpected results. So how do anthropologists learn to speak the languages that they need in the field? How, in fact, does *anyone* learn the complexities of a new language? Many of us try to get a head start by taking formal classroom lessons. Classroom lessons give you lots of information in a short time, but it's often difficult to remember all of that information when you need it, when you are actually trying to communicate in a real situation. Before going to Prague, I took two classes in "Survival Czech," but when I actually got to Prague, most of the forms that I encountered were not what I had studied. How were my Czech teachers to know that someday I would need to order six beers?

My experience learning Shinzwani provides an interesting contrast. There were no Shinzwani classes to take before I went to the Comoro Islands, and there were no Shinzwani-English dictionaries or grammars to rely on. All I had were the basic pattern discovery skills that I had learned in linguistic anthropology class. Daily, and at every opportunity, I made lists of words, analyzed their components, and sorted out the ways they combined into sentences. This turned out to be a phenomenally fast way to learn a language. In six weeks I had a basic understanding of word and sentence building in Shinzwani, and by the end of three months I could answer simple questions without having to stop and look everything up in my notebooks. Complex tenses and sentence forms came later, as did the ability to follow philosophical discussions, to appreciate proverbs, and to guess at riddles with some success. Ever since that experience, linguistic anthropology has been my preferred method of learning a new language.

Using linguistic anthropology to learn a new language means learning how to discover and analyze words ("morphology"), and learning how to analyze phrases and sentences ("syntax"). This chapter gives you some insight into how linguistic anthropologists approach morphology and syntax. It also shows you some of the range of patterns and possibilities that different languages use in word and sentence building.

✳ MORPHOLOGY

"What's the word for beer?" the American students ask the Czech Survival Skills teacher. And the Czech student who is teaching the class obligingly tells the students that the word for beer is *pivo*. If you want to order a beer, you say, *"Jedno pivo, prosím* (one beer, please)," and then, because most of us in the class are college students, she tells us how to order another beer: *"Ještě jedno pivo."* My antennae go up immediately. I have already sorted out that *jedno* is 'one,' so how can *ještě jedno* mean 'another'? Doesn't *ještě* mean something like 'again,' or 'additionally,' or something that combines nicely with 'one'? I interrupt to ask about this and discover that I am on the right track. But I have derailed the class; the instructor has a plan for the day, a list of words and phrases to get through, and she would prefer to get back to the lesson she has prepared for tonight's class. My personal exploration of Czech words will have to wait. I will have to analyze Czech morphology another time.

Morphology is the analysis of words and how they are structured. For most speakers, words seem to be the fundamental units of language. When we look things up in a dictionary, we look for words, not pieces of words or collections of words. When we think about translating between languages, we think in terms of words, not phrases. When we begin learning new languages, we memorize words, not parts of words. So it may come as a surprise to learn that words are not the smallest units of meaning in language.

The English word *helper*, for example, can be broken down into smaller units. Each unit has a meaning that contributes to the word: the unit *help* has to do with providing assistance or aid to others and the unit *-er* has to do with the person who performs the action described by the first unit. Together *help* and *-er* combine to create a word describing a person who provides assistance or aid. The Czech word *piva* can probably also be broken down into two units: *piv-* for the liquid we call 'beer' and *-a* to indicate 'two.' Meaningful units such as these are called "morphemes." A **morpheme** is the smallest unit of meaning in a language.

It is important to understand the difference between words and morphemes. A word can include one or more morphemes. The English word *help* is made up of one English morpheme. The English word *helpful* is made up of two English morphemes. There are three English morphemes in the English word *unhelpful*. Finding the morphemes of a language will take you a lot further in your understanding of how the language works than memorizing long lists of words. Once you know how to find morphemes and you understand how they combine in a language, you can begin to build words in that language, and you can analyze and understand new words as well. You'll begin using dictionaries differently, too.

Dictionaries generally give you just the base forms of words. You are more likely to find the word *help* in an English dictionary than the words *helper* or *helpers* or even *helping* or *helped* or *helpful*. This is because it is inefficient to list every word in all of its forms in a dictionary. It is also because dictionary writers assume that you already know something about the language in question. In particular, they assume that you know how to analyze complex words and how to turn simple base forms into more complex ones. That's why my Czech-English dictionary told me only about *pivo* when I looked up 'beer.' It assumed I would know what to do with that information. Of course, most beginning language learners do not have this kind of understanding yet, which is why beginners in a new language often find dictionaries so *unhelpful*. I'll never forget the exasperated expression that one of the other visiting Fulbright professors blurted out after we had finished going through a Czech language orientation class in Prague. The instructor had just finished explaining some of the many complexities of Czech nouns, and my American colleague's response was "So *that's* why you can't find anything in the dictionary!" The fact that most speakers of most languages think in terms of words, and not morphemes, just slows them down and, in the end, frustrates them in their attempt to use dictionaries. It's much faster, and much more effective, to think in terms of morphemes and structure.

Learning to think in terms of morphemes and structure is much more useful for learning a new language than memorizing long lists of words in that language. It can help you to recognize words that you may not have heard before, and it can help you to create new words that you might need. It helps you to use dictionaries more effectively, but it also frees you from dictionaries in ways you probably have never considered. If you know that a *helper* is 'a person who helps,' then you can also guess that a *farmer* is 'a person who farms.' Even if a *fisher* is not exactly the correct word for 'a person who fishes,' it can get your meaning across. Learning another language means learning how to find and use these kinds of structural details. It means learning how to identify and describe morphemes, and how to understand how they are combined and patterned. It means, in other words, learning how to do "morphological analysis."

Morphological Analysis

There are two parts to **morphological analysis:** identifying (and describing) morphemes and analyzing the way morphemes are arranged in words. Identifying and describing morphemes is fairly straightforward (most of the time), so it is a good place to begin. Then we will move on to discussing some of the ways that morphemes can be arranged. Let's begin with identifying morphemes.

Identifying Morphemes   The trick to identifying morphemes in a language is to find the minimal units of meaning. And the trick to finding minimal units of meaning is to compare words or even short phrases that seem to pattern similarly. Here's an example from Shinzwani (with English equivalents) that will give you an idea of how it works:

Shinzwani	*English Equivalent*
hufua	'to work metal'
hujua	'to know'
hulagua	'to speak, talk'
huloa	'to fish'

First of all, you should note that all the items in the first column appear to be single words (*hufua, hujua*), while all the items in the second column contain two or more words ('to work metal,' 'to know'). This should alert you to the fact that many languages do not build words in exactly the same way. Although this seems obvious, it is something that many of us forget when moving between languages.

The next thing to notice is that all the entries in the first column begin with *hu-* (the hyphen indicates that the *hu-* has been removed from the rest of the word and also shows where it was attached) and that all the entries in the second column begin with 'to.' This suggests that *hu-* is a Shinzwani morpheme meaning 'to' in English (at least in the sense of 'to do something'). It should also help you to identify the rest of the Shinzwani morphemes and to establish approximate English equivalents for each one. Your analysis should look like this:

Shinzwani Morpheme	*English Equivalent*
hu-	'to'
-fua	'work metal'
-jua	'know'
-lagua	'speak, talk'
-loa	'fish'

So far, so good. You have identified your first set of morphemes in another language. Furthermore, you can use them to identify additional morphemes in that language. Suppose, for example, I tell you that the Shinzwani word *hulima* means 'to farm' in English. Would you be able to identify the basic Shinzwani morpheme for 'farm'? Or suppose I tell you that the Shinzwani morpheme -*tembea* means 'walk' in English. Would you be able to form the Shinzwani word for 'to walk'? If you guessed that -*lima* is the morpheme for 'farm' and *hutembea* is the word for 'to walk,'

then you are well on your way to understanding how to identify morphemes. Linguistic anthropologists use this kind of analysis to quickly
learn the basics of new languages in the field. You can use the same kind
of analysis to learn any new language.

Let's try identifying some morphemes in English. Here are a few
words to get you started.

farm	farmer	farmers
walk	walker	walkers
work	worker	workers

As before, if you compare the different sets of words, looking for similarities and differences of forms and meanings, you should be able to identify the morphemes. In this case, there are just five morphemes in the nine
words: *farm, walk,* and *work* (all morphemes describing actions), *-er* (a
morpheme meaning 'person who'), and *-s* (a morpheme meaning 'many').
We can list the morphemes as follows:

English Morpheme	*Approximate Meaning*
farm	'the act of farming'
walk	'the act of walking'
work	'the act of working'
-er	'person who'
-s	'many'

As with the Shinzwani examples, you should be able to use these morphemes to identify additional ones in English. If you heard the word
singers, for example, you would be able to identify the morpheme *sing.*
Given the morpheme *read,* you would be able to form the words *reader*
and *readers.*

Recall the three different words for beer that I learned in the restaurant in Prague: *pivo, piva,* and *piv.* Now that we know something about
identifying morphemes we can take another look at them. Here they are,
with the words for 'one,' 'two,' and 'six' included for clarity:

Czech Words	*English Equivalent*
jedno pivo	'one beer'
dvě piva	'two beers'
šest piv	'six beers'

If you look carefully at the three 'beer' words, you should be able to identify a basic morpheme *piv-* (meaning 'beer') and three other morphemes
that can be tacked on to the basic morpheme to indicate (or go with) the
different numbers: *-o* for 'one,' *-a* for 'two,' and *-Ø* (or silence) for 'six.' As
I learned more Czech, I discovered that for talking about beer, *-a* was the
morpheme to use with 'two,' 'three,' and 'four,' and *-Ø* was the morpheme
to use with 'any number higher than four.' I came to think of these three

morphemes as having English equivalents of 'one,' 'two-three-four,' and 'many.' (More about this later.)

Identifying morphemes is an important first step in working with languages. The next step is describing those morphemes. There are several interconnected ways to do this.

Describing Morphemes   Morphemes are generally described in terms of whether they function as "bases" or as "affixes." **Bases** form the foundations of words, and **affixes** attach to bases. In fact, the word "affix" *means* 'attach to.' In the previous Shinzwani examples, the morpheme *-loa* (fish) is a base and the morpheme *hu-* (to) is an affix. In the English examples, the morpheme *sing* is a base and the morphemes *-er* and *-s* are affixes. In the Czech examples, the morpheme *piv-* is a base and the morphemes *-o*, *-a*, and *-Ø* are affixes.

Bases can be additionally categorized into "roots" and "stems," depending on how they function in word building. A **root** is a morpheme (or word) that serves as the underlying foundation for other words. A **stem** is a word (or a collection of morphemes) that is derived from a root and to which additional affixes can be attached. In the English word *farmers,* the word *farmer* is a stem built from the root morpheme *farm* and the affix *-er.* The fact that we can add *another* affix *-s* to the word *farmer* confirms that *farmer* is a stem, even though we also consider it to be an independent word. Stems can be composed of as many morphemes as a language permits as long as additional affixes can be attached. Figure 4.1 shows the relationship among roots, stems, bases, and affixes.

You have probably noticed that English bases tend to stand alone as individual words (*fish, farm, farmer*), while Shinzwani bases do not (*-loa, -lima*). You have probably also noticed that affixes can never stand alone; they always need (by definition) to be attached to other morphemes. Morphemes that can stand alone are called **free morphemes.** Morphemes that must be attached to other morphemes are called **bound morphemes.** If you know how a language tends to use morphemes in the word-building process, then you will have a better idea of how to learn words in that language. You will know whether words can be analyzed into smaller pieces

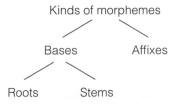

FIGURE 4.1   Kinds of morphemes: roots, stems, bases, and affixes

and, if so, you will know how to build new words. You will know how to find words in dictionaries. You will even have a good idea of how to enter words into a dictionary if you are constructing one. Even though all Shinzwani verbs start with *hu-* for example, would you want to fill up the H section of the dictionary with verbs?

For a while, it was popular to describe languages in terms of whether they used primarily bound morphemes (like Shinzwani), combinations of bound and free morphemes (like English), or primarily free morphemes (like Chinese). Such languages were called agglutinating, inflectional, or isolating. These descriptions were thought to be useful in determining relationships between languages, but in fact most languages use varying combinations of these methods for building words. What is most important, from the standpoint of learning new languages, whether for fieldwork or for tourism, is that, if you can identify and describe the different kinds of morphemes in a language, then you have a good head start on learning and using that language. The next thing you will need to know in order to begin using a language effectively is how to arrange those morphemes into words and sentences.

How Morphemes Are Arranged

It's important to understand some of the ways that morphemes can be arranged to build words. Knowing that English has the morphemes *help, ful,* and *un,* for example, doesn't tell you enough about what to do with those morphemes. Is *unhelpful* the only word you can build with those morphemes? Is *helpfulun* an okay construction? What about *unfulhelp?* Granted, your initial experience in a new language will give you some ideas about arranging morphemes, but proceeding wholly by trial and error can lead you into some glaring errors, especially if you are working in a language that uses different patterns for arranging morphemes than the one(s) that you grew up with. It is better to learn a little about the range of possibilities that linguistic anthropologists have discovered for arranging morphemes so you will be better prepared to decode a new language. There are two interrelated aspects of morpheme arrangement: order and placement of affixes, and derivation and inflection.

Order and Placement of Affixes   Affixes are categorized by where they attach to base morphemes. For English, this is pretty straightforward. Affixes attach either at the beginnings (*un+leash*) or at the ends (*leash+ed*) of base forms. They can attach to roots (*help+s, help+er, help+ful*) or they can attach to stems (*helper+s, helpful+ly, un+helpful*). Other possibilities exist, however. Let's take a moment to survey some of the range of possible ways that affixes can attach to bases.

Prefixes are bound morphemes which attach at the beginnings of base forms. An example from English is the *un-* of **unhelpful;** an example from Shinzwani is the *hu-* that serves to mark the infinitive form of a verb (for example, *huloa* 'to fish').

Suffixes are bound morphemes that attach at the ends of base forms. Examples from English include the *-s* of *hats,* the *-ing* of *singing,* the *-er* of *helper,* and so on. The *-a* at the end of the Czech word *piva* 'two-three-four beers' is also a suffix.

Infixes are morphemes that are inserted into the middle of base forms. Infixes are rare in English, but one good example of something that probably qualifies is the word *bloody* (as in *absobloodylutely*). An example from Shinzwani is the infixation of the reflexive morpheme *-dji-* 'to do something to oneself' into a verb such as *huona* 'to see' to produce the word *hudjiona* 'to be conceited.'

Circumfixes are morphemes that attach simultaneously to both beginnings and ends of base forms. The *m-* . . . *-zi* that builds the Shinzwani word *mlozi* 'fisherman' from *-loa* 'fish' might be considered a circumfix. The French negative *ne . . . pas* is a little like a circumfix because it surrounds whatever verb it is negating (*Je ne vois pas* 'I don't see'). Muskogean languages also use circumfixes to form negatives, so that you have forms such as *chokma* 'he is good' and *ikchokmo* 'he is **not** good,' *palli* 'it is hot' and *ikpallo* 'it is **not** hot' (James Flanagan, personal communication).

Reduplication is a process that creates an affix from part of an existing base form and then attaches that affix to the base form. Reduplicated bits can be prefixed, suffixed, or infixed. In Shinzwani, reduplication of an entire base form confers intensity: If *mpole* means 'slowly,' then *mpolempole* means 'extra slowly' (or 'very carefully'). In this case, you can't really tell if the reduplicated unit has been prefixed or suffixed to the base form. Another example, from Samoan, is the formation of the word *mananao* 'they wish' from the base form *manao* 'he wishes' by reduplicating the next to last syllable of the base form (in this case, *-na-*) and then infixing it into the base form right before the last vowel of the word.

Interweaving is a process in which morphemes are interspersed within base forms. Semitic languages, such as Arabic and Hebrew use this process. The Arabic base form *ktb* 'having to do with writing' is a good example. Weaving *-i-aa-* into this basic root creates *kitaab* 'book,' weaving in *-aa-i-* creates *kaatib* 'writer,' weaving in *-u-u-ii* creates *kutubii* 'bookseller,' weaving in *ma-a-a* creates *maktaba* 'library,' and so on.

Portmanteau [pronounced port-man-toe] is a process in which morphemes blend into one another. Examples include the blending of *smoke* and *fog* into *smog* in English and the blending of *de* 'of' and *le* 'the' into *du* in French. A relatively new example in English is the blending of *web* and *log* into *blog* 'an entry in a log, or diary, that one constructs and publishes on the World Wide Web.'

Hierarchy   You should also note that every language has a specific *order* in which affixes can be attached. Nowadays, this is referred to as **hierarchy.** Knowing the hierarchical relationship among the affixes of a language will keep you from attaching morphemes in the wrong order and creating bizarre words. In English, suffixes are generally added before prefixes. You need to create *helpful* before you can create *unhelpful,* for example. If you add the prefix first, creating the word *unhelp,* it will sound weird to a native English speaker. Also in English, first you "derive" words and then you "inflect" them: *help+er+s,* not *help+s+er.* In most cases, if a language has a particular hierarchy you will encounter it as you learn about derivations. If the hierarchy is not immediately obvious to you, you can experiment a bit, trying different combinations of affixes to see which ones work and which ones get laughed at or corrected for you.

Derivation and Inflection   **Derivation** is the process of creating new words. **Inflection** is the process of modifying existing words. How do you know if you have a new word or just a modification of an existing one? By knowing something about the grammatical category of the word. Essentially this means that words that are used in the same way in a language belong to the same categories. As before, when we were learning to identify morphemes, you can identify categories of words by examining examples. Let's use English.

the cat in the hat   the cats in the hat
the cat in the chair   the cats in the chair
the cat in the basket   the cats in the basket

Comparing these two columns, we can see that *hat, chair,* and *basket* all can be used in the same spot in the phrase *the cat in the ___.* We can therefore say that all three of these words belong to the same category of word. Other words that can fit into the same slot should also belong to that category of word. So if I can say *the cat in the bed,* then *bed* also belongs to this category. Likewise for *car, garden,* and so on.

We can also see that it is possible to substitute *cats* for *cat* in phrases such as *the ___ in the hat* or *the ___ in the chair.* This means that *cat* and *cats* are both words in the same category. If we hear the phrase *the dog in the basket,* we could probably guess that *the dogs in the basket* would also be an acceptable phrase. On the other hand, if we learn that it is not correct in English to say *the **catty** in the chair,* then we have to guess that *catty* is a different category of word than *cat* even though both words seem to share a common root.

The important concepts here are categories and roots. If *cat* and *cats* are related by sharing the same root and both words are in the same category, then we can say that *cats* is "inflected" from *cat*. The word *cat* has been modified, or inflected, to form the related word *cats*. On the other hand, the words *cat* and *catty* are also related, sharing the same root, but these two words are in different categories. This means that the word *catty* is "derived" from the word *cat*. The word *cat* has been used to create, or derive the new word *catty*.

Knowing these basic processes of word formation and applying them to the language-learning process, enables you build (and unbuild) words far more rapidly than memorizing lists of words. It also helps you to find your way through bilingual dictionaries more smoothly. But you have to remember that different languages use affixes differently, inflect and derive words differently, and may even define word categories differently. Knowing about some kinds of patterns can help you to prepare for others. The workbook/reader gives you some practice with the range of possibilities; there you will find exercises for identifying morphemes, defining them, and seeing how they work together to build different kinds of words and word classes.

Allomorphs Suppose you decide to plunge into a language, identify some of its morphemes, work out the patterns by which they are connected, and begin trying to use what you know? And suppose you begin with Shinzwani nouns. Quite often it is nouns that most of us start with when we begin to orient ourselves in a new language. They seem fairly concrete, we can point to the things they describe, and sometimes we can even pick them up and turn them over. In short, we just generally tend to feel more comfortable with learning nouns first. Here's what you are likely to find when you look at Shinzwani nouns.

shiri	'chair'	ziri	'chairs'
shisahani	'plate'	zisahani	'plates'
shikombe	'cup'	zikombe	'cups'
muhono	'arm'	mihono	'arms'
mundru	'leg'	mindru	'legs'

What's going on here? Different prefixes for both singular and plural? Okay. But two different prefixes for singular and two more prefixes for plural? Something else is happening, and we need to sort it out. Let's begin by making a list of the prefixes and their meanings and the words they go with.

{singular}	shi-	used with -ri, -sahani, -kombe
	mu-	used with -hono, -ndru
{plural}	zi-	used with -ri, -sahani, -kombe
	mi-	used with -hono, -ndru

This is helpful, and it should allow us to predict additional plural forms if we hear the singular forms. What's the plural of *shio* 'book,' for example? It should be *zio*, and it is. What's the singular of *miji* 'town'? If you guessed *muji*, you're correct.

But we still have a dilemma. It looks like we have two morphemes for singular in Shinzwani and two morphemes for plural. In fact, what we really have is two variations of the morpheme for singular and two variations of the morpheme for plural. Variations like this are called "allomorphs." An **allomorph** is a variant form of a morpheme. Sometimes allomorphs are predictable; sometimes they are not. In this case, given this limited data, it is tempting to propose that the *shi-* allomorph is used with "useful things," while the *mu-* allomorph is used with body parts. The Shinzwani words *shitswa* 'head' and *muji* 'town,' however, provide exceptions. Still, we have found a pattern by which we can begin to guess at how Shinzwani nouns are inflected for singular and plural.

Here's another example, using English words. In this case there are three different allomorphs of the English morpheme {not}. See if you can describe how to predict which one occurs where.

improbable	illegal	indescribable
impossible	illegitimate	intolerant
implacable	illogical	insensitive

If you sound out these words you will see (and hear) that each variant seems to "go with" a particular kind of sound. The *im-* variant goes with words that begin with [p], the *il-* variant goes with words that begin with [l], and the *in-* variant goes with words that begin with [d], [t], and [s]. In fact, if you think about it, you should notice that each allomorph seems to match up with sounds that are similar (or even identical) to it: [m] and [p] are alike in that both are pronounced with the lips; [n], [d], [t], and [s] are all pronounced with the tip of the tongue a bit behind the upper teeth. We can write this as follows:

{negative}	im-	used with words that begin with [p]
	il-	used with words that begin with [l]
	in-	used with words that begin with [d], [t], or [s]

With this information we should be able to correctly predict the English word for 'not personal.' If you thought of *impersonal*, then you can see how smoothly this works. As with the Shinzwani examples, there are exceptions, but you can see how memorizing a pattern like this, for creating 'not __' from almost any word, gives you the potential for producing lots and lots of new words in a language. Or for explaining the process to someone who is trying to learn your language. The workbook/reader gives you more practice with finding predictable patterns in allomorphs.

Of course, a word in one language might contain enough ideas to translate as a collection of words in another. If you remember the Shin-

Doing Linguistic Anthropology 4.1

ARABIC WORDS FOR 'THE'

One of the first things I noticed when I began learning Arabic was that there were different words for the English 'the.' Or perhaps the Arabic word for 'the' just had a lot of different forms and I didn't understand the pattern. Sometimes I heard *al* and sometimes I heard *as* or *ash*. Sometimes I even heard *at* and *ar* and *ad*. '**The** book,' for example, was *al-kitabu*, but '**the** journey' was *as-safaru*. *Ash-shams* was '**the** sun,' *at-taqs* was '**the** weather,' *ar-rabi* meant '**the** springtime,' and *ad-din* meant '**the** judgment.' It certainly was confusing. The teacher said that it all depended on how the word began. If a word began with something called a "sun" letter, then that letter would double and the *l* would disappear. If a word began with a "moon" letter, then the *l* would be pronounced. Someone in the class asked how you would know which letters were "sun" or "moon" letters, and the teacher said we would just have to memorize them. As usual I started looking for patterns.

It turned out that "sun" letters are those that you say with the tip of your tongue at or near your alveolar ridge, the gum ridge just behind your teeth. They include sounds like *t, d, s, sh,* and even *r*. Most of the other letters are "moon" letters: some in the front of your mouth, like *m* and *b,* and some in the back of your mouth, like *k, g,* and *q* (see Doing Linguistic Anthropology 3.2: Sun and Moon Consonants in Arabic). This made it much easier to remember which version of the word 'the' to use with which word. It's a nice example of how sounds, words, and grammar can all be interwoven with each other. It's also a nice example of how even though we are able to speak a language fluently we don't often know the linguistic terminology to describe how it works.

HJO

zwani words *huloa* 'to fish,' *hulagua* 'to talk,' and *hufua* 'to work metal' that we described earlier, you probably also remember that each Shinzwani word seemed equivalent to at least two English words. This is an important point. It reminds us that different languages mark the boundaries between words and phrases differently. The Shinzwani word *hutsohoa* is equivalent to a fairly lengthy phrase in English 'to collect clams on the beach at low tide' and the Shinzwani word *nitsoloa* is equivalent to an entire English sentence 'I will go fishing.' Although we normally think of working with words as morphology and working with phrases as syntax, it is important to remember that the boundary between morphology and syntax is not as clear as we might like. This is one reason why the subjects of morphology and syntax are best learned as a unit.

❈ SYNTAX

Time flies like an arrow. Fruit flies like a banana.   ATTRIBUTED TO GROUCHO MARX

Knowing about word formation in a language does not automatically tell you how to arrange words into sentences. Sometimes there are surprising differences in the ways that different languages arrange words. And sometimes there are surprising results that you can get just by arranging different words in the same way. **Syntax** is the area of linguistic anthropology that examines and describes the ways that words are arranged into phrases and sentences. Syntax provides the means by which you can learn to arrange words into sentences. And syntax can help to explain why some sentences can look the same but actually be quite different, like the two sentences with which we started this section.

Syntactic Analysis

One of the most productive ways to learn the syntax of a new language is to identify the kinds of "substitution frames" that the language uses. **Substitution frames** are grammatical frames into which you can place related words. In our previous examples of *the cat in the hat/chair/basket*, we were using a substitution frame (*the cat in the* ____), where *hat, chair,* and *basket* were three related words that could all go into the same slot (indicated in this example with an underline, ____). This English phrase contains a number of different substitution frames:

the cat in the hat
the rat in the hat
the dog in the hat
the person in the hat

the cat in the hat
the cat on the hat
the cat under the hat
the cat behind the hat

the cat in the hat
the cat in a hat
a cat in a hat
a cat in the hat

And so on. Each substitution frame that we can find in a language tells us something about the syntax of that language. It tells us first of all about the different grammatical categories that exist in the language. In the case of English, it tells us that *cat, rat, dog,* and *person* are words that fit into a specific grammatical category. It also tells us that *in, on, under,* and *behind* are words that fit into a specific grammatical category. For ease of reference, it is useful to label the different categories that we find. It is easier to say "nouns," for example, than "the cat/rat/dog/person category." Or to say "prepositions" rather than "the in/on/under/behind category." This way, when we find more words that fit into a particular category, we can just use the appropriate label. If we find that we can say *the mouse in the hat* we can add *mouse* to our list of nouns.

We can also note the way that the substitution frames themselves are arranged. In the previous examples, we note that there is a specific order to the frames. First we have the "the/a" category (determiners), then we have the "noun" category, then we have the "preposition" category, then another "determiners" category, and finally the "hat/chair/basket" category. This last category is traditionally also called nouns, and this should make us stop and analyze our examples a bit more deeply. If the "cat/rat/dog/person" category is a noun category and so is "hat/chair/basket" category, then can any of these nouns substitute for any other? Can we say *the chair on the cat,* for example? Or *the basket in the person?* No, we can't, so we need to label the two kinds of "nouns" in some way to indicate the difference between them. In this case, we will label the "cat/rat/dog/person" set of nouns "subject nouns," and the "hat/chair/basket" set of nouns "object nouns." (We will ignore, for the moment, the fact that we can say *the hat in the basket.*)

Learning the different kinds of substitution frames that a language allows, along with the categories of words that can go into each, is one good way of learning a language, especially if you find yourself in a situation where no one speaks any of the languages that you know and you don't speak any of theirs. This is a situation that linguistic anthropologists often find themselves in, and spending some of your time finding and testing substitution frames and word categories is a great way to build vocabulary and learn sentence construction. Of course, you can get into interesting kinds of trouble by following this technique. I am reminded of the time that my husband and I were learning the words for different body parts in Shingazidja, one of the languages of the Comoro Islands. Two young men in the post office next to our apartment were helping us, and in this monolingual situation we were grateful for the fact that they had picked up on the idea of substitution frames so quickly. Here are some of the data they gave us:

Ngamina hitswa	'I have a head'
Ngamina mpua	'I have a nose'
Ngamina kio	'I have an ear'
Ngamina makio	'I have ears'
Ngamina muhono	'I have a hand/arm'

Ngamina mihono	'I have hands/arms'
Ngamina mundru	'I have a leg/foot'
Ngamina mindru	'I have legs/feet'

From these examples, we could tell we were going to have an interesting time of sorting out singular and plural nouns. But that's not the trouble I am referring to. Somewhere along the line, these charming young men decided to use words for body parts that were not so visible. Perhaps it was the procedure we had adopted that inspired them. One of them would introduce a new body part with the substitution frame *ngamina* ____, then my husband would repeat the phrase, and then I would repeat the phrase; and after our instructors had nodded their approval I would write each new word in my notebook. I knew we were in trouble when they started giggling at my husband's response to one of their body part words. Not sure what to do, I decided to try repeating the word as well; they were certainly encouraging me to do so, and a bit more energetically than with the other words. When my attempt was greeted with loud guffaws I had a pretty good idea of what to write in my notebook—something my husband had and I did not!

Using Substitution Frames to Learn Syntax In spite of these kinds of difficulties, linguistic anthropologists have used the concept of substitution frames with great success to begin learning the syntax of new languages. It's an important and useful technique to know and can be applied to any language. It is especially useful if you don't know anything at all about a language. As with discovering words and morphemes, you need to let the language be your guide. Different languages may have very different substitution frames, and they may arrange them in ways that you are not prepared for. It is better, in such cases, to keep an open mind, and to not rush into labeling the substitution frames too quickly. The following example from Shinzwani should give you an idea of the complexities that can be involved.

Nikushiona shiri shangu	'I see my chair'
Nikushiona shisahani shangu	'I see my plate'
Nikushiona shikombe shangu	'I see my cup'
Nikuziona ziri zangu	'I see my chairs'
Nikuziona zisahani zangu	'I see my plates'
Nikuziona zikombe zangu	'I see my cups'
Nikuuona muhono wangu	'I see my arm/hand'
Nikuuona mundru wangu	'I see my leg/foot'
Nikuyaona mihono yangu	'I see my arms/hands'
Nikuyaona mindru yangu	'I see my legs/feet'

We can analyze these Shinzwani substitution frames on two different levels: the level of words and the level of morphemes. Let's begin by looking at the words. Here the substitution frames appear to be "verb" ('I see . . .'), then "object noun" ('chair(s)/plate(s)/cup(s)/arm(s)/leg(s)'), and finally "possessive pronoun" ('my'). At the morpheme level, however, it is clear that there are some interestingly interrelated substitution frames. If you look at how the middle of the verb changes (*nikushiona* vs. *nikuziona* vs. *nikuuona* vs. *nikuyaona*) and you note that it changes depending on how the object noun changes (*shiri* vs. *ziri* vs. **muhono** vs. *mihono*), then you can see that it makes sense to guess that there is a substitution frame in the middle of the verb which is used for matching up with "object pronoun." Likewise, if you look at how the beginnings of the possessive pronouns change, depending on which noun is being possessed, then you can see that there is probably a substitution frame there as well (*shiri shangu, ziri zangu, muhono wangu, mihono yangu*). It is more difficult to give this one an English label because English doesn't have any substitution frames like this. Perhaps we can call it "noun class agreement," and perhaps we can use the same concept to describe the possessive pronoun prefix *and* the object pronoun infix (in the verb).

One of the interesting things about Shinzwani is the way that the different frames relate to one another. If you are going to use a specific noun in a Shinzwani sentence, then there are important grammatical implications for the rest of the sentence. If you choose *shiri* 'chair,' for example, then the *shi-* morpheme that marks the word *shiri* as a singular word will need to be infixed into the verb phrase *nikushiona* 'I see **it**,' and a part of the *shi-* morpheme will also need to be prefixed onto the possessive pronoun *shangu* 'my.' Likewise, if you choose *ziri* 'chairs,' then the *zi-* morpheme that marks *ziri* 'chairs' as a plural word will need to be infixed into the verb phrase *nikuziona* 'I see **them**' and prefixed (at least in part) onto the possessive pronoun *zangu* 'my.' You can also see how it is not so easy to translate words, or even phrases, between languages. How would you translate *shangu* and *zangu* into English? The English word *my* doesn't quite give you enough information; you would want to know 'my *what?*' before you could make a good translation. Likewise, how would you translate the English word *my* into Shinzwani? Again, 'my *what?*' will make a difference. You can also see that if you are trying to learn Shinzwani, you will miss some important grammatical categories if you just stick to looking for standard English categories. You will have much more success if you let Shinzwani itself be your guide.

This brings us back to my difficulties with the Czech words for 'beer.' It turns out that Czech has three different subcategories for nouns. Just like Shinzwani seems to have a subcategory for nouns beginning with *shi-/zi-* and another for nouns beginning with *mu-/mi,* Czech has one subcategory for words ending in *-o,* another for words ending in *-a,* and another for words ending in consonants. In both languages, the different categories are described as "grammatical genders." **Grammatical genders** are different categories into which words (usually nouns) are classified in a language. There are at least eight different genders for Shinzwani nouns, including "useful things," "body parts," "human beings," and more. The three different genders in Czech are called "neuter," "feminine," and "masculine." As with Shinzwani, each Czech word makes its singular and plural differently, depending on its grammatical gender. Czech *pivo* 'beer' is neuter, and neuter words in Czech that end in *–o* make their plurals by substituting an *-a* for the final *-o* of the singular.

Masculine		*Feminine*		*Neuter*	
čaj	'tea'	káva	'coffee'	pivo	'beer'
čaje	'teas'	kávy	'coffees'	piva	'beers'
sýr	'cheese'	houska	'roll'	město	'town'
sýry	'cheeses'	housky	'rolls'	města	'towns'
citrón	'lemon'	voda	'water'	maso	'meat'
citróny	'lemons'	vody	'waters'	masa	'meats'

In addition to grammatical gender, Czech has another interesting phenomenon, which complicates the picture a bit. Nouns in Czech may change depending on whether they function as subjects or objects in a sentence. If a word is the *subject* of the sentence, for example, and you are saying something like 'the beer/coffee/tea is on the table,' then you are fine using the forms listed above. If, however, the word is the *object* of the sentence ('I want (a) beer/coffee/tea' or 'I see (the) beer/coffee/tea' or 'Please drink (the) beer/coffee/tea'), then you may need to use a different form for those words. Finally, if you want to talk about some characteristic quality of the word ('the beer's/coffee's/tea's taste') or about some quantity of the word ('how much beer/coffee/tea?' or 'liters of beer/coffee/tea'), then you may need yet a different form for the word. This phenomenon is known as **case,** and there are seven different cases in Czech. The three that we have been talking about here are called nominative, accusative, and genitive.

	Nominative		*Accusative*		*Genitive*	
sing.	čaj	'tea'	čaj	'(drink) tea'	čaje	'(how much) tea?'
	káva	'coffee'	kávu	'(drink) coffee'	kávy	'(how much) coffee?'
	pivo	'beer'	pivo	'(drink) beer'	piva	'(how much) beer?'
pl.	čaje	'teas'	čaje	'(drink) teas'	čajů	'(how many) teas?'
	kávy	'coffees'	kávy	'(drink) coffees'	káv	'(how many) coffees'
	piva	'beers'	piva	'(drink) beers'	piv	'(how many) beers?'

So as it turns out, when I said *Dvě piva, prosím* I wasn't asking simply for 'two beers'; rather, I was asking for 'two (direct object of the sentence) beers.' Furthermore, when you want to talk about five or more of anything in Czech, you need to use the genitive case; that is why for six beers I needed to say *šest piv.* Given this knowledge of Czech substitution frames, and of the different categories of nouns that fit into each one, you should be able to predict how to ask for 'six teas.' If you guessed *šest čajů*, then you are beginning to understand how to play with grammatical categories in another language. Even if we can't explain *why* these categories exist, we can learn to identify them and use them correctly. And we can get into a new language a bit more quickly.

There is a little bit of grammatical case in English. It is apparently left over from a much more complex set of cases that existed in earlier versions of English. You can see it in the differences among words like *I*, *me*, *my*, and *mine*. *I* is a word that you use in the subject slot in a sentence (*I am here; I see you*), *me* is a word that you use in the object slot in a sentence (*You see me; Give it to me*), and *my* and *mine* are words that you use with possessives (*My book is on the table; This is my book; It is mine*).

Obligatory Categories One of the most interesting things about grammatical categories, from the standpoint of linguistic anthropology, is what they may reflect about the thought processes of the people who use them. If case exists for nouns in Czech but not for nouns in English, do Czech speakers think about the world a little differently than non-Czech speakers? If singulars and plurals are constructed differently in Shinzwani and English, do English and Shinzwani speakers think about those categories differently? Is there a difference, for example, in thinking about 'cups' in Shinzwani and English? In English the singular word *cup* seems to be a base form, while the plural form *cups* seems to be derived from the singular. In Shinzwani both the singular *shikombe* and the plural *zikombe* seem to be derived from some other base form (*-kombe*, perhaps). Grammatical categories that *must* be expressed in speaking are called **obligatory categories.**

It's not clear whether, or how much, obligatory grammatical categories affect our perception of the world, but in some languages you *have* to indicate whether an item is singular or plural, and in some languages you don't; in some languages you *have* to indicate whether an item is masculine, feminine, or neuter, and in some languages you don't; and in some languages you *have* to indicate whether an item is the subject, direct object, or indirect object of the sentence, and in some languages you don't.

For anthropologists, as well as for the rest of us, it is certainly intriguing to wonder about the differences between such languages. I know that some of my difficulty in learning Czech was because I didn't yet know how to *think* in terms of different grammatical cases. And one of the difficulties that American students seem to have with learning French or Spanish is the fact that they are not used to thinking in terms of the grammatical category of gender. I know that one of my Chinese friends has difficulty remembering whether to use the English word *he* or *she* when talking about people, and this makes me wonder about the differences in obligatory categories between Chinese and English. I do know that the more languages I learn, the more ways I learn to think about—as well as talk about—the world.

How Syntactic Units Are Arranged

It's not enough just to identify and describe the substitution frames of a language. You also need to know which ones you can use in which parts of a sentence. French and English both have substitution frames that can be described as "nouns" and "adjectives," for example, but in French the "nouns" typically come first (*chapeau rouge* 'hat red'), while in English the "adjectives" typically come first (*red hat*). In addition, there are restrictions, such as those we hinted at earlier, on which words can be used in which frames. Although both *cat* and *hat* are English nouns, we can't use them in every noun slot in the English phrase *the* noun *in the* noun. We can't, for example, say *the hat in the cat* (unless we know that the cat has just eaten a hat!). English also restricts the ways that certain nouns and verbs go together. Even though *steep, roast, pee,* and *explode* are all English verbs, we can't use them freely in any verb slot. It's okay to *steep a pot of tea,* but it's not okay to *steep a pot of coffee,* for example. You can *roast a chicken,* but you can't *roast a cake.* My cat can *pee on the rug,* but she can't *explode on the rug.* Restrictions such as these are present in every language. In Shinzwani, for example, *hufua nguo* means 'to **wash** clothing,' but *huosa zisahani* means 'to **wash** dishes.' In German, there are two words for 'to go,' one (*gehen*) meaning 'to go by foot,' and the other (*fahren*) meaning 'to go by vehicle (train, car).' Whether it is a matter of sorting out which words can go with which other ones, or one of figuring out the correct order for the different kinds of words (or grammatical categories), the important thing is to be prepared for different patterns in different languages.

Every language seems to have substitution frames for subjects, objects, and verbs, but not all languages arrange those three possible frames in the same order. The vast majority of languages put the subject (S) before the object (O) in a sentence. Examples of SVO languages include English, French, Russian, Swahili, and Thai. Examples of SOV languages include Inuit, Japanese, Persian (Farsi), Quechua, and Turkish. Examples of VSO languages include Classical Arabic, Biblical Hebrew, Irish, and Tagalog. The other three possible combinations, where the object appears before the subject, are much less common but examples of each do exist. VOS languages include Cakchiquel (spoken in Guatemala), Coeur d'Alene (Idaho), Huave (Mexico), and Malagasy. OVS languages include Apalai (Brazil), Barasano (Columbia), and Panare (Venezuela). OSV languages include Apurinã and Xavante (Brazil). Some languages use more than one pattern; German, for example uses mostly SOV, but you can also find some SVO phrases in German. The point is that, if you can identify the basic sentence pattern of a language, then you will have a good sense of how to form most of the sentences of that language.

Doing Linguistic Anthropology 4.2

ANYMORE

Sometimes there are different patterns in different varieties of the same language. Some years ago, Judy Pine (one of my undergraduate students) and I were attending a conference devoted to African linguistics. We were presenting a paper about the work we were doing on Shinzwani. At one of the evening gatherings, the conversation turned to English syntax and, in particular, to some of the more "unusual" syntactic constructions that folks had heard of recently.

"*Anymore*," said one of the linguists. "Has anyone heard any examples of putting *anymore* at the beginning of sentences (instead of at the end)?"

"Sure," said Judy, "that's easy: *Anymore I don't eat pizza, Anymore I like to run in the evenings.* I know it's common in Kansas, but I don't know how much more widely it's distributed." The linguists asked for more examples, so Judy obliged, creating *anymore* phrases, until everyone was satisfied that the construction was stable. Then the conversation moved on to other things.

I reminded Judy of this story recently. Judy has her Ph.D. and is teaching linguistic anthropology now. While I was editing this chapter, she sent me the following email: "Hi! Thought of you the other day when I was ordering coffee from the stand right next to my classroom at the community college. I was describing what [my daughter] Elizabeth was wearing (a pink and red combination, which was eye-catching at any rate), and said, *It's better than my dressing her, but anymore she won't let me do that (anyway).* I realized what I'd said and scribbled a field note on the back of an old check stub, the only paper I could find in my bag at that moment. Now I can recycle that bit of paper. . . ." Not only is this a stable syntactic construction, but anymore I find myself using it too, especially in Kansas.

HJO

In addition, you may also have some clues about other aspects of the language. For example, most VO languages (SVO, VSO, and VOS) tend to put auxiliary verbs *before* main verbs, to put adverbs *after* verbs, and to put prepositions *before* nouns. OV languages, on the other hand, (SOV, OSV, and OVS) tend to do the opposite. English, an SVO language, tends to have prepositions, while Japanese, an SOV language, tends to have postpositions (i.e., morphemes marking place, like 'in,' 'on,' 'beneath,' and 'above' follow the noun). Even this is not a hard and fast rule; Shinzwani, an SVO language (like English), generally uses postpositions (*mezajuu* 'on the table') rather than prepositions. Still, knowing something about the overall tendencies of different kinds of languages is useful if you are trying to learn and describe a language that is new to you. Knowing whether you are working with an OV language or a VO language can alert you to expect certain kinds of tendencies and move you along faster in the language-learning process.

Ambiguities and Other Difficulties

Even if you have identified and described all of the substitution frames, and you have described the general order in which they seem to occur and the restrictions that seem to apply, you may encounter some phrases that are difficult to decode for other reasons. Sentences such as *fruit flies like a banana* or *cow kills farmer with ax* present special challenges to native speakers as well as to language learners. The problem here is that although we think we can recognize the substitution frames in these sentences, in fact there are generally at least two different sets of substitution frames that are possible for each one. In *fruit flies like a banana,* it is possible to think of the word *flies* as either a verb (as in *time flies, the bird flies, the airplane flies*) or as a noun with a modifier (as in *fruit flies, black flies, green flies, biting flies*). Depending on which kind of substitution frame you choose, the interpretation of the sentence is different: if *flies* is a verb, then fruit actually can take off and fly, and we have to think that its method of flight (or perhaps its flight path) might resemble that of a banana (how does a banana fly, anyway?); but if *flies* is a noun, then we are more likely to think that the insects that we call flies like (or enjoy eating) a banana. Every language probably has interesting ambiguities like this, and finding and playing with them can be a source of amusement for native speakers, even though they may be a frustration for new learners.

As you can see, describing the grammar (or the morphology and syntax) of a language can be a complex task. In part, this is because language is a living thing, spoken by real people, rather than a set of word lists and grammar rules that you can learn from a book. Besides, even if you were to memorize an entire dictionary and grammar for a language, you would be stuck just as soon as you heard a new word or construction. I was a bit stuck, for example, when one of my sons began telling me about his *blogs* one day. As I listened to him describe how much he enjoyed *blogging* and how he was in touch with other *bloggers,* it became clear to me that he was talking about an activity and not a disease or a new kind of pet. After a little bit of linguistic anthropological "fieldwork," I discovered the new (to me) set of activities surrounding the creation of *web logs,* or *blogs,* daily entries into a log published on a personal website.

Just as words change in a language, so do the arrangements of substitution frames. A few years ago, one of the office cleaners in my building asked me if my office "needed swept." Before I could answer, I was sidetracked by the new (to me) linguistic construction. What had happened to the *to be* that I was used to hearing in between *needed* and *swept?* Was I in the middle of a linguistic shift? Or was this just a personal play with words that the office cleaner was using? During the next few months, I paid special attention to the *way* the people around me were speaking, and I soon became convinced that a completely new grammatical pattern—one with no *to be* substitution frame in it—had become common in my part of Kansas. Instead of *the dishes need to be washed,* I now regularly hear *the dishes need washed;* instead of *the bed needs to be made,* I hear *the bed needs made.* The fact that language continues to change like this makes it an intriguing challenge to learn and to describe. We talk more about language change in Chapter 9. For the moment, it's important to remember that a description of a language is like a snapshot: It is taken at a particular moment, and it records the language at that particular moment. A snapshot taken a year later may show a slightly different picture of the language.

Kinds of Grammars

Up until the beginning of the nineteenth century, most grammars were "prescriptive." **Prescriptive grammars** are designed to serve as models of proper speech. They tell you how you *should* speak. They determine what is "good" grammar and what is "bad" grammar. From early Sanskrit, Greek, and Latin grammars through medieval Arabic grammars, the tendency was to produce prescriptive grammars. Once a language was analyzed and the structure was made explicit, students and teachers could follow the rules to produce correct sentences. Early grammars of English also took this approach, but with a slight difference. They used Latin grammars as models for English grammars and established English rules based on Latin patterns. The fact that you can't split infinitives in Latin, for example, led to the development of a rule against splitting infinitives in English. (Infinitives are those verb forms that, in English, start with the word "*to*" such as *to be* and *to go*.) The Star Trek phrase, "To boldly go . . . ," is considered "bad" grammar according to this rule, even though splitting infinitives has a long history of acceptance and use in written and spoken English.

The limitations of prescriptive grammars became apparent in the 1700s and 1800s as Europeans began exploring the rest of the world and encountering new (to them) languages and cultures. Most of the individuals who tried to learn or describe these new languages did so by trying to find the patterns that best fit either Latin (the standard model of the time) or the grammars of their own languages. How, for example, do you form the pluperfect in this language, the French explorers wanted to know. Or how do you form superlatives (e.g., *good, better, best*), the English explorers wanted to know. But just as English did not fit well into a Latin standard, most of the other languages of the world did not fit into any European language standards. Remember the Shinzwani noun categories that we discussed earlier in this chapter? Well, even though he lived in the Comoros for two years, from 1821 to 1822, and tried really hard to learn Shinzwani, the English missionary William Elliot never did quite understand the system. It was too different, and prescriptive grammar just wasn't of any use to him in trying to figure it out.

By the late 1800s, American anthropologists such as Franz Boas, working with Native American languages, began to develop a new approach to learning and describing languages. Although it doesn't seem so revolutionary now, the idea of just describing a language in its own terms was an important innovation. Boas and his students and colleagues began to develop "descriptive grammars" for the languages they were encountering. **Descriptive grammars** describe the structure and patterning of languages on their own terms. Descriptive grammars tell you how people actually speak, not how they should speak. Descriptive grammars do not attempt to tell you what is "good" or "bad" grammar, except in the context of how people use the language itself. If it seems acceptable for English speakers to say *to boldly go,* then the task of a descriptive grammar is to explain the patterning that makes this statement possible.

Descriptive grammar was an important breakthrough, and the approach was soon being applied to languages throughout the world. By the early 1900s, Boas was teaching it in the United States and Ferdinand de Saussure was teaching it in Switzerland; and by the 1920s, linguists, anthropologists, and linguistic anthropologists both in Europe and America were focusing on discovering and describing the structures of different languages around the world and learning as much as they could about the different ways that languages build words and sentences.

But descriptive grammars have some limitations too. One of those limitations was the fact that a descriptive linguistic approach expects you to limit your analysis to the language examples that you hear native speakers using. If a native speaker uses a particular sentence construction, then you can include it in the grammar. On the other hand, if you think of a possible new sentence, using substitution frames that you have discovered through your analysis, then you will need to find a native speaker to test your sentence with before you can include it in your descriptive grammar. For some people, this means that descriptive grammars are limited to describing only the surface of a language.

In the 1950s, theoretical linguists, dissatisfied with the limitations of working with actual sentences and with native speakers, began to develop another approach to grammar, one that would allow them to generate an infinite number of theoretically possible sentences from a set of basic rules and components. Following the leadership of Noam Chomsky, a linguist at the Massachusetts Institute for Technology (MIT), **generative**

grammars were designed to provide rules that could "generate" (or create) all of the possible sentences of a language. This new kind of grammar moved away from the concept of substitution frames altogether, shifting the focus of analysis to underlying rules and abstract forms. Where descriptive grammars took the sentence as an end point and explained how sentences were built up out of morphemes and words and substitution frames, generative grammars took the sentence as a starting point and worked to develop rules for getting from the abstract idea of a sentence to the kinds of words that speakers might use in a real sentence.

To describe the mechanism of getting from abstract sentences to real sentences, generative grammars introduced the idea of deep and surface structures, along with different kinds of rules to help you move from the deep (abstract) to the surface (concrete) level. **Deep structure,** in a generative grammar, referred to the underlying grammar that allows people to produce sentences, while **surface structure** referred to the actual sentences that are produced in a language. **Phrase structure rules** were those rules that would generate the deep structure of a sentence. In the deep structure, sentences were thought to be simple and declarative, such as *the dog chases the cat.* Optional **transformational rules** were thought to transform a deep structure sentence to a different kind of sentence. For example, *the dog chases the cat* might be transformed into *does the dog chase the cat?* or *the dog does not chase the cat.* Finally, **phonological rules** would assign specific sounds and produce a pronounceable surface-level sentence.

In the case of our *time flies like an arrow* sentence it would work like this: First, there would be a sentence (S). A phrase structure rule would specify that the sentence should be rewritten as (or should generate) a noun phrase (NP) and a verb phrase (VP), or S → NP + VP. Then, other phrase structure rules would expand the NP and the VP: one rule would specify that the NP should generate a noun (N), NP → N, and another rule would specify that the VP should generate both a verb (V) and an adverbial phrase (AdvP), VP → V + AdvP. Yet another phrase structure rule would expand the AdvP, generating an adverb (Adv), a determiner (det), and another noun, AdvP → Adv + det + N. At this point, the basic outline of our sentence would be complete, and phonological rules would be used to assign actual sounds to the words in the N + V + Adv + det + N sentence that the phrase structure rules had generated. This last step would give us our sentence *time flies like an arrow.* The whole thing would look like the diagram in Figure 4.2, and, per-

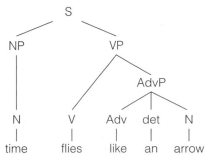

FIGURE 4.2   Tree diagram for *time flies like an arrow*

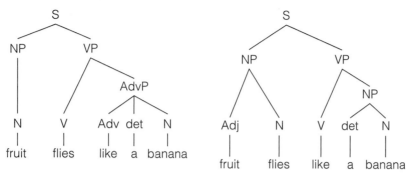

FIGURE 4.3 Two tree diagrams for *fruit flies like a banana*

haps because it resembles an upside-down tree, this kind of diagram came to be called a "tree diagram."

So far, so good. We can see the underlying structure (or deep structure) of the sentence and, if we are native speakers of English, we can confirm that this is, indeed, the most likely structure for *time flies like an arrow*. But what about *fruit flies like a banana?* One of the advantages of generative grammar is the way in which it deals with ambiguous sentences. And indeed, generative grammar trees reveal quite clearly the two alternative underlying structures of *fruit flies like a banana:* one that is identical to *time flies like an arrow* and one that is identical to *house flies* (i.e., the flies that live in houses) *like a banana.* Figure 4.3 shows the two underlying structures for *fruit flies like a banana,* displayed as trees.

Tree diagrams like this reveal the underlying difference between the two interpretations of *fruit flies like a banana,* and they have the advantage of being clear and easy to see. The rules, of course, are a different matter, and we won't get into them here, except to say that they are generally more complicated to read than the substitution frame description that we provided earlier. What is important to remember is that the final tree that the rules generate is called the surface structure of the sentence, while the underlying structure—everything up to just before the surface structure—is called the deep structure of the sentence.

Analyzing sentences this way, to discover their deep structures and explain how their surface structures are generated, seems clear enough, and it is an intriguing way to proceed until you realize that in order to do this sort of analysis with any success you need to be a native speaker of the language that you are analyzing. So, for anthropologists, and linguistic anthropologists, who need to learn unfamiliar languages in field situations, the generative approach to grammar is somewhat less useful than the descriptive approach. Once you have become reasonably fluent in a language, you can certainly attempt generative analyses and use them to construct and test new sentences, but by then you will probably have already been testing new sentences via the substitution frame method.

In fact, most anthropologists and linguistic anthropologists have found ways to combine some of both methods, using tree diagrams to display probable sentence structures and writing morphological rules to explain the way different elements like morphemes and words combine to form phrases and sentences in a language and to display substitution frames.

Another difficulty with generative grammar is the fact that theoretical linguists tend to rely on it to make statements about language universals. If all languages are built from a common grammar, they argue, then analyzing any language should provide enough insight into universal patterns. If we can get deep enough into the deep structure of any language, they argue, then we might be able to say that we are getting to the universally shared core of all languages. And yet every time a linguistic anthropologist analyzes and describes another language, new data emerges to contradict one or another statement about the universals of language. The example of Shinzwani postpositions is just such an example. You can't claim that all VO languages use prepositions if Shinzwani, a VO language, uses postpositions. Whether there are language universals or not, studying, analyzing, and describing a wide variety of languages will probably allow us to get closer to discovering them than analyzing the deep structure of any single language. Every language has the potential to add some new information to what we know about morphology or syntax in language and can help us to revise our ideas about language universals and about language in general.

SUMMARY

Using linguistic anthropology to learn a new language means learning how to discover and analyze words (morphology) as well as phrases and sentences (syntax). Analyzing how words are structured in a language is very useful in learning that language. An important first step is to identify and analyze the morphemes in the language through morphological analysis. This can be accomplished by finding the minimal units of meaning particular to that language.

Morphemes are generally described in terms of their function: They may be free or bound, and they may be bases or affixes. Bases can further be categorized into roots and stems. Affixes can attach to bases in a number of different ways. It is also important to note the order (or hierarchy) in which affixes attach to bases. Affixes function to help derive new words or to inflect (or modify) existing ones. Variations of morphemes are called allomorphs. In many cases, it is possible to predict the patterning among such variants.

Syntax is the study of how phrases and sentences are organized. Substitution frames are one way of identifying the significant grammatical categories of a language. In learning a new language, it is important to identify the substitution frames and the categories that each one signals and to learn which kinds of words can be used in which kinds of substitution frames. In addition, while all languages appear to have substitution frames for subjects, objects, and verbs, not all languages arrange these categories in the same order. Different languages may have very different substitution frames, and these may be arranged in ways that are unexpected by new learners. Obligatory categories in languages are grammatical categories that must be expressed in speaking, and one must learn the substitution frames associated with them. Ambiguous sentences in languages represent situations in which alternative substitution frames can be used to produce the same set of words.

Historically, different kinds of grammars have attempted to account for phrase and sentence structures. Prescriptive grammars describe models and set standards for "proper" speech, descriptive grammars describe the structure and patterning of language as it is spoken, and generative grammars attempt to provide rules that generate all the sentences that are possible in a language. Descriptive grammars make extensive use of the concept of substitution frames, while generative grammars shift the focus of analysis to underlying rules and the tree structures that they generate. In a generative grammar, the underlying structure of a language is called its deep structure and the actual sentences produced are called its surface structure. One goal of generative grammar is to identify universally applicable grammatical rules. Producing a generative grammar for a language appears to require fluent knowledge of that language. Producing a descriptive grammar for a language has proven to be an effective way for anthropologists (and others) to learn new languages in the field.

KEY TERMS

affix
allomorph
base
bound morpheme
case
circumfix
deep structure
derivation
descriptive grammar
free morpheme
generative grammar
grammatical gender
hierarchy
infix
inflection

interweaving
morpheme
morphological analysis
morphology
obligatory category
phonological rules
phrase structure rules
portmanteau
prefix
prescriptive grammar
reduplication
root
stem
substitution frame
suffix
surface structure
syntax
transformational rules

FURTHER READING

About Morphemes and Morphology

Matthews, Peter H. 1974. *Morphology*. Cambridge: Cambridge University Press. This book provides a comprehensive look at the subject.

About Language Universals and Typologies

Comrie, Bernard. 1989. *Language universals and linguistic typology: Syntax and morphology*. 2nd ed. Chicago: University of Chicago Press. This is a basic book about language universals and linguistic typology.

Greenberg, Joseph H. 1977. *A new introduction to linguistics*. New York: Anchor Books. This textbook includes a very readable discussion of subject, verb, and object ordering in languages, but it was written when only three of the possible orders were well described.

Tomlin, Russell S. 1986. *Basic word order: Functional principles*. London: Croom Helm. This is a survey of the basic word orders of the languages of the world.

About Descriptive Grammar

Bloomfield, Leonard. 1933. *Language*. New York: Holt, Rinehart & Winston. This is a classic that continues to influence descriptive grammar as it is currently practiced.

Gleason, Henry A. 1955. *Workbook in descriptive linguistics.* New York: Holt, Rinehart & Winston. This is another classic. Exercises from this workbook continue to be used in many other texts and workbooks.

Hockett, Charles F. 1958. *A course in modern linguistics.* New York: Macmillan. This is still another classic. It provides a solid introduction to all aspects of descriptive linguistics.

About Generative (and Transformational/Generative) Grammar

Chomsky, Noam. 1957. *Syntactic structures.* The Hague: Mouton. This is the book in which Chomsky introduces generative grammar.

Harris, Randy Allen. 1995. *The linguistics wars.* New York: Oxford University Press. This is a lively review of the fallout and fighting that followed the introduction of generative grammar into linguistics and of some of the ways in which generative grammar influenced linguistic anthropology.

 # STUDENT ACTIVITIES

Exercises

A set of exercises in the workbook/reader will give you more practice with analyzing patterns in morphology and syntax.

Web Exercises

The companion website for this book has a series of links designed to help you explore morphology and syntax in greater depth. The companion website also contains study questions that will help you to review important concepts.

Guided Projects

If you are creating a new language, you will need to develop words and sentences for your language. If you are working with a conversation partner, your instructor may ask you to compare the morphological and syntactic systems of your two languages. Your instructor will be your guide.

CHAPTER 5

Language
in Action

"Excuse me," the young man interrupted, as Dr. Stirland and I approached the campus parking lot. "I heard you talking, back there, to Mr. Means, and I wanted to introduce myself."

We turned to face the young man. He looked young, perhaps in his twenties. His glossy black hair was tied back into a low ponytail and he was wearing beads around his neck.

"My name is Harold," the young man continued, "and I just wanted to say that I thought your description of disease in pre-Columbian times in England was really interesting. I'm so glad I got to hear you discussing it with Mr. Means."

"Thanks," said Dr. Stirland. A human skeletal biologist from England, she was visiting Kansas State University as part of a lecture tour. As it happened, the noted Native American activist Russell Means was also on campus at the same time. Dr. Stirland and I had attended his lecture, and after the lecture she had spoken with him at length about her research. She had also mentioned that she was on her way to present that research at a conference in Toronto. Now here we were, in a parking lot, talking to a young Native American student about that conversation. Or so it seemed.

"Toronto is a nice place to be going," said the young man. "My family lives in upstate New York," he continued, "but I haven't seen them for a while. I think of them often, though, especially at this time of the year, when the weather is so nice. . . ." As the young man continued, discussing his family and how much he missed them and how much he had learned from them, it dawned on me that he was asking Ann if she could drop him off in New York on her way to Toronto.

I waited patiently until the young man had finished his narration, and then I said, "It was nice to meet you. But Dr. Stirland isn't driving to Toronto; she'll be flying. I'm taking her to the airport tomorrow morning."

"Oh, I hope you have a nice trip," responded the student with a smile. "It was a pleasure to meet you. Good luck at the conference." And he strolled off into the pleasant March afternoon.

"How did you know he was asking for a ride?" asked Ann, incredulously.

"I had just read an article about Native American indirection as a speech style," I replied, "so I guess I was hyperaware. It's kind of a Kansas-ism too, compared to my more direct New York style, so I've been working at learning to recognize it recently. Plus it's a nice example of how words and sentences can mean different things in different situations," I said, trying not to switch into lecture style with my former student and current friend.

HJO

✳ USING LANGUAGE: CULTURE, ETHNICITY, GENDER, STATUS, AND STYLE

Learning to use a language means learning much more than learning how to pronounce sounds, construct and recognize words, and produce grammatical phrases and sentences. It means learning how to use those words and sentences in actual situations: how to hear intended meanings as well as outright ones and how to use the right words in the right ways at the right moments. It means identifying and negotiating issues of gender, ethnicity, status, and culture as you speak.

The young man asking for a ride never used the word *ride*. Instead, he described his family and where they lived and how he hadn't seen them in a while and how nice it would be to visit them. It was up to us, the listeners, to sort out the fact that if we were driving from Kansas to Toronto we would probably pass by where the young man's family lived. This meant that we could give him a ride, if we had room in our car, or we could explain why we couldn't give him a ride. We might have also been able to ignore his request altogether. On the other hand, had he asked us outright for a ride he could have put us into the potentially embarrassing situation of having to refuse. The young man was using a speech style often associated with Native American speakers. It's called **indirection,** and it involves making a request without directly asking. One point of indirection is to avoid putting people into potentially embarrassing situations. One difficulty with indirection is the fact that not every group of speakers uses it or understands how it works.

Here's another example of indirection. A Japanese student who was studying anthropology at my university came to me one day to ask about how to ask for salt in English. He had been eating in the student cafeteria one day and had decided that his food needed salt. There was no salt on the table at which he was sitting, however. This meant he would have to get up and go to another table to get a salt shaker. He looked around

Cross-Language Miscommunication 5.1

CORN PUDDING

A student from Kansas went to visit her fiancé's family in Boston and was served corn pudding for dinner. It turns out that corn pudding is one of her least favorite dishes, and she avoids eating it whenever possible. But she wanted to be polite, so she ate what she was served. When she was asked how she liked the corn pudding she said, "It's good corn pudding." In Kansas, this kind of answer means something like, 'Well, I guess it's fine, but it's not my favorite dish and I'd appreciate not having to eat it any more.' Her hosts, however, not knowing this Kansas-ism, interpreted the phrase to mean 'I like your corn pudding a lot and would be pleased if you would prepare it for me every time I come to visit.' Of course, this was the opposite of what she had intended to communicate and, much to her dismay, she ended up eating corn pudding at every subsequent visit!

HJO

for a table that had two salt shakers, located one some distance away, and went over to it to get one of the salt shakers. When he returned, his companions wondered why he hadn't just asked the people at the next table to lend them their salt shaker. They also wondered why he hadn't just asked one of them to reach over to a neighboring table to get a salt shaker. He hadn't thought of any of these strategies and had, in fact, taken the trouble to go to a distant table for salt just because it seemed that it would be rude to take a salt shaker from a table that had only one. I asked the student what he would do in Japan if he needed salt in such a situation. He thought about that for a moment and then told me that he would suggest that the other people at his table should taste his food. Having tasted his food, his companions would recognize that it needed salt and would then procure salt for him from a nearby table with extra salt. He asserted that he would do the same for his companions. But asking outright for salt seemed rude to him. It was just too direct, and it put people into awkward or embarrassing positions, requiring them to do things that they might not want to do.

In all of these situations, words are being used in ways that go beyond their dictionary definitions. *Taste my food* does not sound anything like *Please pass the salt*, but that is what it means in this situation. *I miss my family in New York* does not sound anything like *Can you please give me a ride to New York?*, but that is what it means in this situation. *It's good corn pudding* does not sound anything like *I'd prefer not to have to eat this corn pudding.* The important thing to understand is that words and phrases take on different meanings in different situations.

The idea that situations affect the meanings of words is an important one in linguistic anthropology. Anthropologists, and linguistic anthropologists in particular, have been aware of this aspect of language for a long time, beginning at least with the early observations of anthropologist Bronislaw Malinowski (1884–1942). Malinowski researched culture in the Trobriand Islands (in the southwest Pacific Ocean) during World War I. During two extended visits, in 1915–1916 and 1917–1918, he participated fully in Trobriand daily life and culture, becoming fluent in the Trobriand language. Perhaps because his focus was on cultural and social relationships and not specifically on the structure of the language, and perhaps also because he saw the various aspects of culture as closely and complexly interrelated, when Malinowski wrote about language he also wrote about the situations in which language was used. He wrote about how difficult it was to translate between languages, even when you knew the "dictionary" meanings of all of the words. Translation, he argued, meant more than just substituting words from one language for words in another language. Instead you needed to understand the **context**—the cultural and social situation—in which the words were being used in order to understand what was being said. The situation in which you were using the words could signal the difference between asking and telling, between reporting and bragging. According to Malinowski, analyzing language led ultimately to analyzing all of the other aspects of a culture. Language, in short, took on much of its meaning from its culture and, in particular, from the situations in which that language was used.

Applying this insight to the previous examples, we learn that important clues for interpreting requests are embedded in the situations in which people are making those requests. Furthermore, we learn that requests are "made" differently in different cultures. So, it is not possible to translate a request directly from one culture to another. You need to understand both the culture and the situation in order to know whether you are being asked for a ride or to pass the salt or to understand someone's dislike for corn pudding. Being sensitive to the fact that cultures and situations affect language use helps you to be aware of how to use language to interact socially in the most appropriate way for the culture and situation you may find yourself in.

This chapter shows you some of the key insights that linguistic anthropology provides into the ways people use language in real situations. It also gives you some skills for learning how to understand and interpret different situations and how to develop your skills in cross-cultural communication. You will learn how anthropologists approach the task of describing language use in different cultures, and you will learn some specific techniques that have been developed for analyzing specific examples of language use. Finally, you will learn to identify situations in which members of different cultures may miscommunicate because of their different cultural expectations about language use in specific situations, and you will learn how to apply your new descriptive and analytical skills to understanding how to resolve cross-cultural miscommunications.

✳ THE ETHNOGRAPHY OF COMMUNICATION: LANGUAGE, GENDER, AND ETHNICITY

In the 1960s, the American linguistic anthropologist Dell Hymes began to develop an effective fieldwork methodology for studying language in its social and cultural contexts. The new methodology, called the **ethnography of speaking,** was designed to be an ethnography that focused on describing and analyzing the ways that people use language in real situations. If, as Malinowski had suggested, all aspects of a culture were intertwined anyway, then an ethnography that focused on language would provide significant insights into other aspects of a culture as well. Also called the **ethnography of communication,** Hymes's methodology inspired several generations of linguistic anthropologists to go beyond the dictionary-and-grammar approach to learning languages and to pay attention to *how* language was used in everyday situations in different cultures. It encouraged scholars to pay closer attention to specific situations and to try to analyze how they are defined and how access to different situations is also defined (Bourdieu 1977). As the study of language broadened to incorporate research into the social and cultural settings of language use, anthropologists began to develop a much better understanding of the impact of social and cultural contexts on language use. In fact, most of our contemporary understandings of the connections among language, gender, ethnicity, and social power have come from ethnographies of communication. One key concept that has guided this research is the notion of "communicative competence."

Communicative Competence: Real People Using Real Language

Communicative competence is the ability to speak a language well or the ability to use one's language correctly in a variety of social situations. In other words, it means knowing how to have a real conversation in a real situation. It means that knowing the grammar and vocabulary of the language you are speaking is not enough; you also need to know how grammar and vocabulary can change depending on who you are speaking to and in what situation. You also have to understand how to make your voice heard in a conversation and how to make it heard in such a way that people will pay attention, acknowledge your contribution, and give you credit for your ideas. Essentially you have to know how real language functions in real situations. Describing communicative competence in a speech community is one goal of an ethnography of communication. The idea of communicative competence builds on, and contrasts with, the idea of linguistic competence (Hymes 1972a, xxxv, xxxvi; see also Bourdieu 1977).

Speech Communities   It is interesting to note that a "speech community" is not exactly the same thing as a "linguistic community." A **speech community** is a group of people who share one or more varieties of language and the rules for using those varieties in everyday communication. A **linguistic community**, in contrast, is a group of people who share a *single* language variety and focus their identity around that language. While a linguistic community is, by definition, monolingual, a speech community can be multilingual and multidialectal. When I lived in the Comoro Islands, I was part of a speech community in which individuals had access to (and shared) as many as eight different languages and dialects, including Shinzwani, Shingazidja, Shimwali, and Shimaori (the four language varieties of the Comoro Islands themselves), Kiswahili, Malagasy, French, and Arabic. Although I could not speak all of these languages, many individuals could and many were quite proficient at codeswitching and language-hopping, carefully restricting themselves to the linguistic resources of whatever social group they happened to be in at the moment. I was always impressed at how individuals were able to navigate through all of those different languages without becoming confused, but from the standpoint of the ethnography of communication one of most important things to learn from this practice is that there are indeed places where—unlike in the United States—multilingualism is the norm and is highly valued.

Communities of Practice   Related to the idea of a speech community is the concept of a **community of practice**, or a group of individuals who interact regularly, developing unique ways of doing things together (Lave and Wenger 1991). Groups like this may develop around specific activities, such as a choir group that rehearses together regularly or the members of a team that plays together, or they may develop around specific memberships, such as the members of a family group or the members of a sailing club. They may be limited to a particular time frame, such as the group of individuals that participate in an archaeological field school together, the language-creating group that you might have joined as a member of a linguistic anthropology class, or even the conversation-partner dyad that you were assigned to as a member of the same class. Members of a community of practice may stay in touch for years or may never see one another again after the particular activity that they were involved in has been completed. The point is that communities of practice exist in which individuals establish ways of speaking together, at least for a time, and that it is important to understand language use within such communities, as well as within the larger speech community that such individuals also belong to.

Linguistic Competence **Linguistic competence** is a term coined by theoretical linguist Noam Chomsky. It refers to a speaker's underlying ability to produce (and recognize) grammatically correct expressions. The kind of speaker that Chomsky had in mind was an ideal speaker-listener living in a completely homogenous community of speakers, knowing the language of that community perfectly. This ideal speaker would not be distracted by anything in his or her environment when speaking or judging actual sentences. Linguistic competence, in other words, referred only to grammatical correctness and not to what speakers might actually do in real situations. In fact, Chomsky thought of real situations as "distractions."

Most anthropologists have difficulty with such a narrow definition of competence. They know, having read Malinowski and having lived in various field situations and learned various languages, that language varies a lot from speaker to speaker and from situation to situation. They also know that words, as well as utterances, vary in meaning from speaker to speaker and from situation to situation. The word *bad* can mean either 'bad' or 'good,' depending on who is using it and in what setting. The word *yeah* can mean either 'yes' or 'no,' depending on who is using it and in what setting. Do you know the joke in which an English teacher tells the class that, although two negatives should make a positive, two positives never can make a negative? "Yeah, yeah!" comes a negative-sounding voice from the back of the room, thus proving that words take on different meanings in different situations and that speakers need more than just linguistic competence to communicate successfully.

Take, for example, *tu* and *vous* in French, or *tu* and *vosotros* in Spanish, or *ty* and *vy* in Czech, or *du* and *Sie* in German. In terms of the grammar and dictionary of each of these languages, the first of each of these pairs of words (*tu, tu, ty, du*) means 'you-singular' (like the now obsolete English *thou*) and the second of each of these pairs of words (*vous, vosotros, vy, Sie*) means 'you-plural' (like *y'all*, as used in the southern part of the United States). In each of these languages, the verbs change their forms to match the particular pronoun used. So, it is possible to say *vous voulez* 'you-plural want,' and *tu veut* 'you-singular want,' but *vous veut* would be judged to be grammatically incorrect. An equivalent in English might be something like saying *he want* instead of *he wants* or *you wants* instead of *you want*.

A linguistically competent person would know how to put the correct verb forms with the correct pronouns, but, as anyone who has attempted to learn French, Spanish, Czech, or German knows, there is much more to speaking correctly than getting the grammar right. First of all, there is the degree of formality involved in choosing between the two pronouns for 'you.' What we are calling the plural form of 'you' is actually also the preferred form to use between individuals who do not know one another well. It conveys a sense of formality, and perhaps also a degree of respect, that seems more appropriate when people first meet, when students address their professors, or when shopkeepers and waiters converse with customers. The singular form, on the other hand, expresses friendship, informality, and occasionally also solidarity and seems more appropriate when parents speak with children or when professors address students. It is also appropriate among close friends and groups of students. In essence, you use the plural/formal 'you' with acquaintances and the singular/informal 'you' with friends. But how do you know when you have crossed the line from acquaintance to friend? Clearly, this goes beyond linguistic competence. You need more than a knowledge of words and grammar. You need a good understanding of the cultural expectations and social norms and patterns surrounding word choice and language use. You need to know how to make yourself heard in a conversation, to gain the right to speak, and the right to participate in conversations. It is this broader knowledge that Hymes and Bourdieu are describing by the term communicative competence, and it is this kind of knowledge that an ethnography of communication seeks to describe.

Discovering How Language Communicates Identity

How do anthropologists learn about these subtle variations in language use? The same way they learn the basic structure of a language or a culture—by doing fieldwork, by living with a group of people and learning not only how to pronounce words and string them together into meaningful sentences but also the situations in which those words and sentences make sense, are appropriate, or even when they are not appropriate. Living in another culture and paying attention to how that culture influences the ways in which people use their language is the best way to develop the kind of communicative competence that Dell Hymes was talking about. The resulting report, written up for others to read, becomes an ethnography of communication—a description of what communicative competence means in the culture you are studying.

Hymes suggested that students and fieldworkers attend to seven basic areas of research: Setting, Participants, Ends, Act sequence, Keys, Instrumentalities, Norms, and Genres. Together they form the acronym **S-P-E-A-K-I-N-G.** Exploring the depth and range of each of these areas should give you a good sense of how language is used in specific speech communities. Although each aspect is complexly interrelated with all of the other aspects, we will go through them one by one, pointing out some of the interactions. You will probably be able to think of other examples from your own experience.

Setting/Situation **Setting/situation** refers to the place in which the conversation is taking place in its broadest sense and the overall psychological feeling of the place. Where are we? In a house, in a lecture hall, at a Quaker meeting, in a noisy bar? All of this will make a difference in how we speak. In each possible location, a speech community will have specific and unwritten ideas about what is "normal" conversation or discourse, what can be said, what is appropriate or not appropriate, who should be granted entry into the location, who can speak, who should listen, and so on. In a North American classroom, for example, it is generally assumed that the professor will lecture or engage the students in a discussion, and that the students will not interrupt the lecture or each other, nor will they shout obscenities in the middle of the lecture, get up and walk out of the classroom midway through the lecture, or arrive late. Further, the professor will be prepared and will not mutter incomprehensible aphorisims; nor will he or she burst into song.

Some of these seem like obvious expectations, but some may not be. For example, what about students' ability to ask questions? Can they interrupt as needed when they are confused, or must they wait until the professor asks for questions? I have had the experience of teaching exchange students from Japan who do not ask questions out loud in the classroom but, rather, save them for the end of class. These students generally come to the front of the room to ask me their questions after class has ended. I thought these students were just shy until they explained to me that it is considered impolite and wasteful of the other students' time to ask individual questions aloud in Japanese classrooms. Individual questions are not seen as potentially helpful to other students who might have the same questions but, rather, as personal failures to understand, and so they are saved for the end of class and brought to the professor on an individual basis. North American students in classrooms in Japan would probably find themselves being hushed by other students or treated as rude interruptors if they were to try to ask questions, American-style. On the other hand, in Koranic schools in the Comoro Islands students are expected to read aloud, at their own pace, while the instructor circulates around in the classroom listening to the different children to see how well they are reading, and pausing to help or correct students who need specific kinds of help.

Participants **Participants** refers to who can or should be involved in various speech events or conversations and what is expected of the various individuals. Again, this is closely correlated with a number of other aspects. Who is speaking, as well as who is being spoken to, may affect the conversation. In North America, children, even when present, are generally expected not to contribute to adult conversations, as expressed in the folk saying, "Children should be seen and not heard." In addition, in the same speech community adults often are careful about what they

Cross-Language Miscommunication 5.2

FAIS DO DO

In New Orleans, graduate students brought their children with them to dinners and parties and settled them into a separate room from the main action, checking on them from time to time to make sure they were playing quietly or dropping off to sleep as the evening wore on. The practice was referred to as *fais do do* from the French Cajun and the expression meant something like 'put to sleep'; and since we were in Louisiana we all learned to get along with having children around, even at large gatherings. The children would come into the central gathering place if they needed anything, and they would "interrupt" just enough to get the attention of one of the responsible adults, who would then take them back to the children's room and take care of their needs and check on the other children. I liked this idea and adopted it readily, only in part because it promised to save money on babysitters. But a few years later, I was disappointed to discover that it did not transfer easily to my new community in Kansas, where children were expected to stay at home while their parents went out. It only took a few tries to discover the discomfort that my new friends expressed with having young children around as even marginal participants in various events where conversation might be taking place.

HJO

say when there are children in the room, not so much as to avoid offending the children, but to avoid having the children repeat what they hear in other contexts. This concern is reflected in the saying "Little pitchers [meaning the little children] have big ears [meaning that children, even those who are politely silent, are often listening to the adults conversing]."

In some cultures nonhumans are also considered to be conversational participants. In the Comoro Islands, for example, ghosts and spirits are thought to speak through individuals who have entered into a state of trance, and one can have conversations with them. Sometimes the spirits are consulted for help with diagnosing illnesses or suggesting remedies. Deities are also thought to speak through individuals in several West African religious settings, as well as in some African-derived religions in the Americas. Most of the time, the individuals through whom deities, ghosts, or spirits communicate are in a state of religious trance when they serve as mediums of this sort, and they generally claim not to remember what they have said when they awake from their trance.

Sometimes expectations about the participants in a speech situation affect the ways in which hearers understand what is said. In a famous experiment, sixty-two undergraduate native speakers of American English were asked to listen to a lecture that had been tape-recorded by a native speaker of American English from central Ohio, while viewing a slide of the "lecturer." Half of the students were shown a slide of a European American woman lecturer. The other half of the students were shown a slide of an Asian woman lecturer. Both "lecturers" were shown in the same setting and pose, both were approximately the same size, and both wore their hair in the same style. The students who listened to the lecture while viewing the Asian "lecturer" tended to report that the lecturer had an Asian accent, and many of those students scored lower on tests of comprehension of the lecture. Clearly expectations of and attitudes about participants in a speech event can affect the way people hear the speech that is presented to them (Rubin 1992).

Ends **Ends** refers to the reasons for which the speech event is taking place, or the goals that people have in speaking in a particular situation. For example, in some cases a shopper might try bargaining for the purpose of getting a lower price, but in plenty of cases bargaining is seen as a way of establishing a social contact between shopper and seller—establishing an actual purchase price is a secondary consideration.

The young man who engaged Dr. Stirland in conversation, in the story that opened this chapter, had a specific end in mind; he wanted to ask for a ride. Understanding the ways in which people use language to achieve various ends is an important skill. If your goal is to ask for a favor, you need to know how best to make your request, given the specific culture and the specific situation. Should you hint at the favor or come right out and ask for it?

The same cautions apply in asking for directions and giving directions. You might think that asking for directions is a fairly clear-cut situation: You're lost and you need someone to tell you how to get where you want to go. Likewise, giving directions should be equally clear-cut: Either you can provide directions or you can't. Yet most New Yorkers I know will give you directions whether they know the location you are trying to get to or not. Your target might be three blocks to the west, but they will happily send you four blocks to the east. What's going on here? Well, most New Yorkers do not want to seem ignorant. You've asked for directions, so they give you some. *Your* goal may be to get information and to get to your destination, but *their* goal is to appear knowledgeable. They know you will ask someone else around the corner, and someone else again, until you find your destination. Clearly, the ends in this situation are very different for the different participants.

Another example of differing ends in a speech situation comes from research done by linguistic anthropologist Deborah Tannen. Tannen suggests that there are two types of speech styles: "rapport-style" and "report-style" speech. In rapport-style speech, individuals are talking to

Doing Linguistic Anthropology 5.1

BARGAINING IN MEXICO

Two anthropology professors from the United States were shopping at a crafts market in Mexico City. They had just completed an intensive Spanish course and wanted to practice their language skills. They spotted some small saddle-shaped leather stools and inquired, in Spanish, about the price. The shopkeeper gave them a figure and, while they were thinking, another couple of tourists inquired, in English, about the price of the little stools. When the shopkeeper quoted them a price, the English-speaking tourists promptly paid it, selected a pair of leather stools, and thanked the shopkeeper warmly. The shopkeeper turned to the professors and said, in Spanish, something that sounded like "Stupid gringos. They don't ever take the time to bargain." The professors took this as a suggestion that they should "take the time to bargain," and when they did so they found that the shopkeeper became very much more friendly toward them, joking and teasing about the cost of his materials and the state of the world economy. By the time they had settled on a price, they felt like they had not only gotten an excellent price but they had made a friend. As a bonus, they had also gotten a lesson in communicative competence and a recommendation for an inexpensive restaurant nearby.

HJO

establish rapport. People may insert words of encouragement throughout or end one another's sentences to convey how much "in tune" they are with each other. When they tell each other similar stories, they do so to provide encouragement to one another (saying things like "that happened to me, too"). In report-style speech, individuals take separate turns to speak. They rely on eye contact to know when each turn to speak begins and ends. When they tell each other similar stories, they do so in a somewhat competitive environment (saying things like, "I did something like that, but even better"). Of course, each style of speech has different ends, but you can imagine how uncomfortable each type of speaker would be in a conversation with the other type. Report-style speakers tend to feel interrupted by rapport-style speakers and don't quite understand why the stories all sound like "more of the same." Rapport-style speakers miss the encouraging insertions and don't quite understand why the stories seem designed to be "better" than theirs. Some scholars think that the more competitive-seeming report-style is more characteristic of men's speech in the United States, while others argue that it is associated more generally with individuals who have, or are attempting to gain, access to power and status, and that it has little or nothing to do with gender. In fact, the relationship between gender and power is complex, in the United States as well as elsewhere, and it is interesting to see the degree to which language can be used to convey these details. Tannen's 1990 article "Who's Interrupting?" is a classic description of the kinds of misunderstandings that occur when people with these different speech styles converse, and, although it focuses on gender differences in the use of the two styles, it also addresses issues of ethnicity and power and the complexities of assigning a style to a group of people.

Act Sequence **Act sequence** refers to the actual sequence of events. What words are used? By whom? Who begins? Who continues? How are turns taken? What exactly gets said? A classroom in which the professor starts off by saying, "Ladies and gentlemen, . . ." will have a different tone than one in which the professor begins with, "Good morning, everyone!" I have attended lectures in which the speaker begins with a rousing "Good morning!" or "Good evening!" and expects the audience to respond loudly with a similar greeting. In fact, if the audience does not respond loudly enough the speaker will repeat the greeting a few times, coaching the audience on the "proper" response. Speech act scholars call these kinds of greeting and response exchanges "adjacency pairs."

Hymes and others use the term **speech acts** to describe the specific utterances that people make, and some analysts even classify speech acts with reference to the intentions of the speakers (to command, to promise, to apologize, and so forth). The term **speech event** has been used to refer to one or more speech acts involving one or more participants and can include everything from exchanging greetings to making apologies, telling jokes, delivering speeches, ordering meals, having conversations, and more. Much research has gone into analyzing the rules and conventions that different groups of speakers have for how speech events can unfold in different situations. Finally, the term **speech situation** refers to the entire setting or situation in which people speak. For example, a classroom, a conference, a party, a graduation ceremony, a rafting trip, or any other situation you can think of where language might be used could be considered a speech situation. These three concepts—speech act, speech event, and speech situation—provide additional focus and specificity for analyzing language in real situations.

The kinds of act sequences involved in greetings have received much study. Some are fairly restrictive, with formulas guiding who says what and in what order. Others are fairly loosely structured, with the only requirement being that the speech acts occur in pairs (someone offers a greeting and someone responds). As with almost any example of speaking, the degree to which one is expected to follow the formulas depends on the situation and the culture. In Japan, there are certain formulas for expressing condolences and it is widely preferred that people use those formulas. Trying to think of your own words to say to a bereaved family member, as many Americans seem to prefer, generally results in awkward and embarrassing situations (Yamada 1997).

In the Comoros, greetings tend to be formulized fairly extensively. Men and women use different strategies in greetings, as well. For example, on entering a room, a woman is expected to utter the formulaic *mungunahunusuru*, which means something like 'may God bless this place,' and the women in the room are expected to reply with *sontsi*, meaning 'for everyone.' Men generally say that they can't pronounce *mungunahunusuru*, claiming that it is too long a word, but every woman is expected to be able to do so effortlessly, and in order to fit into Comorian daily life I had to learn to pronounce the word and use it appropriately. Men use the much shorter word *kwez*, meaning something like 'respectful greetings to you' with one another; to greet a woman they might say *kwez bweni* 'greetings to you, ma'am'; and both women and men greeting another man can say *kwez mwenye* 'greetings to you, sir.' Beyond this, there is a range of exchanges in which people ask for 'news' (*habari*) and are told that the news is 'fine' (*njema*) or 'excellent' (*njema fetre*). One can ask for news about specific things, such as news of family, work, health, and so on. When I was still learning these formulas, one old man asked me for news of the world, and when I replied with the expected 'fine' he broke out into laughter. Of course, he had led me beyond the normal expected range of items one might ask about, but I hadn't developed enough competency with the language to know how to back out of the situation gracefully.

While in the Comoros greetings can convey information about the gender of the speakers, in Senegal, in West Africa, Wolof greetings seem to convey information about relative status. According to linguistic anthropologist Judith Irvine, among the Wolof when two people meet, the person of lesser status is expected to offer greetings to the person of higher status. This sometimes means that two people, each of whom wishes to be considered higher in status, may try to wait one another out, to see who will break down and begin the greetings. It is considered inappropriate and embarrassing, however, to meet someone and not immediately engage in greetings—the silence is too awkward. So one of the two individuals may try to solve the dilemma by offering a briefer-than-normal greeting and then asking the other person why he didn't greet him (Irvine 1974). This reminds me a bit of when I lived in New Orleans and everyone would rush to be the first to get and respond to a greeting. Often people would greet one another simultaneously with *alright* (as if someone had already asked how they were); but as far as I know, nothing was communicated about status in such exchanges, except perhaps to suggest how "hip" all of the greeters were.

Sometimes silence is the most appropriate form of greeting, and, as such, it should probably also be considered an act sequence. According to linguistic anthropologist Keith Basso (1972), silence is appropriate among Western Apache in Arizona, especially when they are interacting with strangers, initiating courtship, or welcoming children home from school. In each of these situations, people prefer to remain silent, sometimes for extended periods of time, to give the other individuals time to adjust to a new or changing situation. In the case of interacting with strangers or initiating courtship, one doesn't yet know how the new individual will act or want to be treated or spoken to, so spending some time in silence together is deemed a good way to gauge the situation and judge how well the two individuals may get along. Speaking too soon might be taken as a sign of being too pushy or demanding, and people tend to distrust people, especially strangers, who speak "too quickly." In the case of interacting with children returning home from school, parents want to allow their children some time to get readjusted to being at home, and they also want some time to assess how their children have changed before talking with them. You can probably think of how difficult it would be for individuals from cultures preferring silence to interact with individuals from cultures preferring immediate and elaborate greetings. On the other hand, sometimes you can find similar patterns in different cultures. One of my Kiowa students reported enjoying long periods of silent sitting with his Japanese conversation partner. Even though their task was to spend time conversing with one another, the silence seemed, to both of them, like a suitable way to get comfortable with each other.

Contemporary conversation analysts often record and transcribe actual conversations to study act sequences and the ways that people use them. Linguistic anthropologist Deborah Tannen recorded a Thanksgiving dinner conversation that she also participated in and, by analyzing exactly who said what, and when and how they said it, she was able to see how instances of overlapping speech could be heard by participants as being cooperative rather than competitive. By showing this, she also was able to show that overlapping someone's speech (talking at the same time, adding words, completing other peoples' thoughts) was not necessarily the same thing as interrupting someone; it all depended who was speaking and in what situation. Linguistic anthropologist Donald Brenneis (1984) recorded gossip in Fiji, and by analyzing the transcriptions he was able to show how overlapping speech and the rhythms that people used to pace their turns helped to communicate relationships of solidarity among the speakers.

Key Key refers to the mood or spirit in which communication takes place. A funeral in the United States is generally hushed and solemn, with people speaking in low tones. In contrast, some funerals in highland Ecuador involve loud wailing and crying, and there are communities in eastern Europe where professional mourners are hired to sing the loud wailing cries that are necessary to give a funeral the appropriate tone.

Joking and teasing may be appropriate keys for communication among some individuals or in some situations. In the Comoro Islands, teasing is often used among close friends, and strangers may be teased to test their acceptability as members of a group. When my husband was first learning to speak Shinzwani, he was given an obscene word and told—in all seriousness—that it was the word for 'banana.' He was then instructed to go to the market to buy bananas. You can imagine the scene when he asked the women selling bananas in the market for something other than bananas! Both of us soon learned how to recognize when we were being teased (one clue is the mock seriousness used) and to respond appropriately. The example I mentioned earlier, of being asked to evaluate the 'news of the world,' was probably an example of my being teased and tested early in my language learning.

Instrumentalities   **Instrumentalities** refers to the channels that are used (speaking, writing, signing, signaling with flags, etc.) as well as the varieties of language that speakers use (language, dialect, register, etc.). Here we need to pause to define varieties of language. I have been deliberately using the word "variety" because it is a little vague, and it has saved me from having to define whether I am talking about a language, a dialect, or a register. But it is time to address the difficulties involved with using these three words.

The standard way to differentiate a "language" from a "dialect" is to test for what is called "mutual intelligibility." If two or more ways of speaking are **mutually unintelligible**—in other words if the speakers can't understand one another—then they are considered to be different languages. If I speak French to you and you speak Italian to me, and we don't understand one another, then we can be said to be speaking two different languages. If, on the other hand, two or more ways of speaking are **mutually intelligible**—in other words if speakers *can* understand one another—then they are said to be dialects of a single language. For example, if I speak New York English to you and you speak California English to me, and we understand one another, then we can be said to be speaking the same language. We would probably call this language English, and we would call our two varieties of English "dialects" of English. **Dialects of a language** are mutually intelligible varieties of that language.

The problem with all of this is that mutual intelligibility is not always so clear-cut. Politics and attitudes can get in the way. Suppose I refuse to understand your California variety of English, deeming it not worth the effort to overcome the differences in pronunciation, word choice, and grammar. In that case, our two varieties of English would have to be considered different languages. There are some people who think that Czech and Slovak are different languages, and some who think they are dialects of a single language. Up until the 1800s, there were many people who thought that Spanish and Portuguese were dialects of the same language; they called the language Spanish and regarded Portuguese as a minor variation from the norm.

This brings up another aspect of the language-and-dialect difference. Many people act as if languages are real entities and that dialects are lesser varieties of those entities, spoken primarily by splinter groups or lower classes or uneducated individuals, or some other group that varies in some way from "the norm." Generally whatever is regarded as "the norm" is considered to be the "standard" way of speaking, and all other variants are called "dialects," or sometimes even "nonstandard dialects." Typically, the members of the out-group can speak and understand the variety that is considered standard, while the members of the in-group claim not to understand any variety that is deemed nonstandard.

Registers suffer from the same difficulty of definition as dialects. Registers are varieties of a language that are appropriate in specific situations. For example, a language may have a formal register, to be used in making speeches, and an informal register, to be used in ordinary conversation. A language might also have a scientific register, to be used in discussing laboratory experiments, or a joking register, to be used in teasing and taunting. Some registers may enjoy more prestige than others, and some may be looked down on. Some people may be able to shift registers easily, and others may have difficulty understanding registers used by groups that they don't belong to. In some cases, people may actually talk about registers as if they are different, nonunderstandable languages. You can see why all of this makes it difficult to measure mutual intelligibility in real situations of language use and why it makes it so difficult to define such concepts as language, dialect, and register with pinpoint accuracy.

Nonetheless, it is specifically language, dialect, and register that the concept of instrumentalities is concerned with. What languages are being used? Are they spoken or signed or written? What dialects, registers, or other varieties of language are available for speakers to choose from? Especially interesting to anthropologists are questions about the attitudes people have about registers, dialects, and languages. What is being expressed when someone makes a choice among the varieties of language available to him or her? What impressions do we form about people based on the languages, dialects, and registers that they use? And what varieties of language are deemed appropriate to use in what situations? We return to this discussion in Chapter 9. For the moment, it is important to focus on the fact that there are many choices available to us when we use our languages.

Cousin Joe, a blues singer that I worked with in New Orleans, was intensely aware of the ways in which choices could be made between standard and dialectical forms of English. When he narrated his autobiography into a tape recorder he switched speaking styles depending on what he was talking about, using Standard English to describe events, but switching into dialect (particularly African American Vernacular English) to narrate conversations. By switching like this, he gave his characters a folksy down-home quality at the same time that he gave himself a more authorial tone, which seemed appropriate for him as the author of his intended book. Some of the time, he used different pronunciations to signal the difference (*going to* vs. *gonna*), some of the time he used different words to signal the difference (*father* vs. *daddy*), and some of the time he used different grammatical constructions (*you don't have* vs. *you ain't got no*) to signal the difference in voice (Joseph and Ottenheimer 1987).

Differences of pronunciation, word choice, or grammar can signal identity in a number of ways. In the Comoro Islands, for example, on the island of Anjouan, certain sounds are pronounced differently in different towns. In the town of Mutsamudu, on one side of the island, men produce a *v* sound with their upper teeth on their lower lips, and women produce a different sounding *v* by bringing their two lips close together. On the other side of the island, in the town of Domoni, everyone produces the *v* sound with two lips. This means that men from Domoni sound effeminate to speakers from Mutsamudu, and men from Mutusamudu are heard as having a different accent when they travel to Domoni. Women, in this case, can move easily between the two towns without encountering any difference in how they are heard.

Here is another example. Growing up in New York, I learned to drop my *r* sounds and stretch out my vowels so that the words *fourth floor* sounded like *fauth flaw*. This made me sound "in" with my peers, but as it turns out it also gave me a lower-class accent. Moving to Kansas, I discovered that people stretched their vowels and inserted *r* sounds so that *wash* ended up sounding like *warsh*. Most people in Kansas today avoid this *r* insertion and vowel stretching because they feel it makes them sound too "rural." In Boston, leaving out the *r* sound in words like *yard* (so that it sounds more like *yahd*) is a mark of upper-class status. It's actually fairly arbitrary which sounds are used to mark which kinds of things, but it's clear that people do pay attention to different pronunciations and connect them with differences of region, gender, ethnicity, status, degree of education, and much more.

Differences in word choice are also used to signal differences in status identity or to signal something important about the situation people find themselves in. In Java, for example, people are expected to choose their words according to their social status, as well as the social status of the person they are speaking with. There are words for high-, middle-, and low-status speech (Geertz 1960, 248–60). In the United States, someone might choose to say that something is *wonderful* or that it is *def,* thus imparting significant information about the identity of the speaker, as well as the formality or informality of the situation. Multilingual speakers might insert words from one of their languages into sentences spoken in another of their languages; often this is done because the inserted word is "just better" somehow or because it expresses something otherwise inexpressible or because the person wants to sound more worldly. If I decide to use a French word in my English sentence, and I take the trouble to give it an authentic (I hope) French pronunciation, I am probably trying to impress you with my knowledge of, and access to, French. One of the points of noting word choice as an element of "instrumentalities" is to note these kinds of social uses of language and the ways in which speakers take advantage of them or are constrained by them.

There are some interesting examples, too, of ways in which people use different grammatical patterns when they speak. Some Native American languages require that men and women form plurals differently from one another, for example. A study done in the 1950s by linguistic anthropologist John Fischer showed that English-speaking children in New England formed verbs differently according to gender: Girls tended to use -*ing* endings on their verbs, and boys tended to use -*in* endings. He also discovered that degree of formality influenced verb endings as well: Verbs that described informal activities received the -*in* ending more often than verbs that described more formal activities (*runnin, spittin* vs. *sitting, eating*).

Occasionally the instrumentalities chosen may be coded for secrecy. Pig Latins and similar play languages, where words are disguised by manipulating their parts, are often used by children to hide what they are saying from their peers or from their parents. A different example of coding for secrecy is the special language developed by Navajo Code-Talkers during World War II, in which English words were first substituted for other English words and then Navajo words were used instead of the substituted words. In this way, Navajo speakers could relay battle-sensitive information over the radio without fear of being understood. Enemy forces were never able to crack this Navajo code, partly because of the double level of substitution and partly because Navajo was not well known by the enemy decoders.

Of course speakers in multilingual communities have even more choices of speech varieties, and one goal of an ethnography of communication should be to document the conditions and situations in which individuals might choose one speech variety over another, or might choose to mix elements of different speech varieties, and to describe the effects of each of those choices socially and culturally. Paying attention to the instrumentalities that people use when they speak is a major part of understanding language use in real situations.

Norms   **Norms** refers to the expectations that speakers have about appropriateness of speech use. Is it okay to use speech in a particular setting or is silence preferred? Who should speak? Who should listen? How loud is too loud? Should people speak up? Is it okay for specific people to use specific kinds of speech in specific kinds of settings? Are some kinds of language taboo in some situations? The norms attached to speech behavior will affect how someone's behavior is interpreted, judged, and understood in any given situation. In some kinds of religious settings, it is most appropriate to worship in silence, for example, while in others, responding to the preacher with shouts of encouragement is appropriate and expected. In still others, everyone is expected to chant the prayers aloud, each at his or her own pace, or to speak out "in tongues" as the spirit moves them or to take a turn "testifying."

In Madagascar, men are expected to use indirect speech whenever possible, while women prefer directness in speech and are therefore the ones who do most of the buying and selling in the marketplace, where direct speech is more highly valued (Keenan [Ochs] 1974/1989). In Texas, coon-dog sellers are expected to lie about the qualities and abilities of the dogs they are selling; stretching the truth is taken for granted by sellers and buyers alike. The story about corn pudding (Cross-Language Miscommunication 5.1: Corn Pudding) is an example of how young people in the United States find ways to be polite without saying what they really mean. Is the young woman lying when she says, "It's good corn pudding"? If so, is lying justified when the norms of speaking emphasize being polite?

An important subject covered under norms is the question of taboos and avoidances. Are there certain words or expressions that cannot be said in certain situations or in the presence of certain people? Are there certain words or expressions that can't be used at all? In many cultures, children do not call their parents by name; they use kinship terms instead, such as *Mom* or *Dad,* or *Mother* or *Father.* In some places, young people are expected to use special terms of respect for their parents-in-law. In others, young people are expected to avoid talking to their parents-in-law as much as possible. As for outright taboos, many cultures taboo words referring to sexual functions and body parts; some cultures taboo the use of words for supernatural beings or powerful deities. Some cultures taboo the name of a person who has died, others name their children after people who have recently died, and still others name their children after individuals who are still living. In today's global society, when we interact with individuals of many different cultures, it is important to understand the various norms attached to speaking by different groups of people.

Genres   **Genres** refers to different kinds of speech acts or events. Although we can create a long list of genres, such as lectures, conversations, gossip, performances, sermons, jokes, riddles, lies, proverbs, and so on, it is important to be aware of the possibility that different cultures may include different genres in the list. Zen koans have elements of Eu-

Doing Linguistic Anthropology 5.2

S-P-E-A-K-I-N-G IN THE CLASSROOM

I sometimes ask my students to do an impromptu ethnography of the speaking that goes on in our classroom. Here are the kinds of things they come up with. The setting/situation is fairly obvious, but sometimes we describe the physical setting of the room, including the technological gadgetry and the unfriendly "no food or drink" signs posted on the door, as well as the psychological setting, including how the time of day affects our general sleepiness, or how an upcoming exam affects everyone's level of tension. Of course the participants are usually just the students and myself, unless it is conversation partner match-up day. I sometimes joke that my ends are to open their minds and pour in vast quantities of information, while it seems their ends are to find out what will be on the next exam. Act sequences vary from day to day, but there is always a handing back of papers and the making of announcements before we settle down to covering the day's material. The key is generally serious, although I sometimes crack jokes or tell stories to keep things lively and try to keep people awake and engaged. I tend to switch instrumentalities as much as I can, using my New York-ese or my Shinzwani to drive home points about choice. Power Point slides and workbook exercises add examples from other languages and channels of communication. Following the norms of a reasonably standard classroom experience can sometimes prove difficult for us because everyone wants to contribute an experience or an example, and we can get off track fairly easily. Students like to point out that we use a wide range of genres in the classroom, going beyond lectures to include personal narratives and the communal working out of workbook exercises. One of the things we discover by turning the lens of an ethnography of speaking onto ourselves is the degree to which our classroom itself has become a speech community. It's a useful and interesting exercise.

HJO

ropean proverbs, but are not exactly the same thing. Haiku poetry is a specific genre that is different from other genres of poetry. Two genres that people in the Comoro Islands would add to the list are *hale* and *hadisi*. Both are kinds of stories, but they are distinctly different from one another. *Hale* (pronounced ha-lei) are old stories that often have animal characters in them, often have imaginary or fantastic events taking place, and generally have morals at the ends. They begin with the formula, "*Hale,*

hale, hoho" (Once upon a time, a long time ago), and they are a little bit like European and American fairy tales but also include some tall tales as well. *Hadisi* are stories about historical or near-historical events and generally have human or heroic characters. They are more like European and American histories, but they might also include legends as well. An ethnography of communication should attend to the different kinds of genres that a particular speech community identifies and uses.

In the Field, Kansas State University, Manhattan, Kansas, Early 1990s

"Well I started out at . . . where I assisted with . . . and then I was hired at . . . where I developed a program in . . . and then, um, and then I was promoted to . . . so now I was in charge of . . . and oh yes, back when I was at . . . I also managed a special program in . . . and when I was at . . . I did something like that too, but I also have some experience with . . . and with . . ."

The candidate droned on, talking about his background, his career path, his skills, his accomplishments, and whatever else seemed to come into his head. There didn't seem to be any pause.

I looked around the table. My three colleagues on the interviewing committee were sitting there in stunned silence. Their faces showed the same mix of concern and astonishment that I was feeling. At the start of the interview, one of us had asked the routine opening question: "So, tell us a little bit about yourself." Now, twenty minutes later, the candidate was still talking, going back and forth through his career history, filling in details and adding more depth, with no clear pause and no end in sight. We had interviewed three other candidates and nothing like this had happened to us. We were stumped.

And then, as often happens when I am stumped, the linguistic anthropologist in me took over and I was "in the field" again. I spent the next few minutes trying to observe the total scene, making mental notes about everything in it. It didn't take long before I noticed a pattern in the candidate's narration. Each "beginning" seemed to be preceded by a very tiny pause: "[pause] And then . . . [pause] And then . . . [pause] Oh, and back when . . . [pause] But I also . . ." I hadn't heard such tiny pauses since I had left New York City. Living in Kansas, where pauses are significantly longer, I had almost forgotten how to converse in "tiny-pause" style.

I decided to see if I could still use the style. "So!" I said, at the next tiny pause, "Can you give us an example of . . . ?" It was a question one of the other committee members had asked the other candidates. And the candidate answered the question. Then, at the next tiny pause, I tried another committee member's question: "Have you ever had to deal with . . . ?" And then another one: "Can you discuss . . . ?" And so it went for the rest of the hour, with me asking all of the committee's regular questions and the candidate answering all of them in rapid-fire tiny-pause style. When the hour was up, the candidate took off for his next appointment and the committee gathered to prepare its report.

"How did you do that?" was my colleagues' first reaction.

"What?" I asked.

"Get a word in edgewise," they said. "How did you manage to do it?"

"I realized that he was using a different conversational style," I explained. "It goes faster than what we're used to in Kansas, and it has shorter pauses, but it's one I'm familiar with and can use. I'm only sorry it took me so long to recognize it."

HJO

✳ INTERCULTURAL COMMUNICATION: ISSUES AND EXPECTATIONS

Sometimes you find yourself in the field when you least expect it. It's usually when something's "gone wrong" in a speech interaction. In the example above, although we were all speaking English, it is clear that our candidate came from a different speech community than the one that we—the interviewers—belonged to. The fact that I had once belonged to a speech community similar to the candidate's made it easier for me to shift speech styles to accommodate to his way of talking. What happens when you don't already have access to different speech styles? What happens when you are not "multilingual" in this way?

When Things "Go Wrong": Understanding Cultural Miscues

Linguistic anthropologist Michael Agar has a useful answer for these kinds of dilemmas. Agar (1994) uses the phrase **rich point** to describe the kind of moment in which things "go wrong" in a speech situation. Anyone who moves between speech communities is liable to encounter rich points. Interestingly, rich points can't always be predicted. As Agar points out, rich points depend largely on the contrast between the cultures in question and between the expectations of the speech communities involved. This is partly why most of the examples I have given throughout this chapter are so personal. They are rich points that occurred because of the contrast between my particular expectations, learned in my particular speech community, and other individuals' expectations, learned in their speech communities. It is entirely possible that anyone else read-ing this book would not have encountered the same rich points that I did. Rich points are a fairly personal thing.

Of course, each person is a member of a culture, and a speech com-munity, and as such there is a strong possibility that most members of a particular speech community will have the same expectations about speech situations. That's why it's possible to write books and articles about "how to communicate with the X people" or "how people from X and Y cultures misunderstand one another." Books like that can serve as useful starting points, but it is possible to be misled by them as well. It's far better to rely on your own skills in identifying rich points. You will al-ways bring something of your own culture to every experience, but you are still an individual, with individual understandings of your culture and speech community's expectations. That's why it's so difficult to write about rich points. It's just as difficult to write about cultural and linguis-tic relativity.

Using Linguistic Anthropology to Develop Communicative Competence

According to Agar, some people react to rich points by ignoring them and hoping they will "go away." Others react by assuming that the other per-son is behaving incorrectly and that nothing needs to be done, except per-haps for the other person to learn how to communicate better. In the case of the interview, everyone who met that particular candidate reacted more or less in this way, saying things like "I don't know what was wrong with that person; he didn't let me get a word in edgewise." People who know something about linguistic anthropology, however, can do better than this. Linguistic anthropology provides you with the tools to do field work, to analyze the rich points and to use them on your way to devel-oping communicative competence in a new speech community.

How do you analyze rich points? Agar describes the process as tak-ing three essential steps. He sums up the steps with the acronym **M-A-R**, which stands for "mistake," "awareness," and "repair." Let's take each of these concepts in turn.

Mistake refers to recognizing that a rich point has occurred. Some-thing has gone wrong and communication has broken down somehow. In the case of the interview, the rich point occurred when I recognized that we weren't getting our questions answered because—it seemed—the candidate wasn't letting us talk. When I realized that twenty minutes had gone by since our first question, I knew that something was definitely "wrong." In the case of the young Native American asking for a ride, the rich point occurred when I recognized that Dr. Stirland and the young man were "talking" to one another, but not really communicating; he was telling her about his family, who lived over a thousand miles away, and she was smiling and nodding, and I was beginning to wonder what the point of the conversation was going to be. Was he going to ask her about her research? It didn't seem so; he just continued telling her about his family. As I stood there in the warm Kansas sun, wondering what to do next, it struck me that we were in the middle of a rich point and that I was going to have to take steps to resolve the difficulty.

Awareness refers to recognizing that different expectations have caused the rich point to occur. The expectations may involve ideas about settings, participants, ends, act sequences, keys, instrumentalities, norms, genres, or anything else that is covered in the range of communicative competence in a particular speech community. Different expectations provide different "frames of reference" through which we might view our worlds; becoming aware of these different frames of reference is an important step in understanding the rich point, why it occurred, and what to do about it. Awareness makes it possible for you to recognize your own speech community's expectations as just one of a range of possible ways of doing things. In the case of the interview, awareness occurred when I recognized the difference between the candidate's pause style and ours. We expected longer pauses than we were getting. He expected questions in the pauses he was giving us. In our mostly white, Anglo-Saxon, Protestant speech community, we took turns slowly, with minimal overlap and plenty of space between turns. (Sometimes I wonder about the extent to which this style was influenced by interaction with Native Americans in the region.) Our candidate was also white, Anglo-Saxon, and Protestant, but had been raised in Germany and New York and (just as I had adopted Kansas speech styles) had picked up elements of the speech styles associated with speech communities in those places. In particular, he appeared to have picked up the overlapping tiny-pause style that is often associated with Jewish Americans in New York. It is also worth noting that overlapping speech is more often associated with women than with men, yet our candidate was male and our search committee members were all female.

Complications like this are instructive because they remind us that speech styles and competencies can be fairly fluid, that you can develop multiple competencies, and that your gender, ethnicity, culture, and class status do not bind you irretrievably to one specific style of speaking. They do communicate a lot about who you are, and people do make assumptions about you depending on how they hear you speaking, but the interconnections between status and speaking style can be misleading if you leap to conclusions based on stereotypes. We will have more to say about this in other chapters, in particular in Chapter 10.

For the moment, the important thing is to recognize that, when you have encountered a rich point, you know that your next step is to use what you have learned about the ethnography of communication to develop your awareness of the contrasting speech community expectations that the individuals in question are using. In this case, I was lucky. Because I already had communicative competency in two different speech styles, it was easier for me to switch into recognition mode. I could simply identify the two speech styles and the expectations that went with each. I was also lucky in sorting out the contrasting expectations in the case of the young man asking for a ride because I had read an article describing the differing speech styles and could recognize an instance of what I had read about.

In the case of the Japanese student whose food needed salt and of the young woman who detested corn pudding, I didn't know the speech community expectations involved and I needed to spend time with each of these students asking for details about the situations, participants, ends, acts, keys, instrumentalities, norms, and even genres, in order to get enough of a picture of the different speech communities involved and the expectations that worked in each one. In essence, I needed to help each of these students to do a micro-ethnography as we sorted through the rich points, what had happened, and what they could have done about it (or what kinds of repairs they might try in future situations).

Repair refers to developing new sets of expectations to use in communicating. Once you have become aware of the differences in expectations between speech communities, you can begin to experiment with shifting your own repertoire of expectations, adding new ones to your set of communicative skills, and trying new ways of communicating. This doesn't mean that you have to abandon your old set of expectations, any more than learning a new language means you have to give up the one you grew up speaking.

It does mean that you have to try new speech styles, however, and this can be a little intimidating at first. Rest assured that the people you are speaking with will generally be receptive to your efforts. In fact, most of the time they will be relieved that you are beginning to speak more "normally." In the case of the interview, the candidate was visibly relieved when I switched into tiny-pause style to ask him more questions. We spent the rest of the hour in a rapid-fire give-and-take of questions and answers. From time to time, one or both of us would look at the other three interviewers to see if they had any questions, and, probably because I had shifted my frames of reference and my expectations along with my speech style, I was a little surprised to see them just sitting there and watching us. On the other hand, I could empathize with their frustration, having been stuck in a rich point myself for the first twenty minutes.

Students sometimes ask whether switching speech styles to accommodate to the styles of others will be taken as "mocking" rather than as accommodation. I think the answer lies in the "key" area of the S-P-E-A-K-I-N-G model. The tone you adopt in trying out your new style is important. You should be seriously interested in speaking in a manner that fits in, not in a manner that obviously is humorous or makes fun of a different manner of speaking. As you test the water and attempt to develop competency in a new speech style, you need to pay attention to the reactions from members of that speech community. If you fail in some way, then you need to go back through the M-A-R steps and make further adjustments. Keep adjusting until you understand the expectations of the speech community in question and the frames of reference that guide the ways in which language is used in that speech community. It is a never-ending process, of course, and it is one that anthropologists make use of every time they enter a new field situation. The rewards are great as you build your repertoire. The more varieties of language that you learn, the more people you will be able to converse with and the more points of view you will have access to. Just remember that learning a language includes more than learning how to form words and sentences correctly. It means learning how to *use* that language, in all of its varieties, in all kinds of situations, and with all kinds of speakers.

SUMMARY

Learning a language is more complex than merely learning sounds and forming grammatically correct sentences. To really learn a language, you need to learn how the language is used in real situations, by real people. You need to learn how social and cultural contexts can affect the way a language is supposed to be used. Knowing how to form grammatically correct sentences is known as linguistic competence; knowing how to speak appropriately in real situations is known as communicative competence. One of the goals of linguistic anthropology is to describe and analyze communicative competence in different cultures and languages.

Bronislaw Malinowski was an anthropologist who described the contexts of language use in the early part of the twentieth century. Building on the work of Malinowski and others, Dell Hymes took the lead in the 1960s in developing a framework for describing language in social and cultural contexts. Known as the ethnography of speaking, Hymes's framework focuses attention on seven key aspects of language in context: setting/scene, participants, ends, act sequences, keys, instrumentalities, norms, and genres. He proposed the mnemonic S-P-E-A-K-I-N-G to sum up the range of elements that a researcher should attend to in developing a complete description of language use in a community. Contemporary research into communicative competence often focuses on the details of actual conversations in order to analyze how language communicates gender, ethnicity, and power in subtle ways.

Understanding cultural expectations about language use is essential for knowing how to use a language. Misunderstanding those expectations can lead to cross-cultural and cross-language mistakes in communication. Anthropologist Michael Agar has described such mistakes as rich points. Learning how to repair rich points is a key step in developing communicative competence in a new language, as well as enabling you to develop a more cross-cultural awareness of language differences and similarities.

KEY TERMS

act sequence
awareness
communicative competence
community of practice
context
dialects of a language
ends
ethnography of communication
ethnography of speaking
genres
indirection
instrumentalities
key
linguistic community
linguistic competence
M-A-R
mistake
mutually intelligible
mutually unintelligible
norms
participants
registers
repair
rich point
setting/situation
S-P-E-A-K-I-N-G
speech acts
speech community
speech event
speech situation

FURTHER READING

About Malinowki's Ideas Regarding Language in Context

Malinowski, Bronislaw. 1935/1978. An ethnographic theory of language and some practical corollaries. Supplement to *Coral gardens and their magic*. New York: Dover. This is a reasonably readable discussion of the ways in which language takes on meaning in specific situations.

About Linguistic Competence

Chomsky, Noam. 1965. *Aspects of the theory of syntax.* Cambridge, MA: MIT Press. This contains Chomsky's discussion of linguistic competence.

About Communicative Competence

Hymes, Dell H. 1972. On communicative competence. In *Sociolinguistics: Selected readings,* ed. J. B. Pride and J. Holmes, 269–93. Harmondsworth, UK: Penguin Books. This contains Hymes's discussion of communicative competence.

About the Ethnography of Communication

Brenneis, Donald, and Ronald K. S. MacCaulay. 1996. *The matrix of language: Contemporary linguistic anthropology.* Boulder, CO: Westview Press. This is an excellent collection of recent articles on language as social practice, with special emphasis on issues of gender, ethnicity, culture, and power.

Gumperz, John J. and Dell H. Hymes. 1972. *Directions in sociolinguistics: The ethnography of communication.* New York: Holt, Rinehart & Winston. In particular, Appendix 2, "Outline guide for the ethnographic study of speech use" by Joel Sherzer and Regna Darnell, is an excellent and accessible introduction to the methodology.

Hymes, Dell H. 1974. *Foundations in sociolinguistics: An ethnographic approach.* Philadelphia: University of Pennsylvania Press. This is one of Hymes's classic presentations of the approach.

Saville-Troike, M. 1989. *The ethnography of communication: An introduction.* Oxford: Basil Blackwell. This is another good introduction to the ethnography of communication.

About Rich Points

Agar, Michael. 1994. *Language shock: Understanding the culture of conversation.* New York: William Morrow. This is an engaging, well-written introduction to the idea of rich points: how to recognize them and what to do about them. This is also an excellent survey of the history of linguistic anthropology and a good introduction to the field of conversation analysis.

About Issues of Ethnicity, Race, Gender, Status, and Culture in Language Use

Basso, Keith. 1979. *Portraits of the whiteman.* Cambridge: Cambridge University Press. This is a well-written introduction to Native American views of Anglo speech behavior.

Condon, John. 1985. *Good neighbors: Communicating with the Mexicans.* Yarmouth, ME: Intercultural Press. This is about Mexican-U.S. intercultural communication.

Irvine, Judith. 1974. Strategies of status manipulation in the Wolof greeting. In *Explorations in the ethnography of speaking,* ed. Richard Bauman and Joel Sherzer, 167–91. Cambridge: Cambridge University Press. This provides an excellent example of using the ethnography of communication to understand a specific situation.

Lakoff, Robin. 1990. *Talking power: The politics of language.* New York: Basic Books. This is a readable book about how language differences can be attributed to differences in social identity.

Moerman, Michael. 1988. *Talking culture: Ethnography and conversational analysis.* Philadelphia: University of Pennsylvania Press. This is a good presentation of the field of conversation analysis, with examples from Thai and U.S. conversations.

Scollon, Ron, and Suzanne Wong Scollon. 1981. *Narrative, literacy and face in interethnic communication.* Norwood, NJ: Ablex. This book includes interesting material on Athabascan-Anglo communication.

Tannen, Deborah. 1984. *Conversational style.* Norwood, NJ: Ablex. This book includes Tannen's engaging analysis of a Thanksgiving dinner among friends.

Tannen, Deborah. 1990. *You just don't understand: Women and men in conversation.* New York: William Morrow. This is one of the most widely read books on the subject.

Yamada, Haru. 1997. *Different games, different rules.* New York: Oxford University Press. A highly readable introduction to the ways that Japanese and Americans misunderstand one another, from the point of view of linguistic anthropology.

 STUDENT ACTIVITIES

Readings

The workbook/reader for this book has readings that can help you to further explore and understand the issues introduced in this chapter, in particular regarding ethnicity, gender, culture, and language use in different speech communities.

Exercises

A set of writing exercises in the workbook/reader will assist you in understanding the issues introduced in this chapter and in further exploring the intersection among ethnicity, gender, culture, and language.

Web Exercises

The companion website for this book has a series of links designed to help you explore and better understand the complex intersection of ethnicity, gender, culture, and language in greater depth. The website also contains study questions that will help you to review important concepts.

Guided Projects

If you are creating a language, this is the time to develop a social distinction in your group and to mark it using the language. If you are working with a conversation partner, your instructor may assign a writing project to explore issues of language in action. Your instructor will be your guide.

CHAPTER 6

Nonverbal Communication

In the Field, Comoro Islands, September, 1967

'Hurry! Run quickly!' the woman seemed to be gesturing. I looked up, shading my eyes to get a better view of her. She was leaning out of a second-floor window a few hundred feet from where I was standing, and she was waving me away, or so it seemed.

My husband and I had just settled into our first apartment in the Comoros, on the edge of Itsandra Town, and I had decided to take an afternoon walk. Itsandra is an ancient stone city with cool, narrow, winding streets, set on a promontory overlooking the Indian Ocean. A newer suburban section, with a mosque, post office, and restaurant had recently sprung up along the road at the edge of the old town. Our apartment was in the suburban area, facing a sparkling sandy beach.

It was early afternoon and the streets seemed deserted as I headed into the older part of town. Actually, it was a strange time to be taking a walk. In the tropics, most people head indoors at noon to rest and keep out of the hot tropical sun. Maybe the woman in the window was telling me that I should be indoors somewhere and not walking around in the heat?

I stood still, watching. The woman's arm moved up. Then her arm moved down. When her arm moved up she seemed to straighten her hand. When her arm moved down her hand seemed to curve a bit. Her downstroke seemed stronger than her upstroke. It looked like a wave to me, so I tried waving back.

Now the woman waved more energetically. She seemed to be pushing the air away from her as hard as possible. Why the pushing motion? Was she pushing me away? Was she warning me not to come too close? Could she see something dangerous from her vantage point? Was she telling me to get out of the heat? Dozens of questions ran through my mind, but I had just arrived and couldn't speak the language at all. There was no one I could ask for help.

Frustrated, I waved again. Then I turned and walked in the opposite direction. After exploring a few more deserted streets, I returned home to rest. I knew that nonverbal communication systems were different in different cultures. Here I was, struggling with that fact.

Several months passed before I saw the same kind of wave again, but I recognized it as soon as I saw it. I was with a group of women and one of them waved to another woman a short distance away. Not only was it exactly the same sort of wave, but it seemed to have the same sort of intensity. I watched as the woman who was waved to smiled and came over to join our group! As I thought about this, I realized that the curving of the hand on the downstroke of the wave could be seen as a 'come here' kind of gesture, sort of like scooping someone closer to you.

I saw the 'come here' wave a few more times during my stay in the Comoros, and each time its meaning was the same. I tried it out myself a few times and was pleased each time that it worked the way I meant it to. I was beginning to learn the nonverbal communication system of my new language community.

HJO

The waving/beckoning gesture that I encountered in the Comoros is just one example of the ways that different cultures and different speech communities use different kinds of gestures to mean different kinds of things. Anyone who is trying to learn a new language or to interact with people from another culture needs to learn that culture's set of gestures and meanings. Even if you know the words, the grammar, and the socially appropriate uses of the language you are trying to learn, you won't know enough to be able to really communicate effectively. To be fully fluent in another speech community, you also need to know its system of "nonverbal communication." People in every speech community use gestures, postures, facial expressions, and other kinds of nonverbal communication to signal feelings, actions, and even social identities and group membership. Understanding these kinds of communication is one of the goals of linguistic anthropology.

Nonverbal communication is the process of transmitting messages without spoken words. Sometimes called "body language," nonverbal communication is a category with somewhat fuzzy boundaries. Most scholars include facial expressions, gestures, gaze, and postures. Many also include the way we use the space around us to communicate. Still others include hair styles, adornment, clothing, shoes, and other communicative props (purses, briefcases, and backpacks, for example). Many scholars include various kinds of restricted signaling systems (nautical flags and scuba-diving sign systems) and most include the kinds of sign language used by deaf people. A few even include writing, although many scholars argue that, because writing (unlike sign language) represents words that *could* be spoken, writing should not be counted as nonverbal.

Many scholars also include nonword sounds (e.g., *tsk-tsk* and *oooh*), voice quality (e.g., hoarse, raspy, breathy, and whispering voices), and intonation (e.g., the question intonation in *okay?* and the exclamatory intonation in *no!*). Some also include speech substitutes such as drum language, whistled speech, and Morse code.

Finally, a few scholars note that taste, touch, and smell can play a role in nonverbal communication. Anyone who has given chocolates on Valentine's Day, tickled a baby, or appreciated the smell of a new car might be able to tell you the meanings of these examples in their particular cultures. This chapter discusses different kinds of nonverbal communication to help you to learn how to pay closer attention to, as well as to analyze and understand, nonverbal communication in different cultures.

 WEBLINK To learn more about nonverbal communication, go to http://anthropology.wadsworth.com/ottenheimer_language.

✳ LEARNING NONVERBAL COMMUNICATION

Ninety-four percent of our communication is nonverbal, Jerry. KRAMER, *SEINFELD*

Nonverbal communication is a lot more important than many of us realize. Although estimates vary, it is likely that well over 60 percent of our messages get across nonverbally. Some recent research even suggests that nonverbal signals can override verbal signals. Your words may be all about how much you like your friend's new haircut, but your nonverbal signals may communicate to your friend that you really don't like the haircut at all, and your friend is more likely to believe your nonverbal signals more than your verbal ones.

Most cultural and linguistic anthropologists generally believe that nonverbal signals and their meanings are learned by participating in social groups. My own experience with the wave/beckon signal seems to confirm this. As with language itself, the learning of nonverbal signals usually takes place at unconscious levels. However, the interpretation of nonverbal signals appears to take place at even more unconscious levels than the interpretation of spoken signals, in the deepest levels of our brains (Givens 2002). As a result, some anthropologists are intrigued by the possibility that at least some nonverbal communication may be universal and innate.

As with spoken language, encountering different nonverbal communication systems often helps to bring elements of those systems to the level of conscious awareness, making them available for analysis, comparison, and better understanding. Whenever you encounter elements of a nonverbal system different from your own or miscommunicate due to some difference in nonverbal systems, you become more aware of your own system as well as new alternatives. Once you have noticed a difference, you can begin to try to bridge the gap, learning to read and interpret new signals, and adjust your own signals so that you can communicate more clearly. Most important, you can learn ways to avoid embarrassing yourself or your hosts by learning how your own nonverbal signals are seen by others.

In recent years, there has been a spate of self-help, self-improvement, and body-language-across-culture kinds of books. Each tries to list a specific set of postures, gestures, expressions, and so on that are alleged to have specific meanings in specific cultures. As with any dictionary and grammar of any language, however, it is important to realize that memorized lists are not enough. Instead, it is your ability to participate, observe, and analyze—wherever you may be—that will be of most value to you in learning the nonverbal communication system of another culture or speech community. Besides, every guidebook is written for a specific time and place, and nonverbal communication is constantly evolving and changing, so that a gesture that you were told to avoid last year may be exactly the one you will need next year. Finally, a hidden danger of nonverbal guidebooks is the way in which they reinforce stereotypes about people (the X people need more personal space, the Y people enjoy one another's aromas, you should always shake hands firmly with a person from a Z culture, and so on). As with other aspects of language learning, linguistic anthropology can keep you flexible and open to new patterns and new possibilities while avoiding unnecessary stereotyping of others.

※ SMELL, TASTE, AND TOUCH

"Nothin' says lovin' like somethin' from the oven . . ." goes the commercial jingle, and many realtors in the United States believe that if a house smells like freshly baked bread it will sell faster. A few realtors actually believe the opposite: that an odorless house will sell faster. This is a good example of how difficult it is to create concrete rules for what communicates what. For the most part, people do seem to react positively to odors that are familiar to them or remind them of "home," but different smells will communicate this to different people. A landlord I know complained that when he rented to certain ethnic groups his apartments always ended up smelling unpleasant to him! I may like it if my house smells like fermenting sauerkraut, but you may be repulsed.

Smell can sometimes communicate status or even membership in special groups. These days, cigar smoking seems to be making a comeback in the United States, wine tasting seems to have a component for which people talk knowledgeably about the aroma (or "nose") of the wines, and Americans still seem to want their new cars to smell new (even if the odor is due to toxic off-gassing). The key is the association of a particular smell with a particular social group or event. Such associations can change over time and from group to group, probably in response to social and cultural factors. When I was growing up, the scent of pine communicated cleanliness. Nowadays, a citrusy lemony smell sends that message. In the Comoro Islands, sandalwood sends the same message. Americans have a reputation for avoiding contact with odors, and indeed they do buy and use their share of breath mints, room and car deodorizers, and body deodorizers. On the other hand, they also buy and use many products specifically for their smells and for the messages that they seem to send, from citrusy soaps to springlike room fresheners, from coconut-scented sun lotions to perfumes and aftershave lotions. The important thing, as always, is to understand the extent to which aromas can give off nonverbal messages and the messages that different groups associate with those aromas.

It's a little more difficult to talk about how taste communicates. When people give one another sweets to show affection, it's an example of using taste to communicate nonverbally. Another example is the way that particular tastes tend to characterize particular cultures. Europeans frequently comment on the high degree of sweetness of American foods. Americans find most African foods to be spicy compared to what they are used to. When my husband and I ate spicy Comorian curries without discomfort, our hosts told us we were "real Comorians." Indeed, sharing similar tastes can be a strong way to communicate membership in a group, and certain assumptions are made depending on whether you order a beer or a glass of wine or a cup of espresso. Whenever my husband and I order beer and wine, for example, our server brings the wine to me and the beer to my husband even though we tend to drink these items counter to this stereotype, showing that taste is stereotyped and that it is assumed to communicate nonverbally.

Touching can be a way of communicating nonverbal messages. Important considerations regarding touch are the questions of who can touch whom and of what various kinds of touching might signal. Americans tend to avoid being touched, but metaphors of touch abound in the language. Cousin Joe, a blues singer that I worked with in New Orleans, liked to describe someone's skin as "as smooth as a spanked baby's behind," and the expression *as soft as silk* seems also to be widely used to describe something nice. Some toilet paper is marketed as "squeezably soft," and *fabric softeners* are used in laundering clothes. Occasionally we even talk about being *touched* by a particularly poignant event. Shaking hands is a kind of touching as well, and different cultures have different expectations about how firm, how gentle, how long, and how many pumps a handshake should be, as well as what is communicated by a firm hand-

Doing Linguistic Anthropology 6.1

THE TOUCH

Dr. Bell [name changed] was one of those men who would wrap his arm around a woman to greet her. A professor of geography, he just seemed to me to be overly effusive and friendly until I noticed one day that Dr. Bell never wrapped his arm around men to greet them. With men, there was handshaking; with women, there was arm wrapping or, on occasion, elbow squeezing. But always, there was touching. I began to wonder about this and to analyze it. As I watched Dr. Bell over a period of several weeks, I began to think that beyond being "friendly," Dr. Bell was unconsciously signaling dominance through his touching behavior. I decided to test my hypothesis by responding in kind. If Dr. Bell was comfortable with an arm wrap from me, then I could chalk his arm wrapping up to friendliness; if not, then dominance was probably at play. The next time I saw Dr. Bell with a group of colleagues, I approached him, reached out, and wrapped my arm around him. I also delivered the standard *Hi, there, how are you?* greeting that he usually used with me. Poor Dr. Bell tensed up immediately! Clearly startled, he stammered out a greeting, gently edging himself out from my encircling arm. For several months after that, Dr. Bell seemed to avoid me. Eventually, however, he began to greet me with handshakes rather than with arm wraps. He began greeting other women colleagues with handshakes as well. Not only had I tested a hypothesis and found it correct, but Dr. Bell appeared to have reevaluated his nonverbal signals and changed the way he communicated with all of his female colleagues.

HJO

shake as opposed to a relaxed one. Another important consideration regarding touch is the fact that touching is tied up closely with the way we use the space around us, and this brings us to the study of "proxemics."

 PROXEMICS

Developed by anthropologist Edward T. Hall in the 1950s and 60s, **proxemics** is the study of how people perceive and use space. Inspired by earlier studies of animal behavior and territoriality, Hall applied some of the same insights to human behavior in cultural contexts. Hall developed the word proxemics by taking the *prox-* morpheme from Latin and the *-emics* morpheme from linguistic anthropology. *Prox-* means 'near' in Latin, and

-emics refers to that level of cultural analysis that focuses on subjectively relevant, internally verifiable units of culture. (Chapter 3 gives a more detailed explanation of -emics.)

Culture, Ethnicity, and Personal Space

As you might expect, the ways that people perceive and use the spaces around them are different in different cultures. For example, as previously noted, Americans tend to avoid touching one another. Watch a group of Americans in an elevator and you will note that they tend to maximize the space among them. Take an elevator ride in France and you will note that people stand much closer together than Americans do. An elevator that is "full" of Americans would look—to French individuals— as though it still had room for more people to squeeze in. Here's another example. While subway riders in New York might look as though they are being crushed together during rush hour, a careful observer would note that they are not pressed up against one another but rather that each one has a few inches of space to move around in. On the other hand, Japanese subways are said to be much more densely packed during rush hour, with people tolerating close bodily contact at least for the duration of the ride.

Hall proposed four kinds of proxemically relevant spaces, or body distances, that could be compared between cultures: intimate, personal, social, and public (see Figure 6.1). For Americans, he suggested that intimate space ranged from zero to eighteen inches (or zero to one-half meter), personal space ranged from eighteen inches to four feet (one-half to one and one-half meters), social space ranged from four to twelve feet (one and one-half to three and one-half meters), and public space was anything over twelve feet (three and one-half meters). As mentioned, French individuals are more comfortable with slightly smaller personal spaces, and in fact most Europeans, and many Middle Easterners as well, prefer personal spaces ranging from eight to twelve inches. Personal space in England, on the other hand, doesn't seem to begin until you reach approximately twenty-four inches. I am reminded of the story I read recently in which a young American woman living in Russia discov-

| Intimate | Personal | Social | Public |
| (0–1.5) | (1.5–4) | (4–12) | (12+) |

FIGURE 6.1   American proxemics *Source: Coon (2003, 670).*

Cross-Language Miscommunication 6.1

DOWN THE HALL

Some years ago, I was entranced by watching the proxemic dynamics in a conversation between a young graduate student and a professor of veterinary medicine. The student appeared to be from India or Pakistan, and the professor appeared to be from the United States or Europe. Both were males. No matter where they were from, the student's personal space appeared to be considerably smaller than the professor's. As the student moved closer to the professor in order to keep within comfortable discussion range, the professor backed away from the student to maintain his own sense of a comfortable discussion range. It looked like the student was happiest ten or twelve inches from the professor, while the professor seemed happiest at about twenty or twenty-five inches from the student. It was both amusing and sad for me to watch them slowly maneuver their way down the entire length of the hall as they carried on their conversation. I am not sure, and I never asked, the extent to which either one of them was aware of the progression or aware of the mismatch in their proxemic systems.

HJO

---

ered that she needed to stand very close (in her terms) to the person in front her if she was waiting in line. If she stood at the distance that she was comfortable with, other people were likely to assume that she was just standing around waiting for someone else to arrive and they would enter the space that she had "provided" in front of her in the line.

I am told by my students that cowboys in Kansas and Nebraska (and possibly other states) maintain proxemic systems that are different from "standard" American proxemics. Indeed, an interesting article by Joseph Hickey and William Thompson (1988) argues that cowboy proxemics may have developed around the fact that cowboys are frequently seated on horses. Thus, face-to-face personal space between cowboys ranges from six to eight feet (three to four and one-half meters), or the space that would be available if two horses were standing nose to nose, while side-to-side personal space ranges from zero to eighteen inches, suggesting that if the horses are standing side by side the legs of two riders could touch. This proxemic system seems to carry over into nonmounted interactions as well, so that individuals at a campfire or other social gathering tend to arrange themselves facing each other (across the campfire or room) so that they are six or eight feet apart, or they arrange themselves side by side close together, on hay bales or chairs on one side of the fire or room. At first, I thought that Hickey and Thompson's paper was a joke, but my students from ranching backgrounds assure me that it is right on target. It is possible that different ethnic groups in the United States have different proxemic systems as well.

Gender, Status, and Personal Space

One of the problems that American women have with being touched by men that they don't know well is the fact that such touching can be seen as an uninvited violation of their personal space. Indeed, the amount of space one has and one's ability to enter into someone else's personal space without asking are related to one's relative status, at least in the United States. The more powerful you are, the more space you can command and the more easily you can enter someone's personal space without permission. Teachers enter into their students' personal space to help them, but students are considered rude if they enter into a teacher's personal space to ask for help. An unexamined component of Dr. Bell's arm-wrapping gesture (See Doing Linguistic Anthropology 6.1: The Touch) was the way that it expressed his dominance over someone by his ability to enter, unasked, into their space.

American homes and offices often reflect these differential uses of space and communicate, in doing so, the relative statuses of the occupants of those statuses. You are probably aware of the fact that the dean of your college has a larger office than the head of the department that you are majoring in, and that the head of your department probably has a larger office than any of the other professors in that department. If your department has a graduate program, perhaps the graduate students share a single office, with desks arranged in an open bullpen. In contrast, most faculty members have their own individual offices.

Another example of the differential allotment of space can be seen in American houses, where it is fairly common for men to consider at least one room to be "theirs" to use as a den or workshop or office but less common for women to have "rooms of their own" to use for work or hobbies. Occasionally, you might see a sewing room that doubles as a guest room, but it is rare to see a workshop double as a guest room. Another way to look at space in American houses is to note the relative sizes of the bedrooms; parents generally have the largest bedroom, while children have smaller rooms and frequently share bedroom spaces.

In the Comoro Islands, space in houses is often divided into women's areas (courtyards and kitchens) and men's areas (sitting rooms). Although men's and women's spaces are separate, the distinction seems to be along the lines of internal and external parts of the house, with women controlling the core of the house and men occupying the outer rooms. Men and women generally don't enter into one another's areas without asking first.

How we design and arrange and occupy our living and working spaces is an intriguing part of proxemics. As Hall has pointed out, those of us who are used to cities with streets arranged in rectangular grids can find ourselves easily lost in cities where streets meander or are arranged in hub-and-spoke designs. Europeans who are used to the formality of closed doors in office buildings are often uncomfortable with the apparent informality of open doors in American offices. Americans, on the other hand, find the closed doors of European offices formal and off-putting. Comorian women who are used to eating in kitchen courtyards, out of the public view, are often uncomfortable the first time they are asked to eat in public, in a restaurant, for example.

Hall's pioneering work in the area of proxemics has had widespread influence in the years since he introduced the term. Proxemics, and in particular the clash between different proxemic systems, can have a significant impact on our daily lives as well as on our ability to do business across cultures. Countless books, videos, training programs and websites have been developed to help people prepare for overseas assignments. Architects and interior designers make use of proxemics to design contemporary buildings. The United States Department of Defense includes proxemics in its training manuals for personnel going overseas. Proxemics has almost become a common word in the English language rather than one used only by scholars. "Kinesics" is another such word.

✳ KINESICS

The term **kinesics** was originally coined by anthropologist Ray Birdwhistell in the 1950s to describe the study of body movements, facial expressions, and gestures. Like proxemics, Birdwhistell's approach to the subject was strongly influenced by American structural and descriptive linguistics. For example, to parallel the idea of a phoneme as a minimal unit of sound, Birdwhistell proposed the term **kineme** as a minimal unit of visual expression. Just as phonemes had variants called allophones, **allokines** could represent variant forms of kinemes. Finally, just as phonemes might combine into morphemes, or minimal units of meaning, kinemes could combine into **kinemorphs,** or meaningful units of visual expression. Using the methods of linguistic anthropology and working with frame-by-frame analyses of filmed social interactions, researchers worked hard to identify kinemes and to analyze the ways that they combined to form kinemorphs. Over time, however, many scholars, including Birdwhistell himself, found it more convenient to attribute meanings to kinemes, and the word kinemorph was eventually abandoned. Today, people tend to use kineme to mean both a minimal unit of visual expression *and* a meaningful unit of visual expression.

In the 1960s, psychologists Paul Ekman and Wallace Friesen proposed a somewhat different approach. They suggested that gestures could be categorized into five general types.

Emblems, or gestures with direct verbal translations, such as a wave goodbye, or the wave/beckon gesture I learned in the Comoros.

Illustrators, or gestures that depict or illustrate what is said verbally, such as turning an imaginary steering wheel while talking about driving.

Affect displays, or gestures that convey emotion; such as smiles or frowns.

Regulators, or gestures that control or coordinate interaction, such as indicating that it's someone else's turn to talk during conversation.

Adaptors, or gestures that facilitate release of body tension, such as the nervous foot-shuffling of people who would probably rather be leaving.

In the past few decades, linguistic anthropologists and psychologists working in the area of kinesic analysis have greatly expanded our understanding of the ways in which body movement, facial expression, and gestural systems function in different contexts. We now know much more about the ways that different cultures assign different meanings to different gestures. We are also learning how gestures may be broken down into smaller components and how gestures are used as illustrators and regulators, alongside spoken communication. We know that much of a speech community's kinesic system is learned and interpreted unconsciously and perhaps at as deep a level as proxemics.

As with proxemics, there are a great many handy guidebooks to tell you how to move in different cultures, and the same cautions that we mentioned earlier apply here as well. Books and websites that promise instant access to the meanings of gestures often do no more than reinforce stereotypes, so it is important to be careful in how you approach the problem of learning another language community's kinesic system. Note, for example, that Dr. Bell's arm-wrap could have been interpreted as friendly or as dominance-establishing; much depended on the context in which he performed the gesture. As with proxemics, there is plenty of room for intergroup misunderstandings and miscommunication of gestures, facial expressions, and body movements. A few examples should suffice.

Gestures across Cultures

There are lots of gestures, or emblems, that mean one thing in one culture and something else in another. The United States Department of Defense has a website that explains the proxemic and kinesic systems one might encounter in the Middle East, and the rudeness of the "thumbs-up" gesture is noted there. Interestingly, however, the meaning of the gesture has begun to shift in recent years, with almost as many Middle Easterners using it in the American fashion as in the more traditional Middle Eastern fashion. Some of this can be explained by international contact.

Cross-Language Miscommunication 6.2

THANKS FOR THE HELP?

A few years ago, I gave a lecture on the general topic of cultural variations in the language of gesture. An Iranian student came up to me after class and recounted the following story. It happened, he said, just after his arrival in the United States. It was winter and the weather was awful—snow, sleet, ice, you name it. He was standing waiting for a bus when he noticed that the wheels of a nearby car were spinning on the ice and the driver was unable to get the car moving. He offered to help by giving it a push. As he did so, the spinning wheels kicked up sleet and dirt all over his clothes, but the car moved forward. It went to the end of the block, turned and came back past the Iranian. As it did so, the driver gave him a smile and a "thumbs up" sign. The Iranian fumed, furious and humiliated that he got such an obscene gesture from a stranger he had been so nice to! It was only much later, he said, that he learned that "thumbs up" was a good sign in America and that we use the middle finger for the obscenity.

Lelah Dushkin, *Kansas State University*

It helps, of course, to remember that kinesics, like languages, can evolve and change over time and that you need to be open and flexible to possible new meanings, even after you have memorized a set of traditional ones. Another example of this is that the gestures used in New York by Italian-speaking immigrants from southern Italy and by Yiddish-speaking immigrants from Eastern Europe were found to be much less noticeable, and in some cases even absent, in those groups' assimilated descendants (Efron 1941).

Putting your thumb and forefinger together in a circle and extending the other three fingers upward means 'okay' in the United States. In Japan, it refers to money. In France, it may mean that something is worthless. In some parts of Germany, the same sign may be an insult. An episode of *Star Trek: Voyager* (episode 54, part A) revolved around a scene in which a starship commander had put her hands on her hips, thus making a gesture that was taken as obscene and insulting by the alien culture that she was attempting to make peace with. Her second-in-command had to make amends and smooth things over so that the peace-making mission could progress.

Some years ago, American President George H. W. Bush traveled to Australia and, riding in a motorcade, he flashed what he thought was the 'V for victory' gesture: hand up, index and middle fingers extended upward, remaining fingers folded down. Had he kept his palm facing outward that indeed is what he would have signaled; however, he turned the back of his hand out, turning his 'victory' gesture into an obscene gesture instead.

When the Soviet president Khrushchev visited the United States for the first time (in 1960), he clasped his hands over his head and moved them back and forth. He meant it to be a friendly waving motion, as it would have been interpreted in the Soviet Union. For Americans, however, the sign looked more like the kind of gesture that victorious boxers make in a boxing ring, or for cameras, when they have just won a fight. Americans thought Khrushchev was indicating that he was (or would be) victorious over them and did not appreciate the gesture.

Facial Expressions and Eye Contact across Cultures

In addition to gestures, kinesics includes the study of facial expressions, gaze, head movements, and posture. Facial expressions can include winks, blinks, eyebrow movements, smiles, frowns, pursed lips, pouts, lip compression, and more. A recent news photograph showed Tony Blair, British prime minister, talking with French president Jacques Chirac (see Figure 6.2). It was clear from the photo and from the "body language" of the two men (especially Chirac's tightly compressed lips) that they had not really come to any agreement. One year, when I was teach-

FIGURE 6.2 Kinesics in Action: Tony Blair, British prime minister, and French president Jacques Chirac.

ing in Prague, I had a little dictionary stolen out of my purse. When I told this to a Czech friend she said I was probably a target because I "looked like an American." She said that if I didn't "smile so much" I would probably fit in better! "You Americans," she said, "always seem to be smiling for no reason." I took her advice and had no more problems with pickpockets. Winks can communicate a variety of meanings and, as with many kinesic gestures, it is important to assess the context in which the gesture takes place to sort out which of several culturally appropriate meanings is being signaled.

Expectations about gaze can also differ in different cultures and between different ethnic groups. In the United States, for example, European American speakers tend not to look at their listeners until it is time to give up their turns at speaking. Listeners, on the other hand, are expected to look attentively at speakers until they give up their turns. The reverse seems to be common among African Americans, where looking directly at a speaker is considered rude and disrespectful, but speakers are expected to look at listeners while speaking. This can result in conflicts and misunderstandings in classrooms if European American teachers expect African American children to look at them and if those teachers interpret eye avoidance as a sign of guilt or shame. I have actually heard

Doing Linguistic Anthropology 6.2

ANALYZING A WINK

When Dr. Ingle [name changed], a senior administrator at my university began winking at me in meetings, I began to wonder what he was trying to communicate and what I should do about it. A wink seems like a deliberate gesture, so I was sure he was trying to signal something to me. I just couldn't tell if it was 'we're in this together, you and I' or 'you agree with me, don't you?' or something else. I didn't want to wink back without knowing what the message was about. Winks from men to women can sometimes be dominance-assertion signals or outright flirting. Applying my linguistic anthropological observation tools, I began watching Dr. Ingle in different situations, looking especially for winks. I soon discovered that he winked at men as well as at women, usually after he had made a particularly challenging remark. This suggested to me that for Dr. Ingle winking communicated collegiality rather than dominance. Although I relaxed about the winking, I was never comfortable enough to wink back. Instead, I would smile. I guess this was close enough because eventually Dr. Ingle began to seek me out to ask my opinion on important matters.

HJO

teachers address such students with phrases like "Look at me while I'm talking to you!" not realizing that the problem may lie in a clash of kinesic systems rather than in real guilt on the part of the student. Of course, if the student *has* done something wrong, then eye avoidance may also be appropriate; so here too, it's important to know something about the context of the situation in order to interpret the kinesic message. I occasionally encounter some of this avoidance discomfort when I walk through the Orthodox Jewish sections of Brooklyn, New York. Although I know that Orthodox men are expected to avoid looking at women, it always feels awkward the first time I pass a man in the street and he turns his head to avoid making eye contact with me. In contrast, European Americans traveling to Russia report being uncomfortable at the intense amount of staring that they encounter because Russians appear to make much more direct eye contact than Americans do.

OBSERVING AND USING KINESICS AND PROXEMICS

The way you stand, the way you walk, the way you sit, all of these communicate something about you within the kinesic system of your speech community. In addition, your choice of clothing, shoes, hairstyle, and accessories are a part of your culture's kinesic system. And the way you relate to others spatially is an important part of your culture's proxemic system as well.

To experiment with how much can be communicated through kinesics and proxemics, try turning off the sound on your television or on a movie you have rented on video or DVD. You will probably be surprised at how much of the story you can follow just from the proxemics and kinesics used by the actors. Now, try turning the sound down on a foreign film—choose one with no subtitles if possible—and see what a difference this makes. If you don't know the proxemics or kinesics of a speech community, you will be just as lost in that speech community as when you don't know the language. Part of learning to communicate in a new speech community is learning the language, but part of it is also learning to interpret proxemic and kinesic messages.

It's interesting that some kinds of knowledge are best learned nonverbally. This is especially true of things like knitting, cooking, playing an instrument, or repairing machinery, where watching someone else go through the correct motions seems to make all the difference. Somehow book learning doesn't seem to be sufficient for these kinds of technical pursuits; it takes nonverbal instruction and sometimes even apprenticeships to get it right.

✳ GESTURE SYSTEMS AND COMPLEX ALTERNATIVE SIGN LANGUAGES

In some cases, speech is difficult, or impossible, and gesture may be used to replace it. In some of these cases, the gestures become routinized and can develop into a gesture system. In auctions, sawmills, race tracks, or any place where people can see one another but may be too far to communicate effectively by spoken language, systems of gestures can develop. In most of these cases, it appears that gestures that may start out as fairly elaborate illustrators may eventually become simplified enough so that they can be used as a means of basic communication. One example of this that you may be familiar with is the set of signals that pitchers and catchers use in baseball games. Another example is those gestures that people use to help one another when backing up cars, or cars with boat trailers, where one person standing outside and behind the car signals to the driver the direction to turn the steering wheel, and how much space is left for maneuvering, and whether to continue backing up, go forward again, or stop. The more routinized these gestures become, the easier it is to communicate between the guider and the driver. Workers in a sawmill in British Columbia developed a rudimentary sign system to coordinate basic mill operations and found that they could use it to communicate—in a fairly limited way—about some other topics, such as sports, weather, women, and worker-boss relationships (Meissner and Philpott 1975). Also, although they are not exactly gestures, the system of flags used by the navy to signal to distant boats may be included here. A similar communication system is the set of flags and guns used by sailboat racers to signal the start of each race, the changes in course, or the abandoning of the race due to threatening weather.

Complex alternative sign languages are gestural systems that can be used almost as effectively as spoken language. They tend to develop in situations where speech is completely unavailable in all settings. Complex alternative sign languages are more elaborate than gesture systems. Frequently, an elementary syntax develops in a complex alternative sign language to guide word/sign order. A particularly interesting example of a complex alternative sign language is found among certain Australian Aborigine populations where women give up speech for periods as long as a year following the death of a spouse or other close male relative. The complex alternative sign languages that develop in such situations can be used almost as effectively as spoken languages and to communicate almost as many ideas. Another example is the signing that develops among certain monastic orders where speech is given up for religious reasons. Most complex alternative sign languages appear to mimic the syntax of the spoken languages of the communities that use them. In other words, they use the grammar of the spoken language and just substitute signs for all (or most) of the words.

An example of a complex alternative sign system with a grammatical structure that is *not* based on any specific spoken language is Plains Indian sign language. Used widely throughout the Plains region, from what is now North Dakota to northern Mexico, Plains Indian sign language made it possible for people to communicate with one another in spite of differences between their spoken languages. It was even used to communicate with European Americans in the early days of contact. Signs in this system worked as emblems for specific concepts, meaning you didn't need to know the actual spoken words or grammatical systems of the people you were "talking" with. If you wanted to say that six horses went over the hill and you had signs for numbers, horses, movement, and hills you could do it without regard to speech-based linguistic differences. As long as you knew the individual signs and the order in which they were to be combined, you could communicate.

✽ SIGN LANGUAGES

Hearing people—people who can hear sounds—often use gestures as they speak, and sometimes they develop complex alternative sign languages for times when they can't—or don't want to—use spoken language. Still, these alternative sign languages are generally limited to the contexts in which they are used and often are also limited in what they can communicate. The sign languages of deaf people, on the other hand, are as complete and complex as any spoken language. The term **sign language** refers to language performed in three-dimensional space. Sign languages are not alternatives to spoken languages, and they don't depend on spoken languages. Instead, they are complete languages with their own grammars.

For many years, people thought that deaf people just used the grammar of the spoken language around them, substituting signs for spoken words, much like complex alternative sign languages work. Contemporary research, however, has demonstrated that this is not so. This can be clearly seen in the fact that American Sign Language and British Sign Language are mutually unintelligible. If each system was just mimicking the grammar of English in a word-for-word (or sign-for-word) fashion, then signers of either system would be able to understand signers of the other one, and this is not the case.

Each of these sign languages developed separately, without much contact between the two communities of signers. American Sign Language developed from French Sign Language. It was brought to the United States in 1816 by Thomas Gallaudet, a graduate of Yale University, and Laurent Clerc, a French graduate of the Paris school for the deaf. Working together, Gallaudet and Clerc developed a sign language based on Old Signed French. They began teaching their system to students at the American Asylum at Hartford, Connecticut, the first school for the deaf in the United States. Called Old Signed English, this developed into contemporary American Sign Language. It is completely different from British Sign Language; the signs are different and the grammatical bases are different. In fact, American and British Sign Languages are as different from one another as spoken English is from spoken Japanese.

 WEBLINK   To learn more about sign languages, go to
http://anthropology.wadsworth.com/ottenheimer_language.

American Sign Language

In American Sign Language (ASL, also called Ameslan), as in every other complete sign language, signs stand for concepts, not for specific words. For example, in English the word *right* has two meanings: 'correct' and 'the opposite of left.' In ASL, there are two separate signs, one for 'correct' and one for 'the opposite of left.' The sign for 'correct' is made like this: Hold your right hand at waist level with your index finger pointing away from your body, then position your left hand at shoulder level, and, with your left index finger pointing outward, move your left hand down and touch the top of your right hand. To make the sign for 'the opposite of left,' put your right hand in front of your body, about chest high, cross the index and third fingers of your right hand, and then move your hand to the right. These are clearly two different signs for two different concepts.

ASL grammar is not the same as spoken English grammar, either. For example, in ASL a single sign may communicate a short phrase or an entire sentence. For example, using ASL it takes just one sign, I-ASK-HER, to communicate the spoken English 'I ask her.' This single ASL sign includes the subject, the verb, and the object; in spoken English it takes three separate words to say the same thing. English speakers who are learning ASL sometimes make the mistake of relying on their own spoken grammar, making sure that they provide signs for each English word. The result in this case would be the signed I I-ASK-HER HER, which of course seems awkward and repetitive to someone whose first language is ASL, just like using your own English grammar to organize a sentence in French (or vice versa) gives you rather strange results.

Another example of a difference between spoken English and ASL is in the order of words in questions. ASL tends to put the "question words" (in English, words such as *what* and *why*) at the ends of sentences. While spoken English might ask *what did he buy?*, ASL tends to prefer the order HE BUY WHAT?

There is a version of sign language sometimes taught in the United States called Signed English, including SEE1 (Seeing Essential English) and SEE2 (Signed Exact English). Signed English requires that every spoken English word and morpheme be replaced by a sign. For deaf people who have learned ASL, formal Signed English systems are unnatural, awkward, and slow.

Analyzing Signs

The signs used in sign languages are as systematically describable as the phonemes and morphemes of spoken languages. The basic descriptive components of signs used to be called "cheremes," by analogy with the word phoneme, but nowadays they are more commonly called "primes" or even phonemes. **Primes** can be thought of as elements of signs corresponding to the phonological elements of spoken language. Primes are grouped into three categories: "hand shape," "hand placement," and "hand movement." Primes from all three categories are combined to form signs that correspond to the words or morphemes of spoken language. The orientation of the hands can also be important.

Some of the most commonly used primes for *hand shape* are "flat hand," "fist hand," "index hand," and "cupped hand." For **flat hand,** your hand is held flat; for **fist hand,** your hand looks like a fist; for **index hand,** your index finger is extended; and for **cupped hand,** your fingers are arranged in the shape of a C. In fact, each of these primes can also be used to signify a letter of the English alphabet, and many people use those let-

Doing Linguistic Anthropology 6.3

VARIATION IN SIGN

Serious academic study of sign languages started with the work of William Stokoe in the 1960s. In addition to being the first person to describe signs as being made up of parts such as hand shape and hand movement, he noticed that people used different kinds of sign language in different settings. At home people used a casual American Sign Language not much influenced by English, but in more formal settings people used a more English-influenced variety of signing. Stokoe thought that in prestigious settings, such as churches, users saw English as being a bit more prestigious and therefore appropriate. Others saw the use of a pure ASL or a more English-influenced form of signing as having to do with being an insider or outsider of Deaf culture.

When I started working with Pastor Terry Buchholz, currently of Hampshire View Baptist Deaf Church in Silver Spring, MD, I was struck by how much more complex his use of sign language was than anything that had been described before. In one church service, there was English-influenced sign singing, done with large, rhythmic movements that were easy for everybody to see and follow along with; a joke told in ASL done with large hand movements; announcements made with medium-sized hand movements and a form of sign language that was in between English-influenced signing and ASL; prayers done in English-influenced signing with very small, rhythmic gestures; Bible reading done with an intermediate form of signing; and, finally, the sermon was in a fluent ASL done with very large hand movements (see Figure 6.3). This study was done in 1988, just a year after the revolutionary "Deaf President Now" protests at Gallaudet University. When Stokoe studied signing in the 1960s, English might have been

ters to designate the primes instead of the shape descriptor. Thus, flat hand may be referred to as "B shape," fist hand is called "A shape," index hand is called "G shape", and cupped hand is called "C shape." The most common primes for *hand placement* are "near the face," "head," and "upper body." Some common primes for *movement* include "up," "down," "toward the body," "away from the body," "twisting," and "across the body."

As with spoken languages, there are minimal pairs in sign languages. For example, the signs APPLE and CANDY form a minimal pair that contrasts only in hand shape. In both of these signs, hand placement is at the cheek and hand movement is a twist from back to front. The sign APPLE, however, is formed with fist hand (or A shape), while the sign CANDY is formed with index hand (or G shape). The signs SUMMER and UGLY contrast only in hand placement. Both signs use the same hand shape (index finger is extended in a hook shape), and the same hand movement (draw-

seen as necessary throughout the church service, but by 1988 ASL was seen as the right form for the heart of the church service, the sermon. Sign languages, like all spoken languages, are infinitely variable and reflect everything from how to adjust the language so the largest audience can perceive it to political fashions about what language is appropriate when.

Leila Monaghan, *Indiana University*

FIGURE 6.3 Variation in sign: a. English-influenced WILL or FUTURE; b. ASL *FINISH*; c. pastor responding to question in classroom. *Source: Leila Monaghan.*

ing the hand across from left to right), but hand placement in the sign SUMMER is at forehead level, while hand placement for UGLY is at nose level.

When there is no sign in ASL, signers either invent one or use a system called finger spelling. In finger spelling, the fingers are arranged to represent letters of the alphabet. The letters are signed, one at a time, to spell out the needed word. This method is used primarily for spelling out technical terms or personal names, and it can be mixed in with regular ASL, much as hearing speakers sometimes pause to spell out a word or a name for clarity.

As with spoken languages, sign language changes over time. New signs can develop, placement of signs can shift, and different varieties of signing can emerge. Regional variations exist in ASL, for example, with marked differences between northern and southern signers. As with spoken English, it seems that northern signers are perceived as signing more quickly than southern ones. Differences also have been noted with regard to age and gender in sign language. Signs can change over time and new ones can emerge, so older signers may still be using older signs while younger ones may be using signs that might be considered slang by their elders. Distinctions between male and female forms of signing have been studied in Ireland, and some researchers have also noted ethnic variations in signing, particularly between African American and European American signers.

✳ PARALANGUAGE AND SPEECH SUBSTITUTES

Paralanguage (meaning 'alongside of language') is a term developed by linguistic anthropologist George Trager in the 1950s to describe the sounds that accompany speech but that are not directly part of language. Paralinguistic sounds contribute to the meaning of your words, but they are not considered words themselves. In Trager's terms, they are "voice cues." In some cases, paralinguistic features can take the place of speech, as in shushing someone or hissing at someone. Paralanguage refers specifically to *how* something is said rather than to what is said. This is another area where speakers from different language communities can miscommunicate. Because Americans tend to speak more loudly than Britons, Britons often feel as though Americans are shouting at them and therefore are angry. On the other hand, Americans often feel as though British speakers are being secretive because they speak so much more quietly. As with proxemics and kinesics, paralanguage often communicates even more effectively than language. You can *say* you're happy with the grade you got, but your tone of voice may actually communicate that you would have preferred a better grade.

Tone of voice, or voice quality, is one of the most commonly noticed kinds of paralanguage. This includes such features as loudness, pitch, and speed of speaking. Also included may be vocal modifications like whispering, whining, or breathy voice. People may speak loudly or quietly, with high-pitched voice or low-pitched voice, quickly or slowly. In the United States, women who have especially high-pitched voices are often thought of as childlike, while women with lower-pitched voices are heard as businesslike. Whispering is often associated with secrecy and whining with unhappiness. Breathy voice, created by keeping the vocal chords slightly apart, creates a voice that is interpreted as sexy in the United States, but as submissive in Japan. The cooing voice that many adults use with babies in the United States can also be included here. In addition, shifts in intonation can convey different messages. A phenomenon called "rising intonation," in which phrases are ended with a rise in pitch, has become common in the United States in recent years and is variously interpreted to mean uncertainty, questioning, or checking to see if others already know what the speaker is talking about. First associated with teenage girls in California, this style has spread to many other segments of the population. As with spoken language, context is often necessary to help interpret these paralinguistic features.

Of equal importance are those sounds that stand on their own, often as interruptions in the flow of speech. These include sounds like *mhm, shhh, tsk-tsk* and other sorts of clucking, hissing, or grunting sorts of sounds. Called vocal segregates or vocal gestures, they are not quite words, but they are often ascribed meanings and interpreted accordingly. The tongue clucking that is usually written *tsk-tsk* is usually interpreted as a sign of disapproval in the United States. "Backchannel cues" like *mhm* help to provide the kind of feedback that reassures someone that you are still listening. Without such cues, speakers often become uncomfortable and sometimes stop to ask whether you are still listening.

It might also be possible to include ideophones, or sounds that represent other sounds, in the category of paralanguage. These are sounds like *bam, pow*, and *splat* that call to mind the sounds that they mimic. Some languages make extensive use of ideophones in storytelling. Others do not. In some languages, ideophones function like words; in others, they appear to be more akin to paralinguistic phenomena. As with every other part of communication, differences in use and interpretation are possible. Paying attention and keeping flexible are the keys to learning how to use these kinds of nonverbal signals in different cultures and different situations.

Speech substitutes are systems of communication in which sound signals substitute for spoken words or parts of words. In most cases, these sound signals are made either by whistling or drumming. Whistling is found in parts of Mexico, the Canary Islands, Turkey, and Switzerland. Drumming is used primarily in parts of West Africa. The drums most commonly used for this are pressure drums (sometimes called talking drums), where head tension can be altered during drumming to produce different pitches. The different pitches, whether whistled or drummed, reproduce elements of the spoken language. In the case of tone languages, where pitches differentiate between words, it is the pitches of the words that are reproduced by drumming or whistling. In the case of nontone languages, such as the Spanish of the Canary Islands, the whistled tones represent different vowels. In all cases, speech substitutes of these kinds are fairly limited in what they can communicate. Generally they are used to call meetings, make announcements, make bargains, or send warnings. Most of the time, the phrases that are represented are fairly stereotyped and predictable. Still, these kinds of speech substitutes are effective wherever they are used, and take maximum advantage of the fact that spoken words can be represented by other kinds of sound signals. Whether they are truly cases of nonverbal communication, however, is arguable. They are representing words, yet they are doing so by selecting just parts of the words (tones or vowels) to signal, and hearers fill in the blanks to interpret what is being signaled.

SUMMARY

Nonverbal communication is the process of transmitting messages without spoken words. This is sometimes referred to as body language, but it can include more than this. Examples of body language include gestures, facial expressions, eye contact, and the way that people use the space around them. Clothing and hairstyles may also communicate nonverbal messages, as can senses such as smell, taste, and touch.

Proxemics, the study of how people perceive and use space, was developed by Edward T. Hall in the 1950s and 60s. Proxemics notes the difference between how close you might stand with your friends and how far you would stand from a complete stranger. Hall proposed four relevant spaces, or body distances, to compare within and between cultures: intimate, personal, social, and public.

Kinesics is a term coined by Ray Birdwhistell in the 1950s to describe the study of body movements, facial expressions, and gestures. Using terms that parallel structural/descriptive linguistics, Birdwhistell suggested the terms kineme as a minimal unit of visual expression, allokines as the variant forms of kinemes, and kinemorphs as the meaningful units of visual expression.

In the 1960s, Eckman and Friesen proposed a different approach, considering the functions of gestures as emblems, illustrators, affect displays, regulators, and adaptors. Emblems are gestures with direct verbal translations, illustrators are gestures depicting what is said verbally, affect displays convey emotion, regulators control or coordinate interaction, and adaptors facilitate release of body tension.

When spoken communication is hampered for some reason, complex gestural systems or alternate sign languages may develop. Examples include signaling in baseball games or in noisy workplaces. These are generally simple systems and not complete languages. Complex alternative sign systems are closer to spoken language, in that they may develop some rudimentary syntax. Examples include the kind of signing that is used in some religious orders where silence is the norm. These sign systems often mimic the syntax of the spoken languages around them, and they are often limited in what they can convey.

Sign languages, in contrast, are considered to be complete languages. Languages performed in three-dimensional space, sign languages have their own unique grammars and vocabularies. They are not alternatives to spoken languages and they don't depend on spoken languages. Sign languages are different from the spoken languages around them. For example, American and British Sign Languages are mutually unintelligible.

Sign languages also exhibit regional and social variation, much as spoken languages do. The basic descriptive components of signs are primes. Primes may be described in terms of hand shape, hand placement, and hand movement. These three dimensions serve to define and distinguish specific signs within a sign language system.

Paralanguage is a term developed by George Trager in the 1950s to describe the sounds that accompany spoken language but that are not directly part of a language. Examples are grunts and hisses, volume, and tone of voice. Speech substitutes are systems of communication in which certain sounds, such as whistling or drumming, substitute for other ones to convey messages.

KEY TERMS

adaptor
affect display
allokine
complex alternative sign language
cupped hand
emblem
flat hand
fist hand
illustrator
index hand
kineme
kinemorph
kinesics
nonverbal communication
paralanguage
primes
regulator
sign language
speech substitutes

FURTHER READING

About Kinesics

Birdwhistell, Ray. 1952. *An introduction to kinesics*. Louisville: University of Louisville Press. This is a fairly technical introduction to Birdwhistell's concepts.

Kendon, Adam, ed. 1981. *Nonverbal communication, interaction and gesture*. The Hague: Mouton. This is an excellent introduction to the field.

About Proxemics

Hall, Edward T. 1966. *The hidden dimension: Man's use of space in public and private*. London: The Bodley Head. This is a classic and very readable introduction to the field of proxemics.

Hickey, Joseph V., and William E. Thompson. 1988. Personal space: The hidden element of cowboy demeanor. *Midwest Quarterly* 29: 264–72. This is an enjoyable discussion of proxemics on the high plains.

About Sign Languages

Farnell, Brenda. 1995. *Do you see what I mean? Plains Indian sign talk and the embodiment of action*. Austin: University of Texas Press. This is an excellent book on Plains Indian Sign Language.

Lucas, Ceil, Robert Bayley, and Clayton Valli. 2003. *What's your sign for pizza?: An introduction to variation in American Sign Language*. Washington, DC: Gallaudet University Press. This introduction to diversity in the deaf community covers age, gender, and ethnicity.

Monaghan, Leila, Karen Nakamura, Constanze Schmaling, and Graham H. Turner. 2003. *Many ways to be deaf*. Washington, DC: Gallaudet University Press. This is a contemporary study of deafness, including history, the development of sign languages, and a discussion of sign language variation.

Padden, Carol A., and Tom Humphries. 1988. *Deaf in America: Voices from a culture*. Cambridge, MA: Harvard University Press. This is about the culture of Deaf people.

About Paralanguage and Speech Substitutes

Key, Mary Ritchie. 1975. *Paralanguage and kinesics: Nonverbal communication*. Metuchen, NJ: Scarecrow Press. This provides a thorough discussion of the elements of paralanguage as well as kinesics.

Examples of Nonverbal Communication Guidebooks

Axtell, Roger E. 1997. *Gestures: The do's and taboos of body language around the world*. New York: John Wiley & Sons. This is a guidebook to body language in different cultures.

Morrison, Terri, Wayne A. Conaway, George A. Borden, and Hans Koehler. 1995. *Kiss, bow or shake hands: How to do business in sixty countries*. Holbrook, MA: Adams Media Corporation. Here is another guidebook that promises easy answers and quick solutions.

STUDENT ACTIVITIES

Readings

The workbook/reader for this book has readings that can help you to further explore and understand the issues introduced in this chapter.

Exercises

A set of writing exercises is the workbook/reader will assist you in understanding the issues discussed in this chapter. Selected exercises in the workbook/reader will help you to explore nonverbal communication in more depth.

Web Exercises

The companion website for this book has a series of links designed to help you explore nonverbal communication, including kinesics, proxemics, sign language, and paralanguage. The companion website also contains study questions that will help you to review important concepts.

Guided Projects

If you are creating a new language, you will need to develop a nonverbal communication system for it. If you are working with a conversation partner, your instructor may ask you to explore and contrast your proxemic and kinesic systems. Your instructor will be your guide.

CHAPTER 7

Writing and Literacy

In the Field, Tororo, Uganda, August, 1967

"Could be a bathroom break," my husband said, as the bus stopped in a shady grove at the side of the road. Everyone was getting off, including the driver. In fact, it was a crew change, as well, mandated by the fact that we were going to be crossing the border about five miles down the road, but we didn't know that until later. Most people sat down at picnic tables under the trees to relax. A few headed for the small cement building at the edge of the clearing.

The building looked a lot like one of those two-sided public bathrooms that you find at rest stops along interstate highways in the United States. We decided to use it.

"Remind me again," I asked, as we approached the building. "What's the Swahili word for 'women'?"

"*Wanawake,*" said my husband, as we separated to find our "sides" of the building. "*Wanamume* is 'men.'"

"*Wanawake, wanawake, wanawake,*" I repeated to myself, trying hard to remember the unfamiliar—to me—word. Sure enough, the word *wanawake* was prominently displayed on the side of the building facing away from the road. Not only that, but there was also one of those cute little international signs (a stick figure in a skirt; see Figure 7.1) reassuring me that this was indeed the "women's" bathroom.

So why was an old man going into the women's bathroom?! Puzzled and embarrassed, I decided to wait for him to finish before entering to take my turn.

Big mistake! When I came back out I was greeted by the sight of the bus heading down the road! And my husband frantically running after it! Everything we had was on that bus: clothing, books, passports . . . everything we were going to need for a two-year field visit to the Comoros. I started running too. And shouting as loudly as I could. Fortunately, some of the people on the bus saw us and persuaded the driver to stop so that we could catch up and reboard the bus.

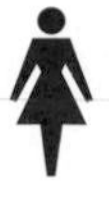

FIGURE 7.1
International symbol for women's bathroom

As we sank into our seats, we reviewed what had happened. Obviously, the old man and I had read the picture sign differently. We had each used our own cultural experience to interpret the sign. I, wearing slacks, had relied on my knowledge of airport signs. He, dressed in a *kanzu*, the traditional Swahili men's long robe, had relied on the fact that the sign looked a lot like the way he was dressed. The inescapable conclusion was that universal signs aren't as universal as we think they are.

HJO

✳ WRITING AND SYMBOLISM

What are universal symbols? Are they really universal? On March 2, 1972, NASA launched Pioneer 10 into deep space. Affixed to its surface was a six- by nine-inch gold anodized aluminum plaque with etched symbols and drawings (see Figure 7.2). Dubbed the Cosmic Postcard by its

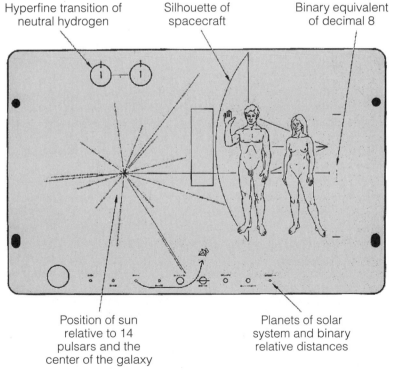

FIGURE 7.2   The gold-anodized plaque carried by Pioneer 10, designed by Carl Sagan, co-founder of the Planetary Society; Frank Drake, now chairman of the board of the SETI Institute; and artist Linda Salzman Sagan *Source: NASA Ames Research Center.*

creators, the plaque was intended to convey basic information about "the locale, epoch, and nature of its builders." The authors hoped that "an advanced civilization would be able to decipher it." Included in the message was a drawing of a man and a woman, the man holding his hand up in a "'universal' symbol of good will" (Sagan, Sagan, and Drake 1972).

 WEBLINK   To get more information about the Pioneer Project website at NASA, go to http://anthropology.wadsworth.com/ottenheimer_language.

Although the plaque's creators hoped that the man's raised hand would be interpreted as a "universal" symbol of good will, my Uganda bathroom experience suggests that you can't reliably predict how symbols crafted by members of one society or culture will be read by members of another society or culture. To me—and presumably many others of my culture—the ♀ symbol brings to mind the idea of a woman in a skirt or dress and, therefore, the idea of a women's bathroom. To the old man in Uganda, the same symbol apparently brought to mind the idea of a man in a *kanzu* and, therefore, the idea of a men's bathroom. These days, as I travel through various airports, I notice that most of the women using the women's bathroom are not wearing skirts at all but, rather, bluejeans or trousers, demonstrating even more clearly that these so-called universal symbols are neither universal symbols nor accurate pictures.

Like the sounds we use to talk about things, the visual symbols that we use to represent those same kinds of things are, for the most part, rather arbitrary. As we pointed out in Chapter 3, different languages have very different-sounding words for the small furry house pet that "meows." From *cat* in English to *mpaha* in Shinzwani, it doesn't matter what sounds you use to represent something. It just matters that everyone speaking that language uses that set of sounds consistently.

Writing systems are just as arbitrary in the way they represent languages. Different characters can represent the same sounds, and different sounds can be represented by the same characters. The sound represented by the IPA symbol [ʃ], for example, can be written in English as <s> (in the word *sure*), as <sh> (in the word *shore*), as <ch> (in the word *machine*), or as <ti> (in the word *motion*). On the other hand, the letter <c> can be pronounced [s] (as in the word *ceiling*) or [k] (as in the word *calling*). And this is just in English. Other languages may write the same sound in other ways. For example, Russian represents the [ʃ] sound with a <ш> and Arabic represents the same sound with a <ش>. So, you need to know which language you are reading in order to know how to interpret the symbols on a page. (Note that we are using angled brackets < > to indicate the letters (or characters) used in a writing system.)

One of the things you will probably want to do when you are learning another language, is to learn its writing system so that you can read and write in that language as well as speak it. Otherwise, if most of the

Cross-Language Miscommunication 7.1

READING ACROSS CULTURES

Dr. Prins, a Dutch anthropologist fluent in Dutch, German, and English, spent time in Israel and learned to speak and read Hebrew. When he moved to New York, he encountered newspapers written with Hebrew letters but found, when he tried to read them, that the words made no sense to him. He could sound out the words, letter by letter, but only a few of the words seemed to be Hebrew. On the other hand, some of the words sounded German to him. Puzzled, he asked some friends, who explained to him that the language he was reading was called Yiddish and that it used both German and Hebrew words. Armed with this information, he was then able to read and understand the newspapers.

HJO

people speaking that language can read and write their language, you will feel foolish being illiterate, especially if you come from a literate culture. This chapter reviews some of the different kinds of writing systems in common use and shows you how to analyze and learn a writing system that is new to you. We will discuss the origins and development of different writing systems and what it means to be literate or to "have writing." We will explore the issues involved in designing or adopting or changing a writing system and the ways that writing things down can convey social and cultural information and reinforce stereotypes. Finally, we will discuss some of the relationships between writing and power, and ask some tantalizing questions about reading, writing, and how these activities are related to culture and identity.

WHAT IS WRITING?

Writing is generally considered to be "a way of recording language by visible marks" (Bloomfield 1933, 21) or "a system of graphic symbols that can be used to convey any and all thought" (DeFrancis 1989, 5). It has also been defined as a "system of more or less permanent marks used to represent an utterance in such a way that it can be recovered more or less exactly without the intervention of the utterer" (Daniels and Bright 1996, 3). Note the comprehensiveness of these definitions. One talks about recording "language," another stresses conveying "any and all thought," and the third reminds us that we record "utterances" so that they can be "read later on." While it is not absolutely necessary to think of writing as representing spoken language, that is generally what we think of when we think of written language. Speech, or spoken language, is considered basic, something all hearing people do naturally. **Writing,** or the graphic representation of language, is considered secondary, something that you have to learn how to do in school, and the same thing is generally true of reading.

Most scholars differentiate complete writing systems from partial writing systems. They argue that a **complete writing system** allows you to record any and all thoughts and words, while a **partial writing system** is limited in what it can convey. "Picture writing" systems, such as the kinds of symbols used on bathroom signs or the NASA space probe, are considered to be partial writing systems. They can only convey what they can picture, and, as we have seen, what they can picture is limited by our cultural understandings of what each picture really "means." A partial writing system may be included as part of a complete writing system, but it generally is not considered a complete writing system on its own. In this chapter, we discuss both partial and complete writing systems, but we will emphasize complete writing systems.

✖ HOW DOES WRITING WORK?

Writing systems work by using symbols to represent sounds as well as ideas or meanings, but there is no general agreement on what to call each of these kinds of symbols. Words such as phonetic, phonographic, and sonographic have been suggested for the symbols that represent sounds. Words like semantic, pictographic, logographic, and ideographic have been suggested for the symbols that represent meanings. In addition, some scholars make distinctions among pictographs, logographs, and ideographs. To avoid getting mired in fine points, we will simply refer to symbols that represent sounds as "phonetic signs" and symbols that represent ideas and meanings as "semantic signs."

A **phonetic sign** is a graphic mark that represents one or more of the sounds of a language. This is a little different from a phonetic symbol. A phonetic symbol, as described in Chapter 3, represents a linguist's hearing and transcription of a specific exact sound, while a phonetic sign represents the mark that you make on paper (or stone or wood or some other medium) to write one or more of the sounds of your language. To keep this distinction clear, and to remain consistent, we surround phonetic *signs* with angled brackets < > and we surround phonetic *symbols* with square brackets [ ]. (Recall that we used square brackets this way in Chapter 3.)

In English (and in many other European languages), the letter <s> represents the sound [s]. In Arabic, the same sound is represented with the letter < س >. Sometimes a particular phonetic sign can be used to represent a group of sounds. In English, the letter <x> represents the combination [ks] (as in the word *box*). In Japanese, the character <サ> represents the combination [sa]. As you will see later in this chapter, there is no requirement that a sign has to be read the same way in every language. The sign combination <ch>, for example, is read as [ʃ] in French (as in the word *chaise*) as [x] in Czech or German (as in the word *Bach*) and as [tʃ] in English (as in the word *chair*).

A **semantic sign** is a graphic mark that represents a specific idea or meaning. Such a sign may or may not also represent sounds, but representing sounds is not the focus of a semantic sign; the primary focus of a semantic sign is to represent meanings and ideas. The semantic sign <2>, for example represents the idea of a specific number in many languages. Note that the actual pronunciation of this idea is not specifically encoded into the sign. The sign <2> can be pronounced *two* in English, *deux* in French, *dvě* in Czech, *mbili* in KiSwahili, and so on. It should come as no surprise that different writing systems may use different signs to express the same idea. In Arabic, for example, the sign used for the idea of <2> is <٢>, in Chinese the sign is <二>, and in Classical Mayan the sign is <• •>.

Some writing systems use phonetic *and* semantic signs in the same written word. We do this in English, for example, with the sign combination <2nd> where we add the phonetic signs <nd> to the semantic sign <2>. Although English speakers generally pronounce <2> *two* [tu], they pronounce <2nd>*second* [sɛkənd]. This makes it seem as though the sign <2> has two different English pronunciations, [tu] and [sɛkə] and that the choice between the two variants depends on whether or not the phonetic sign combination <nd> is present. A similar example, from French, is the combination <2e>, which is read *deuxième* 'second.' In Chinese, the sign <馬> represents the sound combination [ma] in general as well as the Chinese word *ma* 'horse.' As you can see, different writing systems combine phonetic and semantic signs in different ways.

It used to be that scholars categorized writing systems according to whether they stressed phonetic or semantic signs. Chinese, Classical Mayan, and ancient Egyptian hieroglyphic writing systems, for example, were said to use mainly semantic signs, representing ideas rather than sounds; such writing systems were classified together as "ideographic" (idea-writing) systems. English and other European languages were said to use mainly phonetic signs, representing sounds rather than ideas; such writing systems were further classified depending on how, exactly, the sounds were written (one at a time or in groups). It was also assumed that phonetic writing systems were "more advanced" than semantic writing systems, having "progressed" further along a fixed line of development from picture writing to idea writing to sound writing. Recent research, however, reveals that this is a Eurocentric attitude (at best) and perhaps even a racist view (at worst) of the world. Instead, we have come to realize that all writing systems make use of both semantic *and* phonetic signs. The difference between writing systems appears, then, to be the extent to which a system relies on one or the other of these two kinds of signs. English, for example, relies more heavily on phonetic signs, while Chinese relies more heavily on semantic signs. But all writing systems use both kinds of signs to some degree. A lot depends on the specific language and the specific writing system that has developed around it. In the next sections, we will review some major writing systems and some of the languages for which they are used. We will begin with an examination of pictographic "writing" and the role that it played (and may continue to play) in various writing systems. Next, we will explore rebus writing and the way that it made true writing possible. Finally, we will review syllabic and alphabetic writing systems and how they work.

Remember that no matter what symbols and combination of symbols you use, the way that you interpret them depends on how they are used in the language and the writing system that you find them in. You should also remember that the symbols in a writing system are arbitrary, rather than concrete representations, and that they work mostly as mnemonics, or reminders, of what it is their writers want us to remember or read.

Pictographic "Writing"

Pictographic "writing" uses pictures or images to represent things. Generally, the pictures look something like the things they represent. A pictograph like this ☼, for example, looks enough like our idea of the sun that it can represent the sun. Most early attempts at keeping records appear to have been pictographic, using pictures of suns, moons, stars, eyes, arms, sheep, oxen, grains of barley, sheaves of wheat, rivers, crowns, staffs, and so on. 'Two sheep' could be represented by a drawing of two sheep or by a drawing of one sheep and two counting marks. An important limitation to pictographic "writing" is that pictographs can generally only represent what they can picture. It is difficult, for example, to draw a picture of truth or imagination or phonology. Because of this limitation pictographs alone cannot be complete writing systems.

One way around this limitation is to find ways to extend the meanings of pictographs. The easiest way to do this is to extend the idea in the pictograph to an idea that is related to it. For example, in airports and public restrooms, the pictograph ⚲ does not convey the idea 'woman' so much as the idea 'women's bathroom.' Likewise, in ancient Sumeria the pictograph ✳, meaning 'star' was extended to mean 'heaven' as well as 'sky-god' (DeFrancis 1989, 85). In the same way, a drawing of an eye could be extended to represent the idea of 'seeing,' a drawing of a sun could be extended to represent 'warmth' or 'light' or 'daytime,' and a drawing of a moon could be extended to represent 'nighttime' or 'darkness.'

Of course, in all of these cases, assigning and extending meanings to pictographs is a matter of social convention. In other words, there is no guarantee that a pictograph will be read the same way in different cultures. How do you know, for example, whether a drawing such as ☾ is to be interpreted as 'crescent moon,' 'moon (in general),' 'night,' 'darkness,' 'outhouse,' or 'Islam'? How do you know whether a pictograph like ♀ is to be interpreted as 'woman in dress' or 'man in *kanzu*'? How do you know whether a pictograph of a man with an upturned hand is greeting you or telling you to stop? In each of these cases, we rely on cultural and linguistic knowledge to interpret the pictographs that we see. It is important to remember that although no writing system is based entirely on pictographs, all writing systems appear to have evolved from pictographic principles. This extension strategy appears to be one way that the transition to writing began.

Rebus Writing

Rebus writing uses a single picture to represent two or more words that sound the same. By doing this, rebus writing provides a way of moving beyond the concrete limitations of pictographs. It lets you use a pictograph of something that is easy to draw to convey the idea of something that is more difficult to draw. For example, the words *eye* and *I* sound the same in English. This means that a picture of an eye can be used to represent either one of these words for a speaker of English. Likewise, the English words *sun* and *son* sound the same, so a pictograph like ☼ can represent either one of these words. As long as your language has several words that sound the same—and most languages do—you can use pictographs of some items to represent other items. This means that you can write the English phrase *I see you* by drawing a picture of an eye, a picture of the sea, and a picture of a female sheep (ewe). The words that you write just have to sound the same as words you can draw pictures of. Effectively, what you are doing with rebus writing is using symbols as both semantic and phonetic signs at the same time!

The rebus strategy can be applied to any symbol, not just pictographs. For example, in contemporary English the symbol <2> can be used 2 represent the words *two, to,* and *too*. Of course, it is sometimes difficult to know which word is being signaled in rebus writing. You always need a context to help interpret the symbols. As we will see, different writing systems use different strategies to help readers figure out how to interpret symbols that can be read more than one way. In English, one strategy is to rely on word order, or syntax, to help in reading a phrase such as <Please give me 2 apples and 2 oranges, 2, so that I can give some 2 my sister>.

Representing sounds with picture symbols in this way was a major breakthrough in the development of writing. The discovery allowed ancient Sumerians to use the pictograph for 'star' to represent the words 'heaven' and 'sky-god,' for example, because all three words were pronounced [an] (DeFrancis 1989, 85). It allowed ancient Chinese scribes to use the pictograph for 'elephant' to represent the word for 'image' because both words were pronounced [ʃaŋ] (DeFrancis 1989, 104). And it allowed ancient Mayan scribes to use the pictograph for 'snake' to represent the words for 'four' and 'sky' because all three words were pronounced [tʃan] (Coe 1992, 235).

This use of the rebus strategy appears to have been discovered independently in at least three different times and places. It was discovered in Sumeria around 3000 BCE, in China around 1500 BCE, and in Mesoamerica around the beginning of the Common Era (or 0 CE). As we said earlier, no full writing system relies entirely on pictographs but all writing systems emerged out of pictographic systems. They did so by discovering and applying the rebus strategy. After that, different writing systems followed different pathways in developing signs to write sounds and meanings. Some of the differences probably depended on how these different languages were structured; some of the differences probably depended on what kinds of pictographs each one started from.

Logographic Writing

Logographic writing uses graphic signs to represent words, or the ideas associated with those words. Logographs (the signs in a logographic system) are semantic signs in the fullest sense of the word. Some scholars use the word ideograph instead of logograph, and some even try to suggest that ideographs represent ideas rather than words (the word *logograph* actually means something like 'word-sign,' and the word *ideograph* actually means something like 'idea-sign.'). But this is controversial as well as confusing. It is easy enough to show that written signs can bring both words and their associated ideas to mind. But no one seems to be able to prove that written signs can cause you to think of ideas by themselves, without any associated words. This suggests that *logograph* is the most accurate term for a sign that represents words and ideas. Using the term logograph also helps us to remember that writing is, to a large degree, designed to represent spoken words.

While rebus writing allows the use of a single sign to represent more than one word, logographs move beyond this idea to attach individual signs to individual words. Chinese, Mayan, and Egyptian hieroglyphs are generally cited as examples of logographic systems, but recent research suggests that these systems make significant use of phonetic signs as well.

Although some logographs evolved from pictographs, most of them have changed over time and no longer resemble the original pictographs. In fact, most logographs don't look anything like the words or ideas that they represent. They are abstract signs that people have to learn to read. Figure 7.3 shows the development of one Chinese character, from an early Shang oracle bone pictograph (1200–1045 BCE) through Great

Shang   Great Seal   Small Seal   Scribal   Regular   Simplified

FIGURE 7.3   Historical development of the Chinese character for 'horse' *Source: DeFrancis (1989, 96).*

3000 BCE	2800 BCE	2500 BCE	1800 BCE	600 BCE
✳	✳	✳	✳	⊳⊳⟙

FIGURE 7.4   Historical development of the cuneiform symbol for 'star/heaven/sky-god' *Source: Kramer (1963, 302–4).*

Seal (946–935 BCE), Small Seal (221–206 BCE), Scribal and Regular characters (both 206–220 CE), to the Simplified form of the 1950s; Figure 7.4 shows the development of the Sumerian sign for 'heaven' from its early pictographic shape to its eventual cuneiform sign.

Logographs are used in many languages, including English. When the symbol <2> is used to represent the word *two* in English, it is being used as a logograph. The fact that it can also be used to represent the number *deux* 'two' in French and the number *mbili* 'two' in Shinzwani means that, although the same sign can be used as a logograph in different languages, the way it is pronounced can be different, depending on the language in which it is functioning as a logograph. Another sign that is used as a logograph in a lot of different languages is the <@> sign. In contemporary English, it has come to mean *at* and is used as part of an Internet address. It works comfortably in English to say *myname-at-my-internet address,* but this doesn't work as well in some other languages. For example, it is pronounced *zavináč* [zavinatʃ] in Czech (meaning 'rolled up herring snack'), *arobase* in French (referring to an old unit of weight), and *strudel* in Hebrew (meaning 'a rolled up pastry'). In two of these cases, the word chosen refers to the rolled-up look of the symbol, but in none of these cases does the symbol convey any sense of 'at-ness' or of 'being in some location' that it conveys in English. This is a good example of the complexity and arbitrariness of logographs, and a good reminder of the fact that all writing strategies make use of significant amounts of arbitrariness in assigning symbols to words, and vice versa.

 WEBLINK   To read about names for the @ sign, go to http://anthropology.wadsworth.com/ottenheimer_language.

As we have already mentioned, logographs don't generally look much like the words or ideas that they represent. In fact, many don't look anything at all like what they represent. Figures 7.5 and 7.6 show some examples of logographs in Chinese and Mayan.

Syllabic Writing

Syllabic writing uses graphic signs to represent individual syllables. One way to think about syllables is to think of stresses in words. The English word *cat* for example, has one stress and is therefore made up of one syllable. The same is true of the English words *catch* and *scratch*. The English word *caterpillar,* on the other hand, has four stresses, *ca-ter-pil-lar,* so it is made up of four syllables. Generally, syllables are made up of combinations of vowels and consonants. If we label all vowels V and all consonants C, we can describe the syllables of a language by the various kinds of combinations of C and V that the language allows. Some languages use mostly CV syllables. Some use mostly CVC syllables. Some permit V to stand alone as a syllable; a few permit C to stand alone as a syllable (think

一	二	三	上	下	中	力	凸	凹
'one'	'two'	'three'	'above'	'below'	'middle'	'strength' (plough)	'convex'	'concave'

FIGURE 7.5   Some Chinese logographs

FIGURE 7.6   Some Mayan logographs

of the first [m] in the English word *mhm*). Some allow CCCVC, CVCCC, and other combinations where consonants are grouped together. English tends to allow collections of consonants in syllables. Shinzwani (spoken in the Comoro Islands) prefers CV syllables. This means that an English word like *bread* (one syllable in English) is heard and rephrased as *be-re-di* (three syllables) by many Shinzwani speakers.

Using graphic signs to represent individual syllables marks a significant step in the development of writing systems. It means that signs can be used phonetically as well as—or instead of—semantically. It also makes writing a little more efficient. Instead of needing a sign for every word you want to write, syllabic writing lets you use a single sign to represent a single syllable, no matter where it occurs in a word. Using signs to represent syllables can work in just about any language. An example of how it might work in English is if we used the sign <@> to represent the sound of the syllable [æt]. This would allow us to write <c@> for the word *cat*, <c@ch> for the word *catch* and <scr@ch> for the word *scratch*. You can see how this can get cumbersome, however, for a language that allows CCCVCC syllables (as in *scratch*).

Syllabaries (or syllabic writing systems) work best with languages that have mostly CV, VC, and V syllables, such as Japanese, Chinese, Cherokee, Mayan, Inuit, Vai, and more. They work worst with languages that allow clusters of consonants such as English, Czech, and Russian.

Syllabaries have been invented many times and for many languages. One of the best-known recent syllabaries is the one developed for Cherokee by Sequoyah (George Guess) in 1821. It consists of eighty-five symbols: six for vowels that stand alone, seventy-eight for combinations of various consonants with each of the six vowels, and one for an [s] sound that can be used as a prefix or suffix. Cherokee is considered a "pure" syllabary because the signs are all phonetic signs. Figure 7.7 shows the Cherokee syllabary.

Da	**R**e	**T**i	Ꮼo	Ꮳu	**i**v
Sga Ꮖka	**Ᏼ**ge	**y**gi	**A**go	**J**gu	**E**gv
Ꮙha	**Ꭾ**he	**Ꮟ**hi	**Ꮸ**ho	**Ꮧ**hu	**Ꮂ**hv
Wla	**Ꮯ**le	**Ꮅ**li	**Ꮆ**lo	**M**lu	**Ꭱ**lv
Ꮝma	**Ꮉ**me	**H**mi	**Ꮤ**mo	**y**mu	
Ꮎna **Ꮏ**hna **Ꮐ**nah	**Λ**ne	**ʜ**ni	**Ꮒ**quo	**Ꮑ**nu	**Ꮕ**nv
Ꮋqua	**Ꮖ**que	**Ꮖ**qui	**Ꮩ**quo	**Ꮽ**quu	**Ꮾ**quv
Ꮏsa Ꮤ s	**4**se	**Ꮟ**si	**Ꮩ**so	**Ꮖ**su	**R**sv
Ꮣda **W**ta	**Ꮥ**de **Ꮦ**te	**Ꮧ**di **Ꮨ**ti	**Ꮩ**do	**Ꮪ**du	**Ꮫ**dv
Ꮬdla **Ꮭ**tla	**Ꮮ**tle	**Ꮯ**tli	**Ꮰ**tlo	**Ꮱ**tlu	**P**tlv
Gtsa	**Ꮴ**tse	**Ir**tsi	**K**tso	**Ꮷ**tsu	**Ꮸ**tsv
Gwa	**Ꮺ**we	**Ꮻ**wi	**Ꮼ**wo	**Ꮽ**wu	**6**wv
Ꮿya	**Ᏸ**ye	**Ᏹ**yi	**Ᏺ**yo	**G**yu	**B**yv

FIGURE 7.7 Cherokee syllabary designed by Sequoyah in 1821

WEBLINK To read more about specific syllabaries, go to http://anthropology.wadsworth.com/ottenheimer_language.

Japanese uses two different syllabaries. Hiragana is the more commonly used syllabary, and it is used for most informal writing. Katakana is more often used for formal documents or reserved for writing words borrowed from foreign languages (DeFrancis 1989, 135). Both syllabaries contain approximately four dozen signs, representing different combinations of consonants and vowels. In addition, there are small superscript diacritics that can be added to the main signs to indicate such phonetic variants as voicing, devoicing, and final [n]. Figures 7.8 and 7.9 show the two Japanese syllabaries.

Logosyllabic Writing

Some writing systems make use of combinations of logographic *and* syllabic signs. The best known of these are the cuneiform (wedge-shaped) writing of Sumeria, the elaborate system of Mayan glyphs, and contemporary Chinese characters. Until recently, each of these systems had been described by scholars as being entirely logographic, but recent research has revealed that all of them make significant use of both semantic *and* phonetic signs. For example, if you start with the cuneiform semantic sign for 'mouth' (pronounced [ka]) and add the phonetic sign [me] to it, you create the Sumerian word meaning 'tongue,' which is pronounced [eme]. If you add the phonetic sign [nun] instead, you create the word

あ	か	さ	た	な	は	ま	や	ら	わ
a	ka	sa	ta	na	ha	ma	ya	ra	wa

い	き	し	ち	に	ひ	み		り	
i	ki	shi	chi	ni	hi	mi		ri	

う	く	す	つ	ぬ	ふ	む	ゆ	る	
u	ku	su	tsu	nu	fu	mu	yu	ru	

え	け	せ	て	ね	へ	め		れ	
e	ke	se	te	ne	he	me		re	

お	こ	そ	と	の	ほ	も	よ	ろ	を	ん
o	ko	so	to	no	ho	mo	yo	ro	wo	n

FIGURE 7.8 Hiragana syllabary

ア a	カ ka	サ sa	タ ta	ナ na	ハ ha	マ ma	ヤ ya	ラ ra	ワ wa
イ i	キ ki	シ shi	チ chi	ニ ni	ヒ hi	ミ mi		リ ri	
ウ u	ク ku	ス su	ツ tsu	ヌ nu	フ fu	ム mu	ユ yu	ル ru	
エ e	ケ ke	セ se	テ te	ネ ne	ヘ he	メ me		レ re	
オ o	コ ko	ソ so	ト to	ノ no	ホ ho	モ mo	ヨ yo	ロ ro	ヲ wo	ン n

FIGURE 7.9   Katakana syllabary

meaning 'lip,' which is pronounced [nundum]. Note that [ka], or the word for 'mouth,' does not actually contribute to the pronunciation of either [eme] 'tongue' or [nundum] 'lip.' Instead, it is functioning as a *semantic* sign, helping you to think of other words that have to do with 'mouth.' The [me] sign then functions as a *phonetic* sign that (together with 'mouth') helps you to think of the word [eme] 'tongue.' Likewise, the [nun] sign is used as a phonetic sign that helps you to think of the word [nundum] 'lip' (Coe 1992, 27). This is a good example of a **logosyllabic writing** system, in which signs can carry both semantic and phonetic information to help you to decode what is written.

A logosyllabic system is also helpful in differentiating two or more words that sound the same. For example, in Chinese, the words for 'sheep' and 'ocean' both sound like [yaŋ]. This means that you can use the same Chinese phonetic sign to write both words. However, if you add the Chinese semantic sign for 'water' to the phonetic sign [yaŋ], then it is clear that the word intended is 'ocean' and not 'sheep.' Likewise, the Chinese words 'to divine' and 'to moisten' are both pronounced [tʃan] (although with slightly different tones). Adding the semantic sign for 'water' to the phonetic sign [tʃan] makes it clear that the word you are writing is 'to moisten' and not 'to divine' (Coe 1992, 31). One more example: The Chinese phonetic sign [ma] can mean both 'horse' and 'mother,' but, if you add the semantic sign for 'woman' to the phonetic sign [ma], then it is clear that the word intended is 'mother' and not 'horse' (De Francis 1989, 53).

Scholars use the word **determinative** to describe a sign added to another sign to clarify meaning or create new words. Determinatives can be either phonetic or semantic. **Phonetic determinatives** help to suggest related words that are pronounced differently. Our Sumerian example used phonetic determinatives to clarify that the semantic sign for 'mouth' could also be read as 'lip' or 'tongue.' **Semantic determinatives** help to separate different words that might be pronounced similarly. Our Chinese examples show how semantic determinatives can be used to clarify which of several similar-sounding words is meant.

The ancient Mayan glyphs are especially interesting for the way that they combined logographic, syllabic, and logosyllabic strategies all in the same writing system. For example, the name of the Mayan ruler Pacal (born in 603 CE) could be spelled logographically with a glyph that looked like a shield, syllabically with glyphs representing the syllables [pa], [ka], and [l(a)], and logosyllabically with a semantic sign for a shield plus a phonetic determinative [l(a)] to clarify that the shield in question was to be read specifically as Pacal and not as some other shield or ruler (Coe 1992, 207).

 WEBLINK   To read about the Mayan glyphic system, go to http://anthropology.wadsworth.com/ottenheimer_language.

Alphabetic Writing

English clusters too many consonants together to make good use of a syllabic strategy. Words such as *matchbox* and *screwdriver* make it hard to separate out the syllables and assign symbols to each one. Czech words such as *zmrzlina* present the same problem: Too many consonants clustered together for a syllabic strategy to work well. Languages with consonant clusters like these work better with "alphabetic writing."

Alphabetic writing uses graphic signs to represent individual consonants and vowels. Some systems, such as in English, string the signs along one after the other. Others, such as Arabic and Hebrew, place the vowel signs above or below the consonants. In Arabic, for example, you write [ka] with two signs, the <ﻙ> sign (representing [k]) and the < ´> sign (representing [a]) placed above it. The resulting sign looks like this: <ﻛ>. Although the ideal alphabetic system has a clear one-to-one relationship between signs and sounds, this is rarely the case in practice. For example, the sign <x> in English represents the consonant cluster [ks] (as in the word *box*). And the sign <o> in English is sometimes read as [o] as in *so*, sometimes read as [a] as in *box*, and sometimes read as [æ] as in *sow* (or 'female pig'). You can probably think of other pronunciations of the same sign, too. Clearly, the English alphabet, although meant to represent sounds, does not do a very good job of it. Languages vary in the degree to which they achieve the one-sign-one-sound goal.

There is some controversy regarding when and where the first alphabetic writing was used. Some scholars attribute it to ancient Akkadians (or Phoenicians), who borrowed cuneiform signs from the Sumerians sometime in the seventeenth century BCE. Sumerian cuneiform was well suited to a CV kind of language, but poorly suited to the interleaving kind of Semitic language that the Akkadians were speaking, so the Akkadians used the signs to represent individual consonants and vowels rather than whole syllables. Some scholars attribute the first alphabetic writing to the Greeks, who borrowed the system from the Phoenicians in the ninth century BCE. Because Greek had more vowels (and fewer consonants) than the Phoenician did, the Greeks reassigned some consonant signs so that they could be used to represent vowels instead. The Greeks referred to their writing system by the names of the first two letters—*alpha* and *beta*—thus forming the word *alphabet*. But the Phoenician alphabet, from which they borrowed the letters, began with the same two letters. Today in Hebrew, the names of these letters are *aleph* and *bet*. In Arabic, they are *alif* and *bet*. So even the word *alphabet* has roots older than ninth century Greece.

Issues of Classification

Sometimes the vowel signs are omitted from Arabic and Hebrew writing, and because of this some scholars argue that these writing systems should be called consonantal rather than alphabetic. Using a consonantal writing system in English would give you something like <th ct n th ht> to represent the phrase *the cat in the hat*. Some scholars use the fact that vowels are written above and below the consonants, rather than on the same line as the consonants, to argue that these writing systems should be called syllabic rather than alphabetic. But both of these can be seen as Eurocentric arguments. If there are symbols to represent both consonants and vowels, then a writing system should be called alphabetic, even if the vowel symbols are not always used. A similar classification issue occurs with regard to Hindi, where vowel signs are added to the consonant signs in such a way as to form integrated signs for each consonant-vowel combination. In this case, some scholars argue that the system should be called an alphasyllabary, and others think it should be called a syllabary; still others consider it an alphabetic system. Korean also represents consonants and vowels, but the way that the signs are placed makes some scholars consider Korean a syllabary, as well. On the other hand, the fact that some Korean signs appear to represent phonetic features such as voicing or aspiration causes a few scholars to want to call it a "featural" writing system.

Sometimes it seems that the way writing systems are classified tells you more about the classifiers than the systems. The history of writing about writing contains a lot of Eurocentric thinking. Perhaps more important than knowing what to call a system is knowing how to recognize the various strategies that people employ to write their languages. Knowing how a writing system works is what you need most if you are going to learn how to read and write another language.

✳ DECODING A WRITING SYSTEM

Once you understand how writing systems work, you can apply that knowledge to decoding writing systems on your own. To begin with, you need to find out what kind of strategies are in use in the system you want to learn. For example, if the primary strategy is alphabetic, then you will approach your analysis differently than if the primary strategy is syllabic. Mostly, it's a case of knowing whether the different symbols you are looking at are meant to represent consonants and vowels, syllables, or even whole words. Sometimes you'll find that one symbol can represent all three. In English, for example, the symbol <a> represents a single vowel, but that single vowel also can function as a single syllable, either as a part of a word (as in *aha!*) or as a separate word (as in *a boat*). Don't be thrown off by this. Just remember that in English most symbols are meant to represent sounds (consonants and vowels), so the fact that a single sound can occasionally function as a syllable and/or a word should be treated as a coincidence rather than a distraction.

It is helpful to use the word **grapheme** to describe the smallest segment of speech that is represented in a writing system. In English the letter <a> is a grapheme representing a single vowel that, when said in isolation, is generally pronounced [ə]. English is *not* a good language to use as an example because the same grapheme takes on different pronunciations depending on where in a word it is used. The <a> in *apple* sounds different from the <a> in *about* and different still from the <a> in *father*. This is one reason why English spelling is so difficult to learn. Nonetheless, the basic principle of identifying graphemes and the speech segments that they are supposed to designate is still a valid approach. It's just that the more phonemic a writing system is, the closer its graphemes come to having a one-to-one relationship with the sounds that they represent. As you probably realize by now, graphemes can represent single sounds, syllables, and words. In Cherokee and Japanese, for example, each grapheme represents an entire syllable. In Classical Mayan, graphemes represented syllables, but also could represent words. In Chinese, graphemes can represent words or syllables.

Once you know what graphemes are supposed to represent you can begin trying to nail down the correspondences. The process is a lot like using substitution frames (see Chapter 4) or like finding minimal pairs (see Chapter 3). Here's an example from Shinzwani to show you how it works. Shinzwani has been written in Arabic script for several hundred years. In the example, the first column shows a (more or less) phonemic spelling using European letters with a translation into English and the second column shows how the words are spelled using Arabic letters.

koko wahe 'her grandmother'   كُـكُ وَهَ

gari lahe 'her car'   عَـر لَهَ

shiri shahe 'her chair'   شِـر شَـهَ

koko waho 'your grandmother'   كُـكُ وَهَ

gari laho 'your car'   عَـر لَهَ

shiri shaho 'your chair'   شِـر شَـهَ

One way to start is to notice that the second word in each of these short phrases seems to end with either [-he] or [-ho]. As you examine the Arabic letters, note that it is the leftmost letter in each group that stays stable enough to represent these two endings. This should make it easy to identify the graphemes for [h], [e], and [o]. It should also alert you to the fact that the Arabic letters are proceeding from right to left, while the European letters are proceeding from left to right. It should also make it easier for you to identify the other Arabic letters in the example.

The next thing you might notice is that the grapheme for [e] is written beneath the grapheme for [h], and that the grapheme for [o] is written above the grapheme for [h]. Now that you know how to read [he] and [ho], you can examine the remaining parts of these words to decipher the graphemes for [w], [l], [ʃ] (<sh>), and [a]. As you identify each piece, you can use it to sort out the remaining pieces. Notice that [i] and [e] are both represented by a single grapheme and that [u] and [o] are both represented by a single grapheme. As we said earlier, no writing system is perfect in representing sounds. They are all just mnemonic systems that help you to guess at the sounds and words.

You might have noticed that in written Shinzwani words are separated from one another by spaces, much like we separate English words from one another. It is helpful to use the word **lexeme** for a unit of writing that is surrounded by white space on a page. Some scholars prefer to use the word "frame" instead, but the word "lexeme" is a little more intuitive because most of the time a lexeme is the same thing as a word. Chinese is written so that each lexeme takes up exactly the same space as every other lexeme. This means that, if you combine two or more graphemes into a single lexeme in Chinese, then the individual graphemes have to get smaller so that they can fit into the space allowed for the lexeme.

Just like in English, a single grapheme can be the same as a single lexeme in Chinese. An example of this in Chinese is the single character for [ma] 'horse' that we mentioned earlier. Examples of this in English are the letter <a> that we also mentioned earlier and the letter <I> when it stands for the word *I*. It is interesting to note that English dictionaries list the lexemes in terms of phonetic graphemes (<a>, <b>, <c>, etc.), thus giving the impression that sounds are more important in the writing system, while Chinese dictionaries list lexemes in terms of semantic graphemes ('horse,' 'water,' etc.), giving the impression that meanings are more important than sounds. Perhaps this is one reason why so many people write about Chinese as if there were no phonetic component in its writing system?

You can see that decoding or deciphering a writing system becomes possible once you know what the graphemes represent. What happens if you don't know what the graphemes represent or if you think that they represent something else? The story of the decipherment of Mayan glyphs is a good example of exactly this situation. Archaeologists working with Mayan sites figured out fairly early that many of the glyphs represented numbers, dates, and place names, but their certainty that the writing system was entirely logographic kept everyone from deciphering the rest of the glyphs for many years. Eventually a group of linguistic anthropologists discovered that the glyphs could be read phonemically as well, but it was not until the 1970s, when the glyphs were linked with actual spoken languages (Yucatec and Cholan), that real decipherment became possible. Once the code had been broken, the process of decipherment went fairly quickly, until today it is possible to read the ancient glyphs, sorting out which ones are logographic, which are syllabic, and which are logosyllabic, and to read ancient Mayan history.

Constructing a writing system for a language that has not been written presents a similar challenge, but in reverse. Not only do you have to analyze the sounds of the language and decide which ones should be written, you also have to decide whether you are going to use an alphabet or a syllabary or some other system. It is also important to pay attention to how people feel about whichever kind of writing system you are hoping to introduce. Does choosing to use a particular writing system communicate something about perceived identity or political leanings? In the Comoros, using Arabic script can signal a level of traditionalism, using French spelling can signal a level of education, and using phonemic spelling (which looks more like KiSwahili spelling) can signal an anticolonial sentiment. The article "Spelling Shinzwani" (in the workbook/reader) describes my experience with developing a phonemic writing system for Shinzwani and discusses some of the political issues involved as well.

WHAT DOES IT MEAN TO HAVE WRITING?

Humankind is defined by language; but civilization is defined by writing.   PETER T. DANIELS AND WILLIAM BRIGHT

So begins a recent encyclopedic work on the writing systems of the world. It represents an attitude that is widely held, but it also implies that

Doing Linguistic Anthropology 7.1

WRITING SHINZWANI

In the 1960s, when I was in the Comoros, I learned to read and write Shinzwani using Arabic script. Most Shinzwani speakers knew and used the script and the adult population was nearly 100 percent literate so I thought it made sense for me to learn it as well. Following old-fashioned linguistic anthropological tradition, however, I also thought that it would be worthwhile to develop a European-based phonemic writing system for Shinzwani. Such a move would represent the language more clearly, I thought, and would help to bring the Comoros more closely in contact with the Western world. Precious few Westerners take the trouble to learn Arabic script, much less to apply it to non-Arabic languages.

The idea of a European-based phonemic writing system was met with quite a bit of enthusiasm, and several young students helped me to hear and think through various phonemic distinctions and to settle on which symbols to use for which sounds. Most Shinzwani speakers did not like the odd-looking IPA symbols, nor did they want to have to use special characters or extra diacritic marks, such as those on Kenneth Pike's phonetic chart (see Chapter 3 for a discussion of these two kinds of charts and symbols). In the end, we settled on a compromise system that used only the symbols that you could find on a standard European typewriter (French or English, in particular) for sounds and for groups of sounds. We used <tr>, for example, to write a single voiceless retroflex stop (see Chapter 3 for a description of this sound). The system was informally adopted by many young Shinzwani speakers, and formal analyses conducted in later years by Comorian linguists proposed similar phonemic spellings. But Arabic and French spellings continue to be used by many Comorians, for ethnic, as well as political reasons.

HJO

groups of people without writing are "uncivilized" in some way. This attitude may, in fact, lie behind some of the early resistance among Mayanist archaeologists to the idea that the Mayan glyphs represented a real writing system. If the glyphs were just pictographs marking calendrical and mathematical information for the purposes of timekeeping and not a full writing system, then the Maya could be seen as "uncivilized" tribes, and their conquest and "civilization" by Europeans might be more easily justified (Coe 1992).

Interestingly, the determination of whether a group of people *has* writing isn't always as clear as it might seem. The Lahu, in northern Thailand, have several different writing systems that were developed for them by non-Lahu missionaries and government linguists. However, because these writing systems are not seen as ancient or indigenous (like Thai writing), they generally are not regarded as "real" writing, especially by non-Lahu people in Thailand. The Lahu are thus thought of, and many of them think of themselves, as people "without writing" and occupy a minority status in Thailand (Pine 2000). In a similar manner, French colonials in the Comoro Islands treated the Comorians as though they were illiterate because they could not read and write French, in spite of the fact that Comorian had been written (and read) using Arabic script for many centuries. In spite of the fact that there was nearly 100 percent adult literacy in Comorian (using Arabic script), the French colonials introduced French spelling for Comorian and defined literacy only as the ability to read and write Comorian using French script. French spelling fits Comorian even less well than Arabic script. A Shinzwani name pronounced [swafawi], for example, is written in French as <Soifaoui>. This, in part, inspired me to suggest a more phonemic script if people wanted to use a European-based writing system.

✳ WRITING, READING, IDENTITY, AND POWER

Several questions remain that are just beginning to attract attention among anthropologists. The question of how individuals learn to read, long the focus of psychologists and educators, is one example of the new areas of research regarding writing. One thing to take note of is whether there is anything deemed interesting or important to read. Perhaps Bible translators mean well, but if the only thing to read in a newly scripted indigenous language is the Bible how long will interest in reading be sustainable? Shouldn't there also be newspapers, novels, political tracts, and all sorts of other materials written in indigenous languages? Another relevant question is whether reading is considered something that everyone should do, or whether it is seen as limited to a few elites, or to some specific group. In China, for example, during a time when only men were being educated, women are said to have developed their own modified characters for writing personal materials. In addition, does the ability to write cause people to think differently? Are literate people more "literalminded" than their nonliterate peers.

 WEBLINK   To read about Nushu, the Chinese women's secret writing system, go to http://anthropology.wadsworth.com/ottenheimer_language.

Another question that has attracted interest recently, especially among linguistic anthropologists, is the ways in which writing represents actual speech. How exactly do we get spoken words onto paper? The process, called entextualization, involves more than just writing down exactly what people say. If you listen carefully you will notice that most people do not speak in clearly separated words. This is one of the things that makes learning a new language more difficult. For example, in English, most people don't say, *Did you eat yet?*; instead, they are more likely to say [djit yɛt]. How should we write this? <Didja eat yet?> is one possibility, but think about how often you see such spellings in print. Probably pretty rarely. Probably mostly in novels and hardly ever in newspapers. When was the last time you saw someone quoted in a newspaper as having said <gonna>? Yet *gonna* is probably a much more common construction in English than *going to*. On the other hand, every time I see a printed version of a folk tale from the Appalachians or a printed version of a blues lyric, I see written constructions of this sort all the time.

We know that most writing systems are not perfect representations of speech, but how does that explain why some people are represented as having said <going to> and others are represented as having said <gonna>? There's something else going on here, which has more to do with how writers (and readers) expect certain categories of speakers to sound. Writing in dialect like this suggests that a person is more "folksy." And cleaning up someone's "sloppy" speech can make them sound more "educated." Danny Barker, the rhythm guitarist in Cab Calloway's band in the 1940s and 50s, had great difficulty getting his written memoirs published because every publisher he approached asked him to write "in his own words" rather than in the standardized spelling and grammar that he was using. Barker knew that this was a coded message for him to use more examples of words like <gonna> in his memoirs so that he would "sound" (or look on paper) more like the African American musician that he was. But he felt that the publishers shouldn't have the power to change the way he "sounded" because that would change the way people would "read" him and think about him. It took a long time before he finally found a publisher that would allow him to spell words the way he wanted to.

Who really controls writing? Who controls the stereotypes that are invoked by writing one way or another? Who controls the definitions of "correctness" in writing? Who controls the ways that writing changes over time? When will it be acceptable to spell the English word *night* as <nite>? When will <nite> be considered the "correct" spelling? Or will it ever? We address some of these questions in Chapter 9. For the moment, it is important just to remember that writing and spoken language are not exactly the same thing, that they change at different rates, that everyone (with the exception of physically impaired individuals) learns to speak but that only those who work at it learn to read and to write, and that in most cases certain degrees of power and prestige are accorded to those who "have writing" and "know how to write."

SUMMARY

Writing is the graphic representation of language. It is a way of recording language using visible marks. Although everyone can speak (or sign), not everyone can write. Writing is something that has to be consciously learned. It is therefore considered secondary to spoken or signed (gestured) language.

There are complete writing systems and partial writing systems. Complete writing systems allow one to record any and all thoughts or words. Partial writing systems are limited in what they can convey. It is important to understand the difference between phonetic and semantic writing. Phonetic writing uses graphic marks to represent the sounds of a language; semantic writing uses graphic marks to represent specific ideas or meanings in a language. English relies more on phonetic writing, while Chinese relies more on semantic writing, but both languages use both kinds of writing systems to some degree.

Pictographic "writing" is an example of a partial writing system. Pictographic writing uses pictures or images to represent things. It is limited, therefore, to representing what can be pictured. Rebus writing extends the meanings of pictographs to represent words that sound like the items pictured. By moving beyond the limitations of pictographs, rebus writing allows more complete writing systems to emerge. Logographic writing uses graphic signs to represent words or the ideas associated with those words. Although some logographs may have evolved from pictographs, they have changed so much over time that they no longer resemble those pictographs.

Other complete writing systems include syllabic, logosyllabic, and alphabetic writing. Syllabic writing uses graphic signs to represent individual syllables. This works best in languages where the syllables are primarily of the form CV. Because it represents sounds, syllabic writing is considered a phonetic writing system. Logosyllabic writing combines logographic and syllabic signs to represent language. By using both kinds of signs in combination, words that sound the same can be differentiated in writing. Signs that are used to clarify meaning in this way are called determinatives; phonetic determinatives help to differentiate words that are pronounced differently, while semantic determinatives help to differentiate words that sound the same but mean different things. Alphabetic writing uses graphic signs to represent individual consonants and vowels.

If you know how a particular writing system works you can learn to read it more easily. Identifying the system's graphemes is an important first step. A grapheme is the smallest segment of the language that is represented by the writing system. A grapheme can represent a sound, a syllable, or an entire word, depending on the system. Most writing systems separate graphemes into groups that linguists call lexemes (or frames). A lexeme (or frame) is a unit of writing that is surrounded by white space on a page. Dictionaries may list lexemes in order of semantic graphemes or in order of phonetic graphemes.

Creating a writing system for an unwritten language is a serious challenge. You need to go beyond analyzing the sound system and determining whether to suggest an alphabetic, syllabic, or other kind of system. You need to be sensitive to the feelings and wishes of the people who are going to be using the writing system. Gender, class, ethnicity, and nationalism are just a few of the important issues that need to be considered. Different writing systems, and even different spelling systems, can convey different things to different people.

It is also important to understand what it means to "have writing," and what it means to "be literate." Who is expected to become literate? Who is allowed to become literate? How do people learn to read and write? What impact does literacy have on people? Do literate people think differently than others? Ethnographic studies of reading and writing are important recent developments in linguistic anthropology. Ethnographic attention to how writing represents different speaking styles is another important recent area of focus.

No writing system is a perfect representation of language, so it is important to understand the differences between representing a dialectical pronunciation and a "standard" pronunciation in a phonetic writing system. Stereotypes can be created or reinforced by the choices that a writer makes in how he or she portrays someone's speech, whether it be in a novel or a newspaper. It is important to recognize the connections between reading, writing, and power.

KEY TERMS

alphabetic writing
complete writing system
determinative
grapheme
lexeme
logographic writing
logosyllabic writing
partial writing system
phonetic determinatives
phonetic sign
pictographic "writing"
rebus writing
semantic determinatives
semantic sign
syllabic writing
writing

FURTHER READING

About Writing

Coulmas, Florian. 2003. *Writing systems: An introduction to their linguistic analysis*. Cambridge: Cambridge University Press. This is a general text on how to analyze writing systems.

Daniels, Peter T., and William Bright. 1996. *The world's writing systems*. New York: Oxford University Press. This is a comprehensive survey of writing systems.

DeFrancis, John. 1989. *Visible speech: The diverse oneness of writing systems*. Honolulu: University of Hawaii Press. This book contains a clear explanation of how writing systems work, with special attention to the phonetic aspects of Chinese writing.

About Decipherment

Coe, Michael D. 1992. *Breaking the Maya code*. New York: Thames and Hudson. This is an entertaining and informative history of the controversy surrounding decoding Mayan glyphs and of the political as well as the academic struggles. It reads like a well-written mystery story, with clear explanations of how writing systems work.

About Reading, Writing, Power, and Identity

Bender, Margaret. 2002. *Signs of Cherokee culture: Sequoyah's syllabary in Eastern Cherokee life*. Chapel Hill: University of North Carolina Press. This is a fascinating and thoughtful study of how Sequoyah's syllabary functions as a symbol of ethnicity and identity among the Eastern Band of Cherokee.

Boyarin, Jonathan, ed. 1992. *The ethnography of reading*. Berkeley: University of California Press. This book contains fascinating articles about literacy, orality, and the social and cultural aspects of reading.

Goody, Jack. 2000. *The power of the written tradition*. Washington, DC: Smithsonian Institution Press. This book explores the ways that writing may have transformed cultures.

 # STUDENT ACTIVITIES

Readings

The workbook/reader for this book has readings that can help you to further explore and understand the issues introduced in this chapter.

Exercises

A set of writing exercises in the workbook/reader will assist you in understanding the issues introduced in this chapter and in further exploring the intersection among writing, ethnicity, gender, and power. An exercise in deciphering a specific writing system in the workbook/reader will give you practice in working with graphemes to analyze and learn a writing system that may be new to you.

Web Exercises

The companion website for this book has a series of links designed to help you explore the issues introduced in this chapter in greater depth, to better understand them. The companion website also contains study questions that will help you to review important concepts.

Guided Projects

If you are creating a language, you may want to design a writing system for it. If you are working with a conversation partner, your instructor may assign a writing project for you to explore issues of writing in different scripts. Further details about how to proceed are in the workbook/reader and/or on the companion website. Your instructor will be your guide.

CHAPTER 8

How and When Is Language Possible?

In the Field, Comoro Islands, July 1982

"Dagavigi," *one of the girls said, looking at my son, Davi, encouragingly.*

"*Dagavigi,*" said Davi, looking puzzled.

"*Dagavigi,*" the girls repeated, giggling. Then, pleased with their success, they turned to face my other son, Afan.

"*Agafaganigi,*" they said together, with a big smile.

"*Agafaganigi,*" repeated Afan, looking about as puzzled as his younger brother.

"What's going on here?" I asked the boys. I appeared to have stumbled onto some sort of mysterious game.

"We have no idea," said the boys, almost in unison. "These girls have been trying to teach us something, but we're not sure what."

We had been in the Comoros for a few weeks now, and the boys had learned how to say 'please,' and 'thank you' as well as a few simple survival sentences such as 'Can I please have some water?' and 'What is that?' But I had never heard words like the ones I was hearing now.

I had seen, and been subject to, "repeat after me" kinds of games in the Comoros. Often these are lead-ins to some sort of teasing. But the boys seemed open to the possibilities, so I suggested they continue to play the game while I watched.

"*Shigirigi,*" said the girls, pointing at a chair. And then, pointing at a bed, "*Uguligiligi.*" But I knew these words as *shiri* and *ulili!* And then it hit me.

"*Megazega?*" I asked, pointing to a table (*meza* in Shinzwani).

"*Ewa* ('yes')!" replied the girls.

"*Shintiri?*" I asked the girls.

"*Egawaga* ('es-yay')!" replied the girls. "Can you help us teach it to your boys?" And I sat down to learn Comorian "Pig Latin" and—at the same time—to help the girls teach it to my sons.

HJO

172

I had known about the existence of Shintiri since the 1960s when I first lived in the Comoros, but I had never been able to find out much about it. People said it was a "strange language" and that it was spoken by only a very few, highly reclusive people. Speakers of Shintiri were known as Wantiri, we were told, just like speakers of Shinzwani were known as Wanzwani. Someday, if we were very lucky, we might meet some Wantiri, but, we were advised, we shouldn't count on it. At some point, I think we figured out that this was all a joke. But we weren't sure what kind of joke until years later, when I found my sons engaged in Shintiri lessons.

Shintiri is elusive, as it turns out, because only young preadolescent children play with it. Once you are old enough to consider yourself an adult (as all of our field assistants were) you really should be too old to bother with Shintiri; it's just not an adult sort of thing to do. Still, as a way of exploring linguistic structure, it's an outstanding game for children. It has the special value of helping children to turn their own language into an object of analysis as well as of play. Inserting a [g] after every syllable helps them to learn where the syllables are. Reduplicating different vowels helps them to explore variety and contrast in vowel sounds. All this structured language play helps them to develop greater facility and fluency with language in general and with their language specifically.

There are many different kinds of language-altering games around the world, and they are almost always played by children, who abandon the games once they reach adulthood. Can these games teach us something about the way humans apprehend language? Can they teach us something about how language is learned? Can they even teach us something about the origins of language? This chapter explores these issues, discussing the origins and development of language and exploring the complex intersection of language and culture in human evolution and human language learning.

✳ HOW IS LANGUAGE POSSIBLE?

There is remarkably little agreement at present regarding how and when human language may have emerged. This is partly because there is remarkably little agreement among scholars regarding what it means to "have" language. There is even disagreement over whether humans "learn" language or whether they "acquire" it. In addition, there is considerable difference of opinion regarding whether human language emerged all at once, at a single moment in human evolution, or whether it developed gradually over a long period of time, as well as whether human language is qualitatively or quantitatively different from other kinds of animal communication. We will address each of these issues in more detail in the next few pages.

There are two important reasons why there is so little agreement on these issues. One reason is that it is extremely difficult to design ethical experiments with living human children to pinpoint the ways in which they learn/acquire language. The other is that it is impossible to find language itself in the fossil record. So, we are limited to observation, analysis, and speculation, using everything we know about anthropology and even drawing on related fields such as neurology, biology, psychology, and cognitive science to try to solve these puzzles. In spite of these limitations, it has recently become possible to make some educated guesses about possibilities and probabilities.

Theories about Language Beginnings

The subject of language origins was an especially popular topic of discussion in Europe during the 1700s and 1800s. Philosophers and linguists proposed all sorts of fanciful theories and presented and defended them vigorously. They suggested, for example, that language began as people imitated animal calls (*bow wow!*). They suggested that language began as people expressed pain or emotion (*ouch!*). They suggested that language began as people noticed that certain objects had unique imitable sounds of their own (*ding dong!*). They suggested that language began as people worked together (*yo-he-ho*). They even suggested that language began as people agreed among themselves about which sounds ought to represent which items and ideas (social contract). These theories were all speculative, however, and there really was no way to prove or disprove any of them. By 1866, the members of the Linguistic Society of Paris had had enough theorizing, and they voted to ban any further discussion of language origins among their members and any further publication of scholarly papers on the subject.

The question of language origins remains intriguing, however, and in the second half of the 1900s scholars—in particular linguistic anthropologists—reopened the discussion. This time they had a century's worth of research and data to draw on. And this time the data was far more interdisciplinary in nature; data from all four fields of anthropology could be brought together in an attempt to solve the puzzle of language origins. From understanding how language is structured to seeing how it is learned and used in contemporary cultures, from understanding the complex interrelationships of language and culture to interpreting the archaeological record concerning early cultures, from understanding the physical prerequisites for language-production to interpreting the fossil record concerning biological possibilities in early humans, the breadth of scholarship provided new hope for solving this ancient and intriguing puzzle. As a result, many of today's theories, while still speculative, appear more plausible.

Two Approaches: Innateness versus Evolution According to theoretical linguists, language is far too complicated a phenomenon to have evolved slowly over time by a series of random mutations. Instead, they argue, language is a specific human ability, which, once developed, was forever a part of the human brain. The result is that all humans are thought to carry a kind of universal grammar in their brains as part of their genetic makeup. Armed with this universal grammar, a child simply needs to **acquire** language, to map the details of a specific language onto a universal grammar. This means that research into any one language should provide insight into the universal characteristics of language. It also means that, once you understand the universal characteristics of language, you should be able to create meaningful theories about the way that language—as a general capacity—first became possible in humans, as well as how specific languages are acquired by contemporary human children.

Linguistic anthropologists, on the other hand, argue that language is so complicated and so variable that it must have evolved over a long period of time. Furthermore, they argue, language is so complexly intertwined with culture that language and culture must have evolved together, influencing one another in the process and ultimately shaping what it means to be human. The result is that, although human infants may be born with the ability to learn languages, it is social interaction that provides the context in which language is actually learned. Born into a speech community, a child will **learn** language, will discover the details of a specific language by interaction with the individuals who speak it. Each variety of language is differently shaped by the community of individuals that uses it, as well as by the social situations in which they use it, so research into how children learn language in different speech communities provides insight into the general question of how language is learned. As children learn a language, they also learn their culture and develop their cognitive capabilities. This means that research into the fossil origins of humans and the archaeological remains of early cultures, as well as field and laboratory observations of language learning among humans and other primates, all can contribute to solving the puzzle of how and when human language became—and remains—possible.

A Four-Field Approach This is truly an area in which all four subfields of anthropology need to work together. From the standpoint of physical anthropology, we need to ask what makes it physically possible for language to emerge. What clues do we need to look for, and where in the fossil record can we find them? Are there additional clues to be found in contemporary primate communication systems? From the standpoint of archaeology, we need to ask what kinds of evidence exist for the beginnings of culture. As with physical anthropology, we need to identify the relevant clues—tools, fire, burials—and to search for them in the archaeological record. Although physical anthropology and archaeology may help us to identify *when* language became possible, we need to turn to cultural and linguistic anthropology to understand *how* language became possible. How should we define language to be sure we can identify its origins? How, for example, is human language different from primate communication systems? We also need to know more about how children learn and use language in different cultures. What is it about becoming a member of a speech community that helps to shed light on the possible beginnings of language?

The point is to use as much information from as many different research areas as possible to understand how and when the breakthrough to language could have occurred. Contemporary children are born into a language-rich environment and merely need to learn how to use their language to interact with those around them. What was the environment like for the first language users? What was available to them for language creation? And what did they do with it? How, in other words, did humans begin having conversations rather than just issuing alarms and signaling the presence of food? If we can figure this out, then we may be able to solve the puzzle of the origins of language. It's a puzzle that anthropology seems uniquely positioned to solve.

Defining Language

We need to have a definition of language before we can reliably say that we know what we are looking for. To do this, we need to begin by exploring the difference between "language" and "communication." Both of these words are remarkably difficult to define, however. Some scholars define **communication** broadly as the sending of signals. Others define communication more narrowly as the sending and receiving of signals. Still others don't consider communication to have taken place unless a signal is sent, is received, and evokes a response in its hearers. Using even the most restrictive of these definitions, it is easy to see that both humans and animals communicate. For example, vervet monkeys communicate when one of them signals the presence of an eagle and all the others duck and hide. Likewise, humans communicate when a baby screams in pain and its parents stop what they are doing and attend to the baby.

Communication, however, seems somewhat limited in *what* it can transmit. Language, on the other hand, appears capable of transmitting unlimited kinds of information. In addition, communication seems limited in what kinds of response it can evoke, while language appears capable of evoking an unlimited range of responses. For example, vervet monkeys have three specific kinds of warning sounds: one for leopard, one for eagle, and one for snake. If they hear the one for leopard they drop what they are doing and climb up in the trees, if they hear the one for eagle they duck for cover, and if they hear the one for snake they rise up and search the grass around them. In other words, their responses are as limited as their signals. Vervets can be said to have a communication system, but they don't have a language.

Humans, on the other hand, use language for transmitting and responding in a variety of ways. When a child says, "I'm so hungry I could eat a horse," the child probably doesn't mean that she literally needs to eat a horse. The child's parents might respond by making a peanut butter sandwich for the child, telling the child to search in the refrigerator for something to eat, telling the child to wait for supper, or in any other of the possible ways you can think of that would be a reasonable response to the child's statement. Although the child and the parents are communicating, they are also using language.

As clear as this might seem, it turns out that defining the difference between language and communication has been the subject of endless speculation and argument among scholars. Some point out the social nature of language and argue that communication does not require any "real" social interaction. Others focus on the presence of complex grammar in human language and argue that animal communication does not exhibit evidence of grammatical structure. Still others insist that the difference between human language and animal communication resides in the fact that humans use language to tell lies, have conversations, fabricate elaborate hypothetical scenarios, or play linguistic games, while animals do not do any of these things. Can you imagine vervets playing Dungeons and Dragons or creating science fiction narratives or talking about being hungry enough to eat a horse? Probably not.

The Design Features of Language   In the 1960s, anthropologist Charles Hockett helped to provide some clarity to the debate by listing and defining what he called the **design features of language,** or the features by which human language could be identified and distinguished from the more general category of animal communication. There were thirteen features and, as Hockett explained it, all human languages contained all thirteen features. Various animal communication systems might have one or more features, but no animal communication system could be shown to have all thirteen of the basic design features of language. Four of these features, in particular, were unique to human language, and Hockett suggested that, if scholars could pinpoint how these had emerged, then we might be able to describe how human language itself had developed. To this day, anthropologists, linguists, psychologists, philosophers, and cognitive scientists refer to Hockett's design features in their research. Here is a brief discussion of each feature, and how it is important in defining human language.

The **vocal auditory channel** refers specifically to the use of speaking and hearing as a key feature of language. Although we know that human language often uses manual and visual channels for communication, as in sign language or writing, many linguists continue to think of speech and hearing as primary in human language. Other animal communication systems that make use of the vocal auditory channel include birds, whales, dolphins, and nonhuman primate calls. Bee dancing, in contrast, uses space and movement for communication. We will return to this issue later in the chapter, when we discuss sign language.

Broadcast transmission and directional reception means that the sounds of human language are sent out in all directions, but that listeners perceive those sounds as coming from a specific direction. When I lecture, everyone in the room can hear me, and each student can tell, just by listening to me, where in the room I am standing relative to them. If I walk to the back of the room and continue talking, the students can tell, from the sound of my voice, that I am speaking from behind them. Some will actually turn around to watch me as well as listen to me. Broadcast transmission and directional reception appear to be characteristic of just about every kind of animal communication, so it is not particularly useful for defining human language as opposed to animal communication. Still, it is a feature of human language, so Hockett noted it and included it in his list.

Rapid fading (or transitoriness) means that language signals don't last very long. Speech, in particular, fades quickly and when it's gone it's gone (unless, of course, you've made a recording of it). Even when you play back a recording, the sounds of speech disappear almost as soon as you hear them. This is also true for signed language. You see signs while they are being made, but then they are gone unless you've videotaped them. Rapid fading seems to be a phenomenon that is characteristic of all kinds of communication, not just human language. As with broadcast transmission, however, it is a feature of human language and so Hockett included it in his list.

Interchangeability refers to the fact that a speaker can send and receive the same signal. Some animal communication systems only permit certain individuals to send certain signals. A stickleback fish, for example, can only produce the visual signal that goes with his or her specific gender. On the other hand, any human can repeat anything that any other human says, with no limitations. You can say, "I'm a boy," or "I'm a girl," for example, even if that isn't your true gender.

Total feedback means that speakers can hear themselves talk and that they can monitor what they say as they say it. It is possible that this feature is present in most forms of animal communication, but this is difficult to test.

Hockett originally meant **specialization** to mean that language sounds are specialized for communication. In other words, that when humans speak it is generally in order to transmit information. In contrast, when dogs pant it is primarily to cool themselves off. The noise of panting is not intended to transmit information. The dog's owners may realize that the dog is hot because they hear it panting, but that is a secondary matter. This feature could be extended to include signed language in the sense that the primary purpose of a sign is to transmit information rather than anything else.

Over the years some scholars have used the term specialization to refer to the idea that human speech organs are specially adapted for speaking or that parts of the human brain have been specially adapted for language. It is true that the human vocal apparatus and brain are uniquely able to produce language, and in particular spoken language, but this is not what Hockett was referring to.

Semanticity means that specific sound signals can be directly linked to specific meanings. For example, as Hockett pointed out, the English word *salt* refers specifically to salt and not to sugar or pepper or some other substance. Semanticity is present in other forms of animal communication, too. The example we gave before about vervet calls shows that three different signals have three different specific meanings and elicit three different specific responses in vervets. However, animal calls are limited in what they can stand for, rarely seem to change, and are not combined in new and different ways, while human language sounds are not limited in what they can describe, can change fairly rapidly, and can combine in a multitude of ways. No animal appears to be able to combine the signals for food and danger, while human language can combine a variety of words to communicate the fact that the food you are about to eat might be rotten, or poisoned, or likely to induce an allergic reaction, or otherwise potentially dangerous. It is not just the feature of semanticity but the way in which that semanticity is applied that helps to establish a difference between human language and animal communication.

Arbitrariness means that there is no necessary or causal connection between a signal and its meaning. In other words, any signal can be used to refer to any thing. The English word *salt* for example is neither salty nor granular. Nor does the sound of the word *salt* have any particular connection with the sound or taste of salt. The English word *salt* does not resemble actual salt in any way. Such arbitrariness can be further seen in the fact that different languages can assign very different words to the same substance. The Shinzwani word for 'salt,' for example, is *munyo*. Bee communication, in contrast, is not arbitrary. A bee moves in a specific direction and pattern to communicate a specific food location and distance from hive. The further the food from the hive, the slower the movement.

Discreteness means that the units used for communication can be separated into distinct units that cannot be mistaken for one another. Nor do these units blend into one another. In English, the [b] sound is clearly differentiated from the [p] sound. No matter how similar they may sound to speakers of some other language, English speakers will perceive [b] and [p] as discrete, different sounds. Different languages may differentiate different sounds, but all languages rely on the ability to separate sounds into discrete categories. Bee communication, in contrast, is continuous, especially the way in which decreased speed indicates increased distance.

Displacement refers to the fact that you can talk about things that are not present. You can talk about things that are physically absent, such as the planet Mars or your cousin who lives in another country or a place you would like to visit someday. You can talk about different time frames, such as the past or the future or the wished-for or the ought-to-be. You can even talk about things that don't exist, like purple people-eaters. Interestingly, although most animal communication systems lack displacement, bee communication appears to make use of this feature, signaling the existence and location of food that is at a distance from the hive. On the other hand, chimpanzee vocalizations tend to occur only when the relevant item is present. For example, the sight of food can evoke a 'food found' call, but if there is no food present then there is no 'food found' call. Hockett suggested that displacement was one of the four features that separated human language from the communication of other primates.

Productivity is the feature that allows you to produce and comprehend entirely new utterances that you've never spoken or heard before. These utterances can be serious or playful, just as long as you follow the rules that your particular language provides to you for combining units in ways that "make sense" to other members of your speech community. Productivity lets you write poetry and song lyrics and imaginative answers to questions on exams. Productivity let Noam Chomsky write, "Colorful green ideas sleep furiously." It let Lewis Carroll write, "'Twas brillig and the slithey toves. . . ." It let Groucho Marx say, "Time flies like an arrow; fruit flies like a banana." And it let me write this book. If you think about it, most of what you say on a daily basis is not memorized material. Instead, productivity allows you to create utterances as you need them.

Productivity is a key feature in human language, whether it is spoken or written or signed. Not surprisingly, this is one feature that sets human language apart from most other animal communication. Gibbons and baboons have a generally unchanging set of about a dozen calls, but each call has a specific meaning, relating to such things as danger or the presence of food. In addition, the calls do not seem to be combined into novel utterances. New calls are not invented; existing calls are not combined. It does not seem possible, for example, for a gibbon to communicate that there is food present but that the situation is dangerous.

Traditional transmission refers to the fact that language is learned in social groups. Although humans are probably born with an ability to learn language, the learning takes place within social groups. The debate is still raging over what and how much linguistic capacity humans are born with, from a basic grammatical blueprint to simply the capacity to learn language. In any case, it is clear that whatever is learned is learned in social settings. It is also clear that appropriate ways of using language are also learned in social settings. Although there are a few cases in which researchers believe that insects or animals learn or refine bits of their

Doing Linguistic Anthropology 8.1

PLAYING WITH INTONATION

Not long ago I watched a four-month-old baby "learning" intonation patterns from her parents. One parent addressed the baby with the rising intonation typical of questions in English, saying, *Wanna have a bath????* The baby had mastered an [aaaa] sound, but that seemed to be her entire linguistic repertoire for the moment. Nonetheless, she used it to respond to her parents, raising the pitch of her voice exactly as her parents had. It sounded like she was saying, "Aaaaa???" I suggested to the parents that they should try to "declare" something, like *It's time for your bath now!!!*, with a strong falling intonation. Sure enough, the baby responded with "Aaaaa!!!" using a falling intonation just like her parents. As her parents continued the intonation game, it was clear that they were enjoying engaging in an unconscious language-teaching process. Even if all they were doing was activating their baby's innate language-learning capacity, the fact remains that it was taking place in a social setting.

HJO

communication systems after birth, these are relatively rare and are not always clear-cut examples. So traditional transmission is another feature that helps to set human language apart from animal communication.

Duality of patterning is one of the most important features of a language system. It appears to be a combination of the features of discreteness and productivity. Hockett developed the phrase duality of patterning to express the fact that discrete units of language at one level (such as the level of sounds) can be combined to create different kinds of units at a different level (such as words). For example, the discrete English sounds [k], [æ], [t], and [s] can be combined to produced the English words *cat, act, tack, scat, acts, tacks, task, cast, cask,* and more. Every language has rules for which sounds can combine with which other ones and in which orders. English does not allow, for example, a word like *tka* or *kta,* and it generally doesn't use the combination [ts] at the beginnings of words, even though other languages allow words to start with that combination. According to Hockett, duality of patterning was probably the last feature to emerge in human language, and it was critical in separating human language from other kinds of primate communication.

Design Features and the Emergence of Language   As Hockett saw it, the first nine features are shared by all contemporary primates, including humans. This means that they were probably also present in the prehistoric communication system from which human language emerged. He theorized that this early prelanguage communication system must have been made up of a dozen or so distinct vocal calls, each one likely to be uttered in response to a specific situation, such as the discovery of food or the presence of a predator. The last four features—productivity, displacement, traditional transmission, and duality of patterning—are therefore the features that must be unique to humans. So the principal question that Hockett thought needed to be solved was how these calls could have been transformed into language. How, for example, did productivity, displacement, traditional transmission, and duality of patterning emerge and modify the basic call system to produce what we know today as human language?

Hockett suggested that productivity could have emerged through a process that he called **blending,** or the mixing of two signals into one new one. Say, for example, an early human had found some food, but the food was being guarded by another animal or even by another human. Perhaps, rather than uttering two separate calls—one for food, and one for danger—the individual, in his or her excitement, might have uttered some sort of combined call. This would be a little like trying to tell your friend that you had been invited to a late-breakfast-early-lunch event. In your excitement, you might just say you had been invited to a *brunch,* combining the *br-* of *breakfast* and the *-unch* of *lunch.* We combine words like this all the time in English, so, Hockett reasoned, why not imagine the same sort of word blending at the dawn of language?

Productivity could have set the stage for displacement to emerge. If it is possible to create new calls through blending, then it is also possible *not* to create new calls. Suppose, in the previous scenario, that the individual who discovers food and danger in the same place suppresses the urge to shout about it. Instead, in his or her excitement, he or she runs (or tiptoes) back to the rest of the group and *then* utters the appropriate (possibly blended) calls. Productivity and displacement could then set the stage for traditional transmission to emerge because children and others could now be taught to avoid certain dangers without having to actually encounter them first. The newly blended calls could be used in the campsite to "talk" about various possibilities, such as food and danger combined.

The most difficult bit to figure out is how and when duality of patterning could have emerged. How did individuals manage to isolate various bits of calls so that they could be endlessly combined into arbitrary symbols? Hockett thought that, if two calls each had two distinct parts, then perhaps something in the blending process might alert individuals to the existence of discrete units. If you can combine *breakfast* and *lunch* into *brunch,* then does that alert you to the possibility that *br* is a distinct unit of sound that is combinable with other distinct units of sound? Solving this puzzle remains one of the thorniest of the problems in determining how language became possible.

Over time, Hockett revised his feature list and other scholars have added to it and critiqued it as well. Such features as prevarication (lying), reflexiveness (self-awareness and self-monitoring), and learnability (as in learning a second language) have all been suggested as additions to the design feature list, but the four key features of productivity, displacement, traditional transmission, and duality of patterning remain the most important features to consider as we search for the origins of language in human beings.

Since Hockett's design features were proposed, much new research has been accomplished in the areas of primate communication, children's language, neurology, physiology, and human evolution. We will review each of these in turn, exploring what each has to contribute, and then we will return to the question of how and when language might have been possible.

Primate Communication

No matter how many valiant and creative attempts have been made, no one has succeeded in teaching any nonhuman animals to master human language. The most spectacular failures have been in attempts to teach other animals to "speak." Alexander Graham Bell tried to teach his dog to speak by training it to growl continuously while he manipulated its jaws and throat. The best he could get was something like *ow a oo gwa ma*, which was supposed to sound like *how are you, grandma?* Keith and Catherine Hayes had a bit more success with a chimpanzee named Viki in the late 1940s. Vicki could produce a [k] and a [p] with some effort. If she held her nostrils shut with her hand she could even produce an [m]. These limited consonants, together with a rather indeterminate vowel that sounded something like a schwa could be combined to produce utterances that sounded something like the English words *cup* or *mama*. But conversations between Viki and the Hayeses or between Bell and his dog were clearly not possible. This is probably one reason why Hockett assigned such importance to sound (vocal-auditory channel) in distinguishing human language from other forms of communication. As we shall see, Hockett's emphasis on spoken communication may turn out to have been misplaced.

More recently attempts have been made to teach animals to use sign language or even plastic "lexigrams" (or plastic tokens) rather than sounds. Because humans are more closely related to other primates (such as chimpanzees and gorillas) than they are to dogs, most of this work has focused on primates. A variety of experiments with chimpanzees, bonobos, gorillas, and orangutans has had mixed and controversial results. Beatrice and Robert Gardner trained a chimpanzee named Washoe to recognize and use elements of American Sign Language, for example. Penny Patterson did similar work with a gorilla named Koko. Psychologists at the Yerkes Primate Research Center trained a chimpanzee named Lana to use a special computer to recognize and construct simple sentences. David Premack trained a chimpanzee named Sarah to recognize a set of plastic lexigrams representing words and to arrange them into rudimentary sentences. And most recently Sue Savage-Rumbaugh found that a bonobo named Kanzi was even more gifted in the use of lexigrams than Sarah and other chimpanzees.

Some of these animals have been able to learn a number of signs. Washoe was said to have been able to use up to 150 signs; Koko was said to have been able to use over 500. Some appear to combine signs in unexpected ways (productivity). Washoe, for example, combined signs for 'water' and 'bird' when she saw a duck swimming in a pond. Some seem to use the signs to refer to items that are not present (displacement). Koko, for example, continued to use signs to ask for a kitten she had played with and to ask for another kitten after the first one had died. There have even been some examples of traditional transmission. Washoe appeared to pass some signs on to her adopted offspring and others in the group that she lived with. Duality of patterning, however, remains unreachable. Nonhuman primates just don't seem to get the idea of isolating and recombining units at one level into new units at a different level. Bonobos do seem to be able to combine their plastic lexigrams in ways that are tantalizingly similar to this. The lexigrams are, in fact, discrete recombinable units and some recombining seems to take place as the bonobos construct phrases in the lab. But, as Sue Savage Rumbaugh points out, it seems more likely that the bonobos can do this *because* the lexigrams have already been broken into discrete units for them by the researchers who are working with them. Left to their own devices, bonobos, chimpanzees, gorillas, and the like do not seem to analyze signs into discrete units and combine them in ways that clearly indicate duality of patterning. Humans still seem to be the only creatures using duality of patterning, identifying and combining linguistic units into nearly endless combinations.

In general, it remains difficult to prove that animals trained in sign language or in the use of plastic lexigrams are using those signs or lexigrams to do anything other than beg for food or for trainers to play with them or for the chance to go outside or for other kinds of treats and favors. In some cases, it appears that most of their communication is imitative—and intended to please their trainers—rather than initiated for the purpose of conversing. This has caused some scholars to dismiss experiments with nonhuman primates as "trained animal acts" in spite of the fact that they remain intriguing in what they can tell us about language and what it is and is not. Most of these animals learn what they learn with difficulty, and most of them, despite the amount that they learn, never seem to get past the abilities of three- to five-year-old children. The fact remains that human children seem to learn language irrepressibly, while it takes countless M&Ms for chimpanzees or gorillas to learn small bits of languagelike material.

What does this tell us about the beginnings of language? For one thing, it seems that apes and protohumans must have shared some basic abilities for language but whatever adaptation or breakthrough occurred in protohumans to allow for duality of patterning does not seem to have happened among other primates, nor has it evolved since.

Children and Language

In contrast to other primates, human children appear to learn complex languages fairly easily, and most individuals continue to expand their abilities throughout adulthood, sometimes learning additional languages as the opportunity presents itself. Three-day-old babies are able to distinguish their mothers' voices from those of other people. By the time they are three and four months old, many babies start cooing and laughing and experimenting with different-sounding cries. They begin playing with consonants, vowels, and intonation patterns in the fifth or sixth month. Recognizable words start emerging by the end of the first year and a mid-year explosion of naming things (and actions) seems to occur around eighteen months. By the end of the second year, many children are producing two- and three-word sentences. From this point on, children seem to progress in various ways as they develop facility with questions, negative statements, and multiclause sentences. This is also the time period in which they begin to experiment with displacement, using language to refer to things that are not present. Of course, everyone knows of some child who seems to have progressed differently through these stages or who seems to have skipped all of the "baby steps" and just started talking in whole sentences somewhere between the ages of three and five. No matter which way children go through the process of language learning, it is clear that all of them do it, and they do it in ways that far exceed the abilities and complexities present in any other form of animal communication.

Theories about Language in Children   Various theories have been proposed to explain how children develop their language skills, from innatist (children don't learn language, they are born with an internal grammar that they adjust to fit whichever language they are expected to speak) to behaviorist (children learn by imitating and by receiving positive feedback) to cognitivist (children develop their linguistic abilities in fixed stages, as they develop their mental abilities). A recent theory, called "the theory theory," suggests that children analyze language as they hear it, forming and refining ideas (theories) about grammar and structure as they go. This ties in nicely with anthropological observations that note the importance and impact of the speech community in early childhood language development. As anthropologists have been pointing out for some time now, language is generally learned in social groups and learning to use a language also means learning how to use it in socially appropriate ways. Let's look at each of these theories briefly.

Innatist theories tell us that language is already hard-wired into the human brain at birth. In this view, a genetically built-in "core grammar" provides a universal set of rules. These rules allow the brain to function as a "language acquisition device," enabling children to develop their linguistic abilities. This **language acquisition device** compares specific languages with the core grammar and helps children to make the necessary adjustments as they acquire specific languages. If a language uses an element of the core grammar, for example, children include that element in their linguistic toolkit. If a language omits an element of the core grammar, children can ignore that element or delete it from the toolkit. Gradually children polish their ability with whichever specific linguistic varieties they are expected to use. Proponents of innatist theories point out that children demonstrate competence with language in such a short time that there must be some innate grammar present.

Behaviorist theories tell us that children need to hear language from others around them (stimulus) and to receive praise (positive feedback) from parents and/or caretakers in order to develop their linguistic abilities. In other words, children hear words, are encouraged to imitate those words, and are praised for correct performance. If this were so, however, then English-speaking children would never produce such odd-sounding plural forms as *sheeps* or *mouses* when the "correct" plural forms for these words are *sheep* and *mice*. Although there is no ethical way to test this theory, occasionally a child is found who has had little or no social stimulation and who also appears to have few linguistic skills. Generally, these are adolescent or preadolescent children who have been abandoned or kept locked away from contact with other humans. Interestingly, none of these children seems to develop much ability with language after they are found. This has led some researchers to suggest that there is a critical age by which language must be learned; otherwise, it is not possible to learn language at all. But it is also possible that these children had significant difficulties with language from the beginning, leading their caretakers to isolate or abandon them. Since there is no ethical way to test this, the answer will probably never be known.

Cognitivist theories tell us that as children develop their intellectual abilities their linguistic abilities follow suit. In other words, children must first comprehend concepts relating to quantity before they are able to use words such as *more* and *less*. Or they must first have a sense of permanence before they use words like *gone* or *all gone*. As with behaviorist theories, it is difficult to design experiments to test the idea that cognition precedes language. Nonetheless, some recent observations are provocative in this regard. It seems that eighteen-month-old children can be observed using words such as *gone* and *all gone* just at the moment at which they also demonstrate awareness of concepts such as permanence. In addition, children of approximately the same age begin using words such as *uh oh* at just about the same time that they can be shown to be aware of concepts of success, failure, and the outcomes of actions. In all of these cases, it is clear that the linguistic concepts appear at the same time that the intellectual concepts emerge. However, in many other cases it appears that word use comes first. This suggests that the interaction between language use and cognitive abilities (such as thinking about categories and actions) is more complex than cognitivist theories indicate.

The theory theory argues that children observe and interact with the world around them and form theories about their experiences. Language, according to this idea, is the result of a complex set of theories that children create about the linguistic stimuli that they are exposed to. Researchers using this approach observe children interacting with their caretakers and note the ways in which they appear to analyze and generalize about the language around them. Such observations reveal that by the age of eighteen months (or even earlier) most children seem to realize that language is an important source of information about the world around them and begin to pay more attention to the kinds of objects and events that are marked by language. Children therefore seem to be building theories about the language they encounter, and they begin using their growing linguistic abilities to develop, extend, and modify their theories.

Because different languages draw children's attention to different aspects of the world, it is also possible that differences in the ways that languages are constructed may also affect the order in which young children build their theories and develop their linguistic and cognitive abilities. Korean, for example, stresses verbs in ways that English does not, and Korean-speaking parents tend to name actions for their children much as English-speaking parents tend to name objects for their children. As a result, Korean children appear to master concepts related to actions earlier than English-speaking children, while English-speaking children tend to master concepts related to objects earlier. Both sets of children seem to have mastered both sets of concepts by the age of two or three, suggesting that the different languages merely provide different pathways and sequences for cognitive categories to emerge. Most important, it is not the differences in the two languages, as such, that appears to affect the differences in the children's awareness but rather the ways that those differences are presented to the children by their parents. It is language in use, in other words, that affects language learning. Such observations make it clear that children acquire much of what they need for linguistic analysis, and for theorizing about language, by becoming members of their speech communities (Gopnik and Choi 1990, 1995; Gopnik 2001).

Anthropological Observations of Language Learning   Research by linguistic anthropologists further highlights the importance of the social and cultural contexts in which children learn language and demonstrates that children need to interact with parents and other caregivers in order to become fully competent with their language. As linguistic anthropologists Elinor Ochs and Bambi Schieffelin (1982) point out, becoming a competent speaker of a language is complexly wrapped up with becoming a competent member of a culture. Not only do individuals need to learn the vocabulary and grammar of the language surrounding them, they also need to learn how to use that language in socially acceptable ways. When is it okay to utter certain words? When is it not okay? When is it okay to talk and when is it more appropriate to remain silent? How do you use language to get what you want? How do you use language to get other people to do things? Most important, how are children expected to learn such things?

As Ochs and Schieffelin point out, the task of learning how to use language can be markedly different in different cultures. For example, infants can be talked to or not. "Baby talk" can be encouraged by caretakers or not. Americans, for example, tend to encourage a period of "baby talk," using words such as *doggie* and *horsie* that are not really a part of adult speech. Kaluli (New Guinea) adults, on the other hand, tend to bypass such "baby talk," waiting instead for children to begin using adult-sounding words before interacting with them linguistically. Adults then begin "perfecting" their children's speech by correcting their pronunciation and grammar. In other words, expectations about children's language use can affect the specific ways that children actually develop their abilities with language.

Even different attitudes about language learning can be unconsciously transmitted and learned in different speech communities. In the United States, most children routinely grow up in monolingual speech communities; as a result, they get the idea that it must be difficult to learn to speak more than one language successfully. In many other countries, however, children grow up in multilingual speech communities; as a result they understand that it is possible to become competent in more than one language, and many of them do become fluent in several languages. In the Comoro Islands, I often encountered teenagers who appeared to be fluent in six or seven different languages. If linguistic competency is defined in your speech community as knowing how to use a variety of languages then it is likely you will learn a variety of languages. If members of your speech community believe that learning a second language will confuse you, then you are likely to have difficulty learning a second language. In short, it seems clear from anthropological observations of language learning that humans are not only socialized through language but to language.

Doing Linguistic Anthropology 8.2

EXPERIMENTING WITH INTONATION

We had noticed that, earlier, our older daughter, in trying to identify an object, would point at it and try to name it while using a rising intonation. But the reply, to be normal, should have been falling in pitch. She was, in fact, mimicking our own speech, which we used when we asked her if she could name the object. Therefore, for our second child, we decided to distort our question by using a declarative intonation, hoping that by mimicking us she would learn an appropriate intonation to identify objects. (We were the only English speakers in a small village in Mexico, so ours was the only English our daughter heard.) It worked! (See Evelyn Pike 1949.) The child's first words used an adult intonation for naming or calling rather than the normal baby expectancy of rising pitch to mean "Can you say 'X'". We then had to leave her with friends for a few days. The friends were not trained in intonation, and we had made no attempt to instruct them how to carry on the experiment. When we came back, the child's typical question (rising) intonation had replaced the 'adult' (falling) intonation!

Kenneth L. Pike

A Linguistic Pilgrimage (1998, 154)

 WHEN IS LANGUAGE POSSIBLE?

Research into *how* language is possible is complexly interconnected with research into *when* language may have been possible. So our next step is to review some of the recent data that might allow us to speculate on the question of when language might have begun. Such an endeavor takes us more firmly into biology, neurology, physical anthropology, and archaeology, as we attempt to sort out the development of the physical possibilities. Most of the research to date on this aspect of our question has focused on two key areas: the human brain and the human vocal apparatus. Research on the brain has made it clear that the ability to handle complex symbol systems such as language resides in this organ. Research on the human vocal apparatus is a bit more controversial, in part because it has become clear in recent years that language is more than just speech, that the human facility with language includes signed as well as spoken language. Nonetheless, in view of the body of data surrounding the origins of spoken language, we will present and discuss that evidence and assume that it will help us to understand the larger picture as well. Let's begin with the brain.

Language and the Brain

Whether the human brain is hard-wired with a universal core grammar or just set up to facilitate learning and using language, it is clear that the human brain makes language possible in important and intriguing ways. Although the human brain weighs only three to four pounds, it is probably one of the most complex of human organs. Research into how the brain works has been plagued by the same kinds of ethical dilemmas facing research into child language acquisition/learning. Much of what we know about the brain has, until recently, been the result of the close observation of individuals with various kinds of impairments due to brain damage, followed by autopsies after those individuals' deaths, to examine their brains in detail. The advent of electronic scanning and imaging technologies in the late twentieth century, however, has dramatically advanced our ability to map the brain and to determine where specific activities and abilities are controlled.

The human brain contains over a trillion cells. One hundred billion of those cells are neurons, or nerve cells, linked in networks related to memory, intelligence, creativity, emotion, consciousness, and—of most interest to us—language. These neurons reside in the **cortex,** which is the convoluted surface of the brain (the word comes from the Latin word for 'bark') (Fishbach 1992, 51). The cortex is only about two millimeters thick, but it is so convoluted that it actually has a total surface area of more than 1.5 square yards. The oldest part of the cortex, evolutionarily speaking, controls such things as long-term memory and emotions. The **neocortex,** or the younger and larger part of the cortex, is where we must look to understand how language is possible. The neocortex is divided into frontal, temporal, parietal, and occipital lobes, or sections, which are separated by especially deep folds, known as sulci. Note that the neocortex accounts for nearly 80 percent of the human brain but less than 60 percent of a New World monkey brain.

Lateralization and Language   One of the most striking aspects of the human brain is its division into two somewhat symmetrical hemispheres, or halves. Sometimes these are called **cerebral hemispheres.** The two hemispheres, one on the left and one on the right, are joined in the middle by the **corpus callosum,** a membrane made up of over two million fibers connecting the cells of the two hemispheres. The interesting thing about these two hemispheres is that each one controls the opposite side of the body. The left hemisphere controls the right side of the body and the right hemisphere controls the left side of the body. There's an American children's game that demonstrates this nicely. First, you extend your arms outward in front of you; then, you cross one wrist over the other and turn your thumbs downward so that the palms of your hands are facing each other. Fold your hands together, interlacing the fingers as you "normally" do when you're folding your hands. Now bring your folded hands downward, pulling your elbows apart, and then bring your folded hands up and in front of your face, dropping your elbows downward. Ask a friend to point to (not touch!) any one of your fingers and then see if you can wiggle it. Chances are high that you will wiggle the finger on the opposite hand. This is because your fingers are visually reversed compared to their usual left-right configuration; what looks like "left" to you is actually on the right and vice versa. This little experiment should help to convince you of the complex relationship between the left and right cerebral hemispheres and the right and left sides of your body.

The two hemispheres also control a lot more than just the two sides of your body. Language and spatial perception are also controlled by the two hemispheres, with language handled by the left hemisphere and perceptual pattern recognition handled by the right hemisphere. It's actually a little more complicated than this, as contemporary research is beginning to show, but for the most part, language can be mapped to the left brain in about 99 percent of right-handed people and 66 percent of left-handed people. In general, it is fair to say that for most people the left brain is better with language, rhythmic perception, and mathematics, as well as with making judgments about time and about the order of events. It is also fair to say that for most people the right brain is better at matching patterns, recognizing faces, and helping out with spatial orientation.

Damage to either hemisphere of the brain will result in weakness in the opposite side of the body, as well as the impairment of specific functions controlled by that particular hemisphere. In particular, damage to the right side of the brain will result in perceptual difficulties, while damage to the left side of the brain causes language disorders of various sorts, depending on the specific site of the damage. This is true for signed as well as for spoken language. Even though signing may seem more like a gestural or visual or spatial skill, and therefore controlled by the right hemisphere, studies of deaf signers suggests that signing is, in fact, controlled by the left brain, just like spoken language. In fact, if the right brain is damaged, coherent signing is still possible, but, if the left brain is damaged, people have difficulty signing coherently, just as hearing speakers have difficulty speaking coherently. This suggests that it is language in general, and the ability to communicate using language, that is controlled by the left side of the brain rather than just speech or spoken language.

Some years ago it was discovered that people with severe epilepsy could be stabilized by cutting the corpus callosum. Once this pathway has been split, there is no further communication between the two sides of the brain. This makes for some interesting situations because each half of the brain is now functioning independently from the other half. It means that, if you put an apple into the left hand of a person with a split-brain (and you don't let them see it), the person can sense the presence of the apple but can't name it. If you let the person see the apple using the left eye (and only the left eye), then the person can point at the apple and gesture at it but still can't name it or talk about it. If, instead, you put something—let's say an orange—into the same person's right hand, the person can name it as well as describe it and talk about it. Clearly, language is located in some way in the left half of the brain and not in the right half.

The evidence is even more dramatic when you compare individuals from whom the left or right hemisphere has been surgically removed. Removal of the right hemisphere impacts visual and spatial ability, but language remains normal. Removal of the left hemisphere impairs language ability but allows people to continue developing normal visual and spatial abilities. Finally, studies of children with damage to the left hemisphere show that they have difficulty learning/acquiring language, while children with damage to the right hemisphere seem to learn/acquire language normally.

Language Areas of the Brain For many years, the only way to know about how language mapped onto the brain was through the study of individuals who had suffered from strokes or other kinds of damage to the brain. Most of the time, it was autopsies of such individuals after their death that revealed the specific damage that had led to the specific impairments observed while they were alive. Thus, brain research has been difficult, particularly with living beings, until fairly recently. Nowadays, it is possible to use magnetic resonance imaging (MRI) to find the damaged areas of the brains of living people. In addition, positron emission tomography (PET) scans make it possible to experiment with living people and to see which parts of their brains respond when different stimuli are introduced.

In August 2003, after ten years of research scanning 7,000 human brains, a comprehensive computerized atlas—or map—of the human brain was released online. Coordinated by the International Consortium for Brain Mapping (ICBM), the atlas is available to researchers at the UCLA Laboratory of Neuro Imaging. The atlas provides unparalleled access into brain functioning and makes it possible to map speech functions in the brain with the most remarkable detail. Even though every individual brain is unique, it is still possible to map the general areas of the brain that are involved in using language. The most important of these appear to be Broca's and Wernicke's areas, both located in the left cerebral hemisphere.

 WEBLINK To read more about language and the brain, go to http://anthropology.wadsworth.com/ottenheimer_language.

Broca's area, an area of the frontal region of the left cerebral hemi-sphere, is named for Paul Broca, the medical doctor who first located it and proposed its connection with language. Broca had a patient who could only utter one syllable (*tan*). A postmortem dissection of this patient's brain revealed damage to the front part of the left hemisphere. Autopsies performed on eight more patients with similar speech impair-ments revealed similar damage to the frontal region of the left hemi-sphere. Broca presented his findings to a scientific conference in Paris in 1861.

Today we know that damage to Broca's area affects clarity of speech, and in particular the area seems to be responsible for coordinating facial, tongue, palate, and larynx movement. People with damage to Broca's area have difficulty pronouncing words clearly, they pause a lot while try-ing to compose and produce words, they seem to have difficulty with function words (e.g., *of, and, if, but*), and sometimes they even have dif-ficulty with correct word order. For the most part, however, they seem to understand what is said to them, although they sometimes have difficulty with more complex syntactic structures.

In 1874, Carl Wernicke presented the results of autopsy dissections with patients who had had different kinds of speech disturbances than the ones that Broca had observed. In contrast with Broca's patients, Wer-nicke's patients could pronounce words clearly but they couldn't put their words together into meaningful sentences. Their sentences were garbled, and they also had difficulty understanding spoken language. The affected area, Wernicke discovered, was also in the left hemisphere but in the temporal lobe, further back than Broca's area. The area is now known as **Wernicke's area,** and it is understood to control understanding words and the ability to converse with others.

Recent research with brain mapping through MRI and PET scans suggests that still more is involved than just Broca's and Wernicke's areas. Neurolinguistic research is a rapidly evolving field. Some scholars sug-gest that in order to fully understand the way that language functions in the brain it will be essential to also understand how linguistic symbols (such as words for things) come to represent objects and thoughts and feelings. Neurolinguists Antonio and Hanna Damasio are currently en-gaged in researching these pathways through the brain. They propose a model in which both the left and right hemispheres of the brain are en-gaged in identifying and classifying concepts, while the left brain con-trols both the linguistic naming of those concepts and the connection of linguistic forms (sounds, words, grammar, and so on) with the corre-sponding concepts. In addition, they suggest that words and sentences are formed in areas such as Broca's area, that nouns appear to be handled in a large area surrounding Broca's area and including Wernicke's area, and that verbs appear to be handled in yet another area just forward of Broca's area (Damasio and Damasio 1992, 89). Clearly, this is a rapidly evolving field of study and there is still much to be learned about the ac-

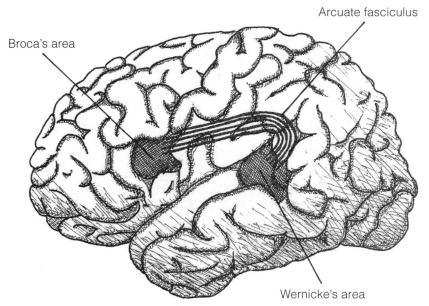

Arcuate fasciculus

Broca's area

Wernicke's area

FIGURE 8.1A Broca's and Wernicke's areas *Alan Joseph, 2004. Used by permission.*

tual way that language is mapped onto the brain. Figures 8.1a and 8.1b compare the mapping of Broca's and Wernicke's areas with the mapping of speech areas in the brain more generally.

Knowing when these complexities could have evolved can help us to better pinpoint when language might have evolved in humans, and for this we need to turn to archaeology, to physical anthropology, and to the fossil record. As it turns out, it is possible to get an idea of what a particular brain might have looked like by examining the skull that contained it. This means that we can tell quite a bit about the evolution of human and prehuman brains just by examining the fossil record. We can see when the neocortex gets complexly convoluted, and we can see when Broca's and Wernicke's areas begin to appear. An individual with evidence of Broca's area must certainly have been capable of language, whether spoken or signed. What does the fossil record tell us about these things?

Language Areas of the Brain in the Fossil Record   The primate lineage is believed to have split into two branches between ten and four million years ago, with one lineage leading to African apes and the other leading to humans. *Australopithecus* is currently considered the earliest genus on the human—or hominid—line. Some time between 2.5 and 2 million years ago, a second hominid genus emerged, splitting off from the *Australopithecus* genus. The first species in this new genus was dubbed *Homo habilis* because its remains were found with crude stone tools such as scrapers and choppers. The Koobi Fora region of Kenya is particularly

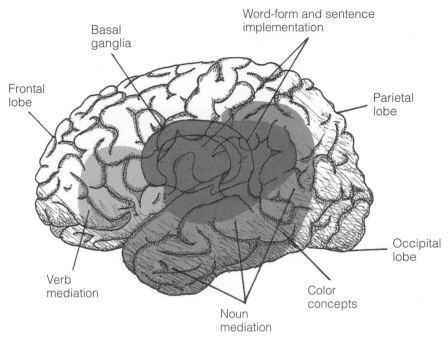

FIGURE 8.1B   Brain systems for language *Alan Joseph, 2004. Used by permission.*

interesting because individuals of both genera—*Australopithecus* and early *Homo*—have been found at the site, and both are from approximately the same time frame. By comparing the reconstructed skulls of both genera, it is possible to see differences in what their brains must have looked like.

The Australopithecine brain, dated between 1.26 and 1.8 million years ago, appears apelike (pongid) both in basic overall shape and in the imprint of the frontal-orbital lobes of the brain. In contrast, the *Homo habilis* brain, dated between 1.8 and 2 million years ago, is different from the Australopithecine brain, both in overall shape and in having distinct frontal and parietal lobes with a clear sulcus (fissure) separating the two. In addition, the lower parietal lobe appears more convoluted and enlarged in the *Homo habilis* brain. Similar brain development can be seen in other *Homo habilis* individuals from other sites, such as Olduvai Gorge in Tanzania (Tobias 1987; Falk 1983). This development suggests the presence of Broca's as well as Wernicke's area. Thus, *Homo habilis* seems to be the earliest species to have a humanlike brain structure and to be capable of spoken or signed language.

Language and the Human Vocal Apparatus

It is possible that signed and spoken language developed at roughly the same time. Once the brain mechanisms for language were present, there is no particular reason to imagine that both of these forms of language did not develop. Perhaps early *Homo habilis* was using both signs and speech. Signs would have been more useful during hunting, and speech would have been more useful during times when one's hands were busy. Both could have been used in tandem at moments of leisure. Or signed language could have developed first and been gradually replaced in prominence by spoken language.

We mentioned earlier that nonhuman primates can be taught to use simple sign language, but that they are unable to reproduce human speech. In the 1960s, linguistic anthropologist Philip Lieberman showed that the main reason for this is the difference in shape of the human vocal tract. In particular, the larynx (where your vocal cords are located) is lower in humans than in other primates. What's especially important about this is the fact that a lower larynx makes for a longer pharynx (the space above the vocal cords in which air resonates on its way to the mouth and nose). As Lieberman's research demonstrated, having a longer pharynx means that it is possible to produce a greater variety of vowels. Much of this is done by moving the tongue backward and forward in the space available, thus changing the shape of the pharynx as well as the shape of the oral cavity. Changing the shape of the pharynx, which is the resonating chamber for vowels, allows us to produce such different sounding vowels as [i], [u], and [a]. The more flexible human tongue also produces a wider variety of consonants than most other animals are capable of.

The human configuration of larynx, pharynx, and tongue has advantages and disadvantages. Humans can talk, breathe, and swallow at the same time, but we also run an increased risk of choking or inhaling our food, as you know if you have ever "swallowed something wrong." Animals, with higher larynxes and flatter tongues, don't have these problems. A higher larynx facilitates breathing while eating without risk of food "going down the wrong pipe." Located higher up in the neck, closer to the bottom of the skull, a high larynx helps to form a gasket that keeps the pathway for air separate from the channel for swallowing food and liquid. The human larynx, on the other hand, is much lower in the neck, which means that air, food, and liquid share a common pathway above the larynx (see Figure 8.2). It also means that if you are not careful, liquid can pass through your larynx and enter your lungs or bits of food can fall into your larynx and shut off your breathing! Interestingly, human babies are born with high larynxes and are able to breathe comfortably while suckling. At around three months of age, the human larynx begins its gradual descent, reaching its final location when a child is about three or four years old. A second, smaller descent takes place at puberty for males. So, although a high larynx seems safer, a lower larynx makes speech possible. One of the things that Lieberman was able to demonstrate in his 1960s research was that human infants, as well as nonhu-

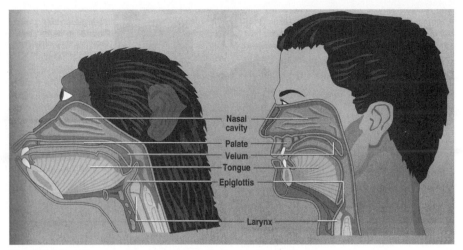

Nasal cavity
Palate
Velum
Tongue
Epiglottis

Larynx

FIGURE 8.2 The price that humans pay for spoken language *Source: Haviland (2002, 93). Used by permission.*

man mammals, are limited in the range of vowels and consonants they can produce because of the higher placement of the larynx.

The supralaryngeal vocal tract (or the vocal tract above the larynx) is made up of soft tissue and cartilage, so it is never present in fossil remains. Still, Lieberman and his colleagues have succeeded in reconstructing fossil supralaryngeal vocal tracts using the methods of comparative anatomy. Key in these reconstructions are the basicranium (the base or bottom of the skull) and the lower jaw. A more curved basicranium indicates a lower larynx; a straighter basicranium suggests a higher larynx. Here is what they have discovered: The ape-like Australopithecines (as late as 1.5 million years ago) appear to have had supralaryngeal vocal tracts similar to those of modern, living apes, and therefore are assumed to have had larynxes high in their throats as modern apes do. Because there are no well-preserved basicrania of *Homo habilis* (2 million years ago), it is not possible to reconstruct the vocal tract, but early *Homo erectus* basicrania (for example, KNM-ER-3733 from Lake Turkana in Kenya, 1.6 million years ago) show a degree of curvature that suggests the possibility of somewhat lower larynxes. It is possible to reconstruct a nearly modern-looking supralaryngeal vocal tract for an early *Homo sapiens* fossil found at Broken Hill, Zambia (dated 125,000 years ago). Finally, a fully modern supralaryngeal vocal tract is likely in *Homo sapiens* fossils (dated 100,000 years ago) from Jebel Qafzeh VI and Skhul V in Israel (Lieberman 1994, 125–26).

According to Lieberman and his colleagues, the basicrania of Neanderthals (130,000–30,000 years ago) are flatter and straighter than those of modern humans and their palates are longer. This means that the Neanderthal larynx would have been higher than in modern humans and that Neanderthals would therefore have been limited in the variety of sounds they could produce (Lieberman and Crelin 1971; Laitman et al. 1996). Some recent research into other mammals indicates that it is possible to lower the larynx when producing sound. Dogs, pigs, goats, and tamarind monkeys, for example, move their larynxes downward when vocalizing (Tecumseh Fitch 2000). This suggests that Neanderthal speech might not have been as limited as the reconstructions indicate.

HOW *AND* WHEN IS LANGUAGE POSSIBLE? PUTTING IT ALL TOGETHER

Putting all of this material together can be a daunting task. But it is an excellent exercise in drawing from all four branches of anthropology. From physical anthropology, we learn that language was possible, in terms of brain structure, for *Homo habilis,* 2 million years ago. From contemporary research in sign language, we know that signing is controlled by the same regions in the brain as spoken language. So we can infer that signed language could have been possible 2 million years ago in *Homo habilis* groups.

From linguistic reconstructions of fossil vocal tracts, we learn that articulate speech was possible, by means of a lowered larynx and a larger more flexible tongue, approximately 125,000 years ago with early *Homo sapiens*. But because partially lowered larynxes appear as early as 300,000 years ago, in *Homo erectus,* we must conclude that the transition—from the time when language was possible to the time when speech became the dominant form of linguistic communication for our human ancestors—had to have been a long slow process.

From cultural and linguistic anthropology, we know that language and culture are intimately connected in complex ways, both in how language is learned and how it is used. We know that children learn language as members of a speech community. We know that each speech community lays down "rules" for appropriate use of language. We also know that language, culture, thought, and perception are interrelated in complex ways. Because language and culture are so elaborately intertwined, it seems difficult to escape the conclusion that language and culture would have evolved together. This means that evidence for one should indicate the presence of the other.

For the origins of culture, we generally turn to archaeology. Archaeological analyses of early tools indicate that right-handedness (which indicates the development of dominance in the left—or language—side of the brain) was likely to have been present at early *Homo habilis* sites in Ethiopia 2.5 million years ago. Marking the beginning of the paleolithic (or old stone age), these early tools include choppers that appear to have been used for butchering meat. Similar tools have also been found in

East and South Africa. Early evidence of fire appears with early *Homo erectus* 1.6 million years ago in Koobi Fora in Kenya, and early evidence of more complex and sophisticated tools appears by 1.5 million years ago. Sometime after 1 million years ago, *Homo erectus* began to spread out of Africa. By 800,000 years ago, cleavers, scrapers, and flake tools were being used in Africa, Southeast Asia, China, and Europe, suggesting that *Homo erectus* groups were clearly beginning to use culture—and probably language—to adapt to differing environments.

Putting everything together, it appears that signed language must have been possible some 2 million years ago and that fully articulated spoken language must have been developed and refined by 125,000 years ago. As Lieberman notes, "A hypothetical archaic hominid that was able to produce human speech would have had *both* a functional, human-like Broca's area and a human-like supralaryngeal vocal tract" (1994, 119). How, then, did early *Homo habilis* change a closed sign system into the open system that we call language? How was duality of patterning discovered?

Recall that Hockett was thinking primarily of spoken language when he suggested that a closed call system had to become open through the process of blending. But it is entirely possible—indeed it is likely—that the same process took place for signed language as well as for spoken language. In fact, it is even possible that the transition from closed to open signs took place before spoken language was fully developed. Recent research into the development of sign language in populations for which there is no spoken language context suggests that the mental ability to manipulate fully structured language is a human capability and that whether it is exhibited in signed language or in spoken language is not as important as the fact that it exists. The difficulty is in developing a reasonably plausible scenario for the occurrence of the breakthrough to signs that can be endlessly combined and recombined in the way that Hockett described as duality of patterning.

Given the fact that children generally learn language in existing speech communities, the questions are: What might that first community have been like? From whom might those first language users have learned? What materials were available to them for learning or for manipulating into language? And what manipulations were necessary to transform the available material into language? Hockett suggested that situations that required uttering two different calls at the same time might have focused attention on the possibility of blending distinct calls; he thought that the act of blending calls could have helped open up the call system. Another possibility is that children could have been play-mimicking the calls of their elders, thus developing the ability to have a sound (or perhaps a gesture) stand as a *token* of the real thing but not be the real thing at all. In this way, a sound that *pretends* to be a closed call becomes in fact an open call, or a symbol of the closed call. Likewise a movement that *pretends* to be a closed gesture becomes an open sign. The elusive duality of patterning looks a lot like the kind of language play that contemporary children engage in when they develop and use disguised languages such as "Pig Latin." Could the early identification of discrete recombinable units of language have been a product of children playing with the gestures and calls available to them? Of course, this is sheer speculation, but it is speculation that is assisted by reference to the kinds of knowledge that can be gained by studying all four fields of anthropology. Solving complex puzzles generally requires interdisciplinary cooperation, and anthropology's holistic interdisciplinarity seems uniquely suited to solving the puzzle of how and when language could have begun.

SUMMARY

We don't really know how humans first developed the capacity for language. Some theories stress a gradual development, while others seek to find a single defining moment. Did language evolve slowly over time, in tandem with cultural evolution, or was it an innate biological feature that developed suddenly, marking the emergence as well as the definition of human beings? Anthropology's four-field nature makes this a particularly well-suited discipline for exploring the question of language origins. Anthropologists combine research into language structure and process with research into language use in cultural and social settings, with research into archaeological evidence for early language use, and with research into evidence from the fossil record for the physical ability to produce language to put together a holistic picture of when and how language could have begun.

Language can be defined as a kind of communication. Many animals communicate, but only humans appear to have language. Charles Hockett's design features help us to see how language is distinct from other forms of animal communication. Animal communication systems use some of Hockett's design features, but only human language uses all thirteen of the features that Hockett identified. Humans share nine features with contemporary primates, suggesting that those nine may have been part of the prehistoric primate communication system from which language emerged. The remaining four features—productivity, displacement, traditional transmission, and duality of patterning—are unique to humans. Key to understanding how and when human language evolved, then, is determining how and when these four features could have developed. Hockett suggested that the blending of distinct primate calls may have been a key factor in the development of human language.

Because humans and primates share much biologically and evolutionally, recent research has focused on attempting to distinguish more precisely the differences and similarities between human language and primate communication systems. Attempts to teach nonhuman primates to use various forms of language, from sign language to combinable plastic lexigrams, have been suggestive but problematic. Duality of patterning appears to remain a language feature uniquely possessed by humans.

In contrast to other primates, human children appear to learn complex languages easily. Various theories have been proposed to explain how children develop their language skills. Innatist theories argue that children don't learn language but are born with an internal grammar that they adjust to fit the specific language they hear around them. Behaviorist theories argue that children learn by imitation and feedback. Cognitivist theories suggest that children develop language simultaneously with their mental abilities. The theory theory suggests that children analyze language as they hear it, building theories about grammar and structure as they go. Anthropological theories stress the importance of understanding the impact of the social group, and in particular the speech community, on the ways that children learn to speak and to use their language in socially appropriate ways.

Research into how language is possible is complexly interconnected with research into when language became possible. Recent research has focused on discovering when the human brain was evolutionarily capable of language and on when spoken language was physically possible. Broca's and Wernicke's areas of the brain appear to be two key areas in which language is processed. Both of these are present in the left hemisphere of the brain, and so language is understood to be a primarily left-brain activity. This is true for both spoken and signed language. Damage to the left hemisphere of the brain, such as from a stroke, can affect an individual's ability to communicate using language. Recent technologies such as MRI and PET scans make it possible to learn even more about how the brain functions and how language is mapped onto the brain. The discovery of evidence of Broca's and Wernicke's areas in *Homo habilis* fossils dating 1.8–2 million years ago suggests that language was indeed possible at an early date. What is not known, of course, is what that language might have looked or sounded like. Analysis of the positioning of the larynx in various primates suggests that fully modern speech may not have been possible until 100,000 years ago, in *Homo sapiens*.

Although we still don't know how the transition to language occurred, it is important to include an understanding of the ways in which children learn language. It is possible that children playing with the discrete calls of their elders may have been key in making the transition to duality of patterning and, therefore, to the beginnings of complex language.

KEY TERMS

acquire language
arbitrariness

behaviorist theories
blending
broadcast transmission and directional reception
Broca's area
cerebral hemispheres
cognitivist theories
communication
corpus callosum
cortex
design features of language
discreteness
displacement
duality of patterning
innatist theories
interchangeability
language acquisition device
learn language
neocortex
pharynx
productivity
rapid fading
semanticity
specialization
the theory theory
total feedback
traditional transmission
vocal auditory channel
Wernicke's area

FURTHER READING

About Nonhuman Primate Communication

Savage-Rumbaugh, Sue, Stuart Shanker, and Talbot J. Taylor. 1998. *Apes, language, and the human mind.* New York: Oxford University Press. This provides a summary and defense of various projects to teach chimpanzees to communicate.

Goodall, Jane. 1986. *The chimpanzees of Gombe: Patterns of behavior.* Cambridge, MA: Belknap. This is a book on chimpanzees in the wild.

About Children and Language

Schieffelin, Bambi. 1990. *The give and take of everyday life: Language socialization of Kaluli children.* New York: Cambridge University Press. This is a readable study of language socialization among Kaluli (New Guinea) children.

About Language and the Brain

Gazzaniga, Michael S. 1970. *The bisected brain.* New York: Appleton-Century-Crofts. This is a classic introduction to studies with split-brain patients in the 1960s.

Poizner, Howard, Edward S. Klima, and Ursula Bellugi. 1987. *What the hands reveal about the brain.* Cambridge, MA: MIT Press. This is a study of the biological bases of language based on an analysis of the breakdown of the ability to use sign language caused by damage to the brain; it also includes good diagrams of minimal pairs in sign language.

About the Evolution of Language

Corballis, Michael. 2003. *From hand to mouth: The origins of language.* Princeton, NJ: Princeton University Press. A psychologist suggests a gestural origin for language.

Deacon, Terrence. 1998. *The symbolic species: The co-evolution of language and the brain.* New York: W. W. Norton, and Co. A biological anthropologist presents a clear and engaging discussion of the evolution of language, the brain, and culture.

Hockett, Charles F. 1960. The origin of speech. *Scientific American* 203(3): 88–96. An accessible article in which the original design features were proposed and explained.

Lieberman, Philip. 1984. *The biology and evolution of language.* Cambridge, MA: Harvard University Press. This is a detailed discussion of the physical requirements for language in humans.

 # STUDENT ACTIVITIES

Readings

The workbook/reader for this book has readings that can help you to further explore and understand the issues introduced in this chapter, in particular with regard to language origins and language learning/acquisition.

Exercises

A set of writing exercises in the workbook/reader will assist you in understanding the issues introduced in this chapter and in further exploring how and when language is possible.

Web Exercises

The companion website for this book has a series of links designed to help you explore the issues introduced in this chapter in greater depth and to better understand them. The companion website also contains study questions that will help you to review important concepts.

Guided Projects

If you are creating a language, you may want to design a "Pig Latin" for it. If you are working with a conversation partner, your instructor may assign a writing project that asks you to explore and compare "Pig Latins" in your two languages. Your instructor will be your guide.

CHAPTER 9

Change
and Choice

In the Field, Manhattan, Kansas, July 1974

"Oooh, look! A butterpillar!" said my four-year-old son, examining a large green creepy-crawly thing with yellow spots.

"*Cater*pillar," I corrected, without thinking.

"No, *butter*pillar," insisted my young son, annoyed at my correction.

"Why is that?" I asked.

"Well," said my son, "it's a baby butterfly, isn't it?"

"Sort of," I replied, not wanting to start a biology lesson.

"Then it's a *butter*pillar," he said. "It's going to be a *butter*fly when it grows up, not a *catter*fly!"

"Ok," I retreated, not wanting to spoil his fun. Besides, I thought it was a cute analysis.

In the Field, Manhattan, Kansas, July 1981

"Wow, that's so . . . , so . . . , bogus!" said my ten-year-old son, just back from summer camp and hearing about the plans for our upcoming sailing trip.

"Bogus?" I repeated. What's bogus about a sailing trip?

"It's just . . . , *bogus!* You know . . . , like . . . , *cool*," he responded.

"Cool?" I said. "What's cool about *bogus?*"

"That's what bogus *means*," he said, exasperated. "It means cool, or even *extra* cool."

"Where'd you hear that?" I asked.

"At camp," he responded. "It's the latest word. You like to keep up with language change, don't you?"

"Yes I do," I said, "but this isn't a new word. It's an old word with a new meaning."

"What's the old meaning?" he asked.

> "It used to mean *phony*," I said. "I don't remember it having any-
> thing to do with *cool*."
> "Okay, okay, let's look it up in the dictionary," he said.
> So we did, and there it was. *Bogus* meant 'false' and 'spurious.'
> "Hmmmm," we both said together. And the next thing I knew he
> was phoning his friends from camp to talk about how *bogus* might not
> be so 'cool.' This time I really *had* spoiled his fun!
>
> HJO

One of the interesting things about getting older is that you can observe changes in your own language. Sometimes the changes stick, and sometimes they don't. One of my students told me that her young granddaughter had decided that the singular form of *clothes* was *clo* and that none of the adults wanted to correct her because it sounded so cute. I doubt if that one stuck for long. Even if adults do allow new words like *clo* and *butterpillar* to become "family words," most of the time these kinds of "invented" words eventually get stamped out, corrected by play-mates or teachers or other folks from outside of the family.

Sometimes, however, the new words do stick and, as more and more people adopt them, the language gradually changes. The English word *terrific* is an example of just such a word. It was invented in the 1940s by a newspaper reporter to express the idea that something was both *terrible* and *awful* at the same time. The new word spread quickly, but over time its meaning shifted from 'terribly-awful' to 'great, wonderful, superb.' Another example is *up-tight,* which in the Stevie Wonder song of the 1960s meant 'ready to go, cool, looking sharp.' The words "up-tight, everything is all right, up-tight, outta sight" make this clear, but over time the meaning of *up-tight* has shifted to convey 'tense, nervous, overly con-cerned about correctness.' Although the two sets of meanings may be loosely related, they do seem to be at opposite extremes of a continuum. My son's encounter with *bogus* is another example of this kind of change. Still another example is the way some people use words like *bad* and *sick* to mean 'great' or 'wonderful.'

This last example brings up another interesting aspect of language change: Different people use words in different ways to set themselves off as unique or up-to-date or otherwise "different" in some way. So lan-guages change not only in response to children's mistakes or mishearings or deliberate inventions but also in response to social pressures, and, as languages change, the choices that individuals and groups make about which words to use, and which ways to use them, can come to have po-litical, social, and even economic value. The idea that "you are what (or how) you speak" is more widespread and deep-seated than most people realize. This chapter discusses these issues and shows how they are re-lated to one another. We will begin by exploring some of the ways that languages change. Not only do words change, but sounds and syntax and spellings also change. We will explore some of these dynamics as well. We will explore how languages evolve into dialects and how dialects in turn become distinct languages. We will also explore the effects of language contact on language change and explore the concept of "genetic" relationships among languages. We will learn how scholars use contemporary knowledge about language change to reconstruct ancient languages and to analyze ancient population movements. Throughout the chapter, we will pay special attention to the complex relationships between language choice and social/cultural identity.

HOW LANGUAGES CHANGE

Linguists talk about two general ways that languages change: "external change" and "internal change." **External change** refers to the kinds of changes that occur due to language contact and borrowing between speakers of different languages. **Internal change** refers to the kinds of changes that occur due to the way speakers of a language gradually modify their language over time. External change is generally more rapid than internal change. Examples of external change are the borrowing of words such as *rouge* and *garage* and *au jus* from French into English and the borrowing of words such as *hot dog* and *computer* from English into French. Examples of internal change are the shift in English from *bad* meaning 'bad' to *bad* meaning 'good,' and the gradual loss in English of the *-ly* ending on adverbs such as *quickly* and *slowly* and *excellently,* and the way that the *a* in the word *another* is starting to feel like a separate word, as in the expression *a whole nother.* Both internal and external change can affect any part of a language: phonology, morphology, syntax, and even spelling. Let's take a look at some examples.

External Change

Words are the most easily borrowed items between languages. As the speakers of languages come in contact, it seems only natural that items will be borrowed between them, and, in most cases, when an item is borrowed so is the word that describes it. Nonetheless, some languages seem to be resistant to borrowing, making up their own words for new items, while others appear to do lots of borrowing. English, in particular, seems to do a lot of borrowing from other languages. It has words like *chocolate* and *chipmunk* from Native American languages. It has words like *pork* and *beef* from French. It has words like *safari* from Bantu languages, words like *pajama* from Hindi, and words like *alcohol* and *algebra* from Arabic. *Sputnik* comes from Russian and *sayonara* from Japanese. *Robot* comes from Czech, and *schlep* comes from Yiddish. The list of words borrowed by English from other languages is large and continues to grow.

Because different languages have different sound systems, you might wonder what happens to a word's pronunciation when it is borrowed from one language into another. In some cases speakers of the borrowing language take care to pronounce the words the same way as in the donor language, but in most cases the new words are just pronounced according to the sound system of the borrowing language. You can see the difference in these two approaches by comparing American and British pronunciations of the French word *garage*. Americans pronounce this word [gəraˈʒ] (with a "soft" <g> and a stress on the final syllable), as in the original French. British speakers, in contrast, pronounce the same word [gæˈradʒ] (with a "hard" <g> and with a stress on the first syllable). American speakers, it appears, have borrowed the French [ʒ] sound along with the word. British speakers have repronounced the word, adding a [d] to the [ʒ], so it sounds more British. Interestingly, speakers of American English use the [ʒ] sound only in words borrowed from French, such as *garage, mirage, rouge, negligee*, and so on.

Actually, it's fairly unusual to borrow sounds from one language into another. Most of the time, borrowed words with new sounds or sound combinations are just modified to fit the sound system of the borrowing language, like in the British example. Sometimes, if the word was borrowed long enough ago, it becomes almost unrecognizable to speakers of the donor language in its new pronunciation. The following examples will give you an idea of the way sounds can be changed in the process of borrowing.

Word	*Original Pronunciation*	*Borrowed Pronunciation*
sputnik (Russian)	[ʃputn̩ik]	[spətnɪk] (English)
Bach (German)	[bax]	[bak] (English)
tomato (Native American)	[tomatɬ]	[təmeito] (English)
beef (French)	[bœf]	[bif] (English)
bread (English)	[bɹɛd]	[bɛrɛdi] (Shinzwani)
flask (English)	[flæsk]	[falasika] (Shinzwani)

In addition to changing the pronunciation of words, speakers change the way borrowed words are used. Absorbing words into your own grammatical system helps to make them more familiar and perhaps easier to use. The French phrase *au jus,* for example, means 'with gravy.' In English, however, it has come to mean just 'gravy.' The result is sentences like *Would you like your meat served with au jus*? and *Could I have some au jus on my meat, please?* The combination *with au jus* actually means 'with **with** gravy,' but *meat served au jus* just doesn't sound like ordinary English so the extra *with* gets thrown in to make the whole phrase fit more smoothly into English syntax.

Another way that borrowed words are changed to fit into the new language is in the ways that plurals are made out them. Most of the time, the original way of making the word's plural is not borrowed along with the word. Rather, the word is made plural in the same way that other words in the borrowing language are made plural. Take, for example, the way English makes its plurals. Generally we think of adding an [-*s*] to the end of an English word to make it plural. (Of course, it's a bit more complicated than this, but that's not important here.) Adding an [-*s*] to the end of a word means that for English speakers the plural of *safari* becomes regularized as *safaris*. But *safari* was borrowed from KiSwahili (a Bantu language), and in KiSwahili the plural of *safari* is *safari* (or occasionally *zisafari*). You can see the same sort of regularizing process going on in other languages, too. In Shinzwani, for example, one common way of making plurals is to add [*ma-*] to the beginnings of words. This means that a borrowed word like *beredi* (from English *bread*) becomes *maberedi* in the plural. (It's more complicated than this in Shinzwani, too: The plural of *pulisi* (from *police*) is *mavulisi*, for example, and the plural of *falasika* (from *flask*) is *zifalasika*.)

Sometimes people reanalyze the words that they borrow. **Reanalysis** is the process of analyzing (or perhaps even misanalyzing) unfamiliar words into familiar-looking components and assigning familiar meanings to those components, even if those components have no meaning or function in the original words. A good example of this is the way that the German word *hamburger* seems to have been reanalyzed after it was borrowed into English. In German, the word was divided into *Hamburg* (a city) and *-er* (from, or in the style of). A *hamburger* was something 'from or in the style of the city of Hamburg.' (Similarly, a *frankfurter* was something 'from or in the style of the city of Frankfurt.') In the United States, however, the word *hamburger* was redivided into *ham* (a common meat) plus *burger*, even though there was no ham in a hamburger. Now, *burger* had no particular meaning in English (although it does resemble the old English word *burgher* 'townsperson'). Still, the fact that *ham* was a familiar morpheme for English speakers is what probably led to the use of *burger* for the bready bun used in hamburgers. Once this shift was made, English speakers (and perhaps clever marketers) began to create all sorts of new words using the English morpheme *burger*. Almost anything served on a bready bun became some sort of burger, including *cheeseburger* (hamburger with cheese on top), *baconburger* (hamburger with bacon on top), *chickenburger* (chopped chicken patty on a bun), *fishburger* (breaded fish filet on a bun), and *veggieburger* (vegetarian patty on a bun). Another example of this sort of reanalysis is the way that the French word *histoire* 'history' was borrowed into English and then reanalyzed into *his* and *story* making it possible to create the English word *herstory* to refer to women's history.

Internal Change

Internal change, in contrast to external change, tends to be a slower process. It also tends to be somewhat more predictable because existing structural patterns in a language can be seen as exerting more pressure in certain directions than others. A good example of this is the increasing use in American English of the third-person plural pronouns *they, them,* and *their* in place of their singular counterparts *he/she, him/her,* and *his/her.* This shift was actually predicted in the 1960s by linguistic anthropologist Michael Silverstein, based simply on the observation that English had already undergone a similar structural shift with regard to its second-person pronouns. The plural pronoun *you* had replaced the singular form *thou* as well as the singular form *thee* and the plural pronoun *your* had replaced the singular form *thy.* By the 1960s, the older singular forms *thee, thou,* and *thy* sounded archaic, quaint, and obsolete and were generally only heard in religious contexts, marriage vows, and other formal sorts of contexts. If the singular forms *thee/thou/thy* could be replaced with their plural forms *you/your,* it seemed reasonable to predict that the singular forms *he/she, him/her,* and *his/her* could also be replaced with their plurals *they, them,* and *their.*

Pressure from proponents of women's rights helped move the transition along, making it clear that *he* did not always include *she* and that a more inclusive term was needed if people wanted to express gender-neutrality in English. For a while, people tried using a variety of gender-neutral terms such as *he/she, s/he,* and *he or she,* but now, nearly forty years after Silverstein's prediction was made, the plural forms *they, them,* and *their* seem to be the most comfortable to use in just about every situation where the singular ought to go. So, for example, it is common to hear the phrase *Someone left **their** book in the classroom* rather than *Someone left **his** (or **her**) book in the classroom.* Or *I gave the book to **them*** rather than *I gave the book to **him** (or **her**).* Or *If anyone wants to go with us tonight **they** should be in the lobby at six o'clock* rather than ***he or she** should be in the lobby.* Try it yourself. Listen to people around you and see how many times you hear the plural forms *they, them,* and *their* being used in phrases where the singular forms would be "correct." This is an excellent example of internal change in language, and because it is still ongoing it is easy to document. It is also an excellent example of the ways in which understanding something about patterns and something about social pressures can help you to understand, and even to predict, language change.

Here's another example of a kind of ongoing change in English. Recall that *you* in English is both singular and plural. Nonetheless, two new words for 'you plural' have begun to enter into common use. *Y'all* seems to be used a lot in the South and central parts of the United States, while *youse* is becoming firmly established in New York, especially in Brooklyn. Now, *youse* is one of those words that people used to tell me not to use when I was growing up in New York. People thought that using it made us sound "uneducated," "lower class," or just plain "stupid." *Y'all* has overtones of the "old" South, and some folks feel that it signifies a similarly "uneducated," "low-class," or "dumb" speaker, as well as someone who continues to believe in an outmoded "Southern" value system. But nowadays more and more people are using these words, and their formerly negative meanings have begun to diminish a bit. They are definitely handy words for addressing more than one person without ambiguity, and perhaps people really do want to have a way of doing this. Does that mean that it is becoming more important to use a grammatical plural form for *you* than to fret over sounding "uneducated" or "regionally based"? Perhaps. It certainly seems as though more and more people really are overcoming whatever social pressures were keeping them from using *youse* and *y'all*. There is always some balance between social pressure and structural (or grammatical) pressure in language change, and it's important to understand both parts of the process. If being able to distinguish between singulars and plurals is important enough in English, then perhaps in another 100 years or so, when *he* and *she* have disappeared from daily speech, a new plural form of *they* will emerge to fill the need for an unambiguous plural. Perhaps it will be one of the two existing forms or perhaps one that is a bit more "standard" and less "regional" in social overtones. *They-all* anyone? Or *theys?* In fact, as linguistic anthropologist Jill Brody has noted, *theys* is already being used among some groups of college students in Louisiana. How long before the rest of us begin to follow suit?

Another way that words can change over time is through a kind of misanalysis. An example of this is the English-speaking child who thought that the singular of the word *clothes* (pronounced [kloz]) had to be *clo*. The child was simply observing the parallel between [kloz] and similar words like [toz] (*toes*) and drawing structural conclusions about the similarities of the singulars. If the singular of [toz] is [to], shouldn't the singular of [kloz] be [klo]? An example of this sort of misanalysis that actually has entered contemporary English is the shift from *a napron* to *an apron*. The fact that *napron* was the correct form of this noun is confirmed by other English words having to do with pieces of cloth such as *napkin* and *napery* (a generic, if nearly obsolete, word for household linen and especially table linen such as napkins and tablecloths). It seems, in the case of *an apron*, that the [n] was heard as part of the word *an* rather than as part of the word *napron*. A similar sort of misanalysis is currently taking place with regard to the word *another.* Although the word derives from *an other*, many people today are separating the *a* from the rest of the word (since *a* is a word on its own in English) with the result that *nother* is becoming a new English word.

These sorts of shifts go on all of the time in language. The fact that languages are spoken by real people in real life means that language has to change. Some of the changes are due to misanalysis, some to social pressures, and some to the need for words to express new concepts or emotions. *Blog* is a new word formed from *web* and *log* to refer to an Internet-based daily diary, published on a website for everyone and anyone to read. But the *log* in *blog* has already become a productive morpheme, spawning such additional words as *phlog* (from *phone log*), and *moblog* (from *mobile-phone log*). *Smog* is an English word constructed from *smoke* and *fog*. Recently, I saw the phrase *data smog* used to mean 'too much information.' The letter <e> was first added to the word *mail* to produce *e-mail* (originally—and sometimes still—hyphenated), which was a short form for *electronic mail* or 'mail sent over the Internet.' By now the hyphen has all but disappeared, so the word is most often written <email>, and the *e-* has become a productive morpheme, spawning new words like *ezine* for 'magazine on the Internet' and *ecommerce* 'business conducted on the Internet.' The word *hardware* has spawned new words like *software*, *spyware*, and, most recently, *malware*, 'a program designed to spread email viruses and worms.'

Sometimes morphemes can be analyzed into completely new words. An example of this is *dis*, which moved from being the negative prefix in words like *disrespectful* to taking on the meaning of the whole word, so that the phrase *Don't dis me* now means 'Don't be disrespectful to me.' And sometimes the edges of words can get "worn away," as in the case of the adverbial suffix *-ly* in English. When I was growing up, the answer to *Can you do that?* was *Surely, I can.* Now the answer is *Sure, I can,* and people talk more and more about doing things *quick* (rather than *quickly*) or *slow* (rather than *slowly*). Another example of loss of endings in English is the disappearance of the suffixes that used to mark grammatical case on English nouns. Grammatical case tells you whether a word is the subject or object of a sentence (see Chapter 4), and it also tells you that an item belongs to someone. Just about all that's left of case marking in English are pronouns such as *I* (the subject form, as in *I am going*), *me* (the object form, as in *give it to me*), and *mine* (the possessive form, as in *it's mine*). Because language is always changing, it can sometimes be difficult to understand things that were written as little as a few hundred years ago in your own language. It's fun to watch these kinds of changes in language, but it's also important to understand how language changes and the social and structural pressures that speed and slow those changes.

Sounds also change over time, but this is a slower process so it is a little more difficult to see (or hear). Still, it is possible to find examples of contemporary sound change if you know what you are looking for. One example is the changing pronunciation of the words like *fourth* and *floor* in New York. In the early 1900s, most New Yorkers pronounced these words with no [ɹ]. They also lengthened and centered the vowel somewhat, so the words ended up sounding more like *fouath* [fɔːəθ] and *flooooah* [flɔːə]. Sometime during the mid-1900s, around the time of World War II, middle- and upper-class New Yorkers began to insert an [ɹ] sound into these words (they also began to shorten the vowel sounds so the words sounded more like [fɔɹθ] and [flɔɹ]). By the late 1900s, dropping your [ɹ]s

Doing Linguistic Anthropology 9.1

BTA DQMOT

During the 2003–2004 academic year, I noticed a strange phenomenon in the exams I graded. I was used to seeing an occasional <@> or <&> sprinkled through the essays that students wrote because, frantic due to the limited time they had to answer the test questions, they often resorted to easily understood abbreviations. I knew that <@> meant *at* and <&> meant *and*. However, this year, I saw multiple cases of an unfamiliar combination of letters: <ppl>. My training in linguistic anthropology came in handy. Since there were multiple cases in the exams of multiple students, this clearly wasn't just nonsense. Rather, it had a source. The questions became: What did it mean and where were my students learning it? There were a number of clues. Since <ppl> had no vowels, it couldn't simply be a word I didn't know. Since it wasn't capitalized, it wasn't an acronym for a named organization. The fact that it was lowercase made me think of a trend in communication through electronic media (e-mail, instant messaging, etc.) toward eliminating capitalization completely. "Ahha," I thought. I know that many of my students spend a lot of time sending instant messages on computers, mobile phones, and PDAs (Palm Pilots, for example). Perhaps this was an abbreviation, commonly employed in order to cut down on keystrokes and to appear "in the know" in digital environments, that was bleeding over to more formal, and nondigital, settings. I googled "ppl abbreviation." (This is another example of the impact of the Internet on language. The company name Google has become a commonly used verb since its founding in 1998.) My search results showed me lists of common Internet chat abbreviations, including <ppl> for *people*. The puzzle was solved. The widespread use of Internet chat, especially among those who are growing up with it, makes it reasonable to predict that I will be seeing more instances of similar crossover. bta, dqmot (but, then again, don't quote me on this). Perhaps the formalness of the exam setting will prevent 2 much crossover.

Laura Bathurst, *University of California—Berkeley*

and lengthening your vowels had become an indication of lower-class status or of lack of education or of isolation in a working-class community or just of advanced age. I mentioned this to an aunt of mine once and, as she was over sixty and increasingly conscious of her age, she began deliberately shortening her vowels and inserting [ɹ] sounds into her words, hoping that it would help to make her sound "younger."

Of course, the idea that you can use a specific sound such as [ɹ] to evaluate a speaker's degree of upper-classness or access to education or age is completely arbitrary. A good example of this arbitrariness is the fact that an [ɹ] after vowels conveys exactly the opposite meaning in parts of the central plains states. In Kansas, for example, if you insert an [ɹ] into the word *wash* (so it comes out sounding like *warsh* [wɔɹʃ]), you are judged to be older, more rural, and/or less well-educated than folks who do not use [ɹ] in such words. Just as some people make fun of New Yorkers by mimicking their (now-mostly-abandoned) pronunciation of [fɔːəθ flɔːə], others make fun of Kansans by mimicking their (equally mostly abandoned) pronunciation of [wɔɹʃ] and [wɔɹʃɪŋtən] (*Washington*). The fact that these pronunciations are nearly abandoned in each place does not seem to matter as much as the fact that people are aware of the sounds and have attached some sort of social significance to them. Perhaps by way of reaction, and perhaps to demonstrate regional loyalty, some young New Yorkers are beginning to reemphasize the use of these "old-fashioned" pronunciations. So the changes are not complete yet. But they probably will be in another generation or so.

✳ THE IMPACT OF LANGUAGE CHANGE

If the account of language change in the Comoros (see Cross-Language Miscommunication 9.1: Losing Shinzwani) surprises you, perhaps it is because you know that these are small, somewhat isolated islands in the western Indian Ocean. Shouldn't languages that are spoken in relatively isolated areas change more slowly? Apparently the answer is no. There are many factors influencing the rate at which language changes, including the attitudes of the speakers towards borrowing and change. When most members of a speech community value novelty, for example, their language will change more quickly. When most members of a speech community value stability, then their language will change more slowly. Many people think that if a language has a written form then it will change more slowly, and this is indeed possible, but change it will, if it is being spoken. In the case of written languages, if the writing system doesn't change along with the spoken language, then it will become out of date, no longer fitting the spoken forms and making it more difficult to read. This is why it is so difficult to learn to read English. A word like *knight,* for example, came to be spelled that way back when the word was pronounced [knixt]. Now that it is pronounced [nait], it is difficult to see what the letters <k> and <gh> are doing in the word.

The important thing to remember about change is that, as long as people are using a language, that language will undergo some change. This means that if you leave a particular speech community for a while, you will miss out on the changes that take place while you are gone. Imagine, then, what could happen if a group of individuals moves far enough away

Cross-Language Miscommunication 9.1

LOSING SHINZWANI

My anthropologist husband and I had learned to speak Shinzwani fairly fluently living in the Comoros in the 1960s, but when we moved to Kansas in 1969 we were the only two Shinzwani speakers in our new community. To keep from forgetting our Shinzwani, we spoke it with each other as often as possible. We also visited Shinzwani-speaking friends in France one summer, and we hosted some Comorian friends in Kansas for two summers. And we listened—as often as we could— to tape-recordings of Shinzwani folktales, songs, and interviews that we had made during our fieldwork in the Comoros. So when my husband returned to the Comorian town of Domoni in 1974, he was surprised to learn that his Shinzwani was already out of date. According to his young Comorian friends, he now spoke Shinzwani "like an old man." Had the language changed that much in just seven years?

Of course it had, and by being away we had missed many significant changes. The Shinzwani word *mongo* (a ten-day period in the old Shinzwani calendar) was gone, for example. People now talked about *mezi* 'months' instead of *mengo* (*mengo* is the plural of *mongo*). In addition, a distinction had developed between two kinds of /v/. Women were still using the older bilabial [ʋ], but men had begun using a labiodental [v] variety of the sound, thus introducing a distinction between men's and women's pronunciations. Ways of making words plural were shifting as well. The plural prefix [zi-], for example, was being used with more and more words, sometimes replacing older ways of making plurals, so that *zibakuli* was replacing *mabakuli* 'bowls.' We quickly realized that the Shinzwani that we had learned seven years earlier had been no more than a snapshot of the language at that particular time and place. If we were going to continue to be a part of this speech community, we would need to find ways to keep in touch on a regular basis.

HJO

from its original speech community to be out of contact with it for a while. Perhaps the individuals move across a river or beyond a mountain range or across an ocean or even (in a science fiction scenario) to Mars. As long as the distance is large enough, travel is difficult enough, or communication "back home" is infrequent enough, at least two distinct varieties of the original language will gradually develop over time: the variety spoken by the folks "back home" and the one spoken by the folks who have moved away.

From Language to Dialect

When a language splits into two or more varieties in this way, each variety is referred to as a dialect of that language. A dialect is best defined as a specific variety or subdivision of a language. Another good definition of a dialect is that it is a way of speaking that is characteristic of a particular group of people. Recall also from Chapter 5 that dialects are mutually intelligible varieties of a language. All of these definitions are part of a complete understanding of the concept of dialect. In the scenario just presented, it's really not possible to say which of the two dialects is "better" or "more correct" because there will have been ongoing changes in both varieties of the language. They are just different—that's all. Of course, people may want to assign relative value to one or another dialect, but that's just a matter of social or political preference. Sometimes people want to believe that the language that they left behind was "purer" or "more authentic." Alternatively, they might want to think of it as "old-fashioned" and "out of date." Of course, neither of these assertions is really true, but it is important to us, as anthropologists, to understand that people do make these kinds of assertions. It is also important to know that people often make decisions about one another based on the associations that they have made with their dialects.

The changes that lead to different dialects are fairly random, depending on where different groups of speakers of a language end up and what external and internal influences are exerted on each variety of the language as it develops. An example of external influence is the borrowing by American English of a lot of words from Native American and African languages. Words such as *coyote, toboggan,* and *chipmunk* (Native American) and *gumbo, okra,* and *tote* (African) are common in American English but not British English, for example (except where they may have been borrowed secondarily from American English). An example of internal change is the preservation of a large number of older English words in American English that—over time—were replaced by newer ones in British English. Americans use the word *period,* for example, to name the little dot that ends a sentence. Although *period* was a common word in Shakespeare's time, it eventually fell out of favor in England and was replaced by the words *full-stop.* There are differences of grammar as well. Whereas Britons say *the house wants painting,* for example, Americans say *the house needs painting* (or, in the Midwest, *the house needs painted*). Whereas Americans say *that's different from,* Britons say *that's different to.* Whereas Britons say *transport,* Americans say *transportation.* Differences in pronunciation (or stress) provide additional examples of internal change. Whereas Americans say [skedjul] (*schedule*), Britons say [ʃedjul]; whereas Americans say [gɔɹɑ'ʒ] (*garage*), Britons say [gæ'ɹadʒ]. We even spell some words differently: Americans write <color>, for example, and Britons write <colour>.

Over the years, the various changes have resulted in two quite different versions of English. An important point to remember, however, is that none of the changes has been better than any of the others. They have just been different, that's all. Although purists or nationalists might argue otherwise, both American English and British English are perfectly acceptable varieties (or dialects) of English. Neither dialect is "better" than the other. They are just different from (or should we say different to?) one another. Recognizing the differences can help you to shift gears when you encounter other dialects of English, whether they may be Australian, Canadian, Indian, Jamaican, Kenyan, or some other variety that has developed through time and separation.

From Dialect to Language

Varieties (or dialects) of language, such as American and British English, that have developed through time and separation in this way are often said to be "related" to each other. This is because they can be shown to have descended from a single original language. **Related dialects,** then, are dialects that have developed from a single parent language. In this case, the various dialects of English are separated by only a few hundred years. Given enough time—say 1,000 years or so—related dialects will gradually evolve into distinct languages. Because the new languages will have evolved from related dialects they will also be related to each other, even if a bit more distantly. **Related languages,** then, are languages that have developed from a single ancestral language.

What's the difference between a dialect and a language? It's something that linguists call mutual intelligibility, or the ability of speakers of two language varieties to understand one another. (See Chapter 5 for a more detailed discussion of mutual intelligibility.) Dialects are said to be mutually intelligible; languages are not. You can understand someone who is speaking a related dialect, much as speakers of American English can generally understand speakers of British English, and vice versa. You may have to learn a few different words or expressions or pronunciations, such as substituting *flat* for *apartment* or *rubber* for *pencil eraser,* or [ʃedjul] for [skedjul], but for the most part you can make the transitions fairly easily. You can't do this with someone who speaks a completely different language. There's no way you can understand a Shinzwani sentence such as *nikusoma shio shini* by relying on your knowledge of various dialects of English. You need someone who speaks both Shinzwani and English to translate for you. (The sentence means 'I am reading this book.')

Of course, like everything else about language, issues related to identity are involved here, too. In some cases, you may not *want* to understand someone else, just because you feel they are "beneath" you or really "different" in some way. You erect internal barriers and really come to believe that you don't understand the way "those people" speak. This kind of thing happens in cases of social inequality, but it also happens in cases where national or ethnic pride is connected to pride in one's own language. If your language or dialect is a source of your identity, then you might want to insist that the variety of language you speak really is "different" enough from related varieties that nobody can understand it or that you can't understand related varieties. I've seen this happen in the Comoros, where people of one island say that they really can't understand people of the next one, and in the Czech Republic, where people who speak Czech often say they can't understand the neighboring Slovak. In each of these cases, the linguistic varieties in question can be demonstrated to be closely related, having separated so recently that people speaking one variety should be able to understand people speaking the other one. In each of these cases, political and ethnic concerns weigh more heavily in determining whether people will make the effort to understand one another. There have been a number of fascinating studies of these kinds of situations in language communities around the world, and they all point to the fact that there is more to mutual intelligibility than formal measurements of linguistic similarities and differences. As always, the fact that language is used by people means that people will bring all sorts of social and political interests to the table whenever they use their language or encounter a different one.

Nonetheless, languages do evolve into different—but related—ones, linguistically as well as socially speaking, so let's look more carefully at some examples of how this can happen. We can use English as an example, since there are written records to help us. It turns out the English of 1,000 years ago is quite different from the English of today, and it doesn't really matter whether you are talking about American or British English. If you examine the following list of words carefully, you can see both the differences and the similarities.

Old English	Modern English
bairn	son
bat	boat
ece	forever
fisc	fish
fold	earth
ful	foul
gar	spear
ic	I
manian	admonish
manig	many
mece	sword
mid	with
mus/mys	mouse/mice

nu	now
of	from
onfon	accept
cwen	queen, wife
rostian	roast
scyp	ship
snoru	daughter-in-law
unhold	faithless
wer	man

If you didn't know that these words represented two different stages of the same language, separated only by 1,000 years, you would most certainly want to conclude that they were words from two different but related languages. A few look familiar, such as *mus : mouse, mys : mice, nu : now, manig : many, cwen : queen, fisc : fish, scyp : ship,* and so on. These familiar-looking pairs help us to see the similarities between the two varieties (or, in this case, stages) of English and to conclude that they are related. We can see, for example that a <c> in Old English has often become a <sh> in contemporary English and that a lot of the vowels have changed as well: *Mus* has become *mouse, mys* has become *mice,* and so on. Historical linguists call this particular shift in vowels "The Great English Vowel Shift." This shift in the way that vowels were pronounced seems to have begun sometime in the 1400s and continued on through the 1700s (or perhaps even later if you consider some of the shifts that are happening today). Although theoretical linguists tend to emphasize the structural aspects of this shift, it is likely that there were some significant social aspects as well. Remember the shift in the use of [ɹ] in New York and Kansas? Similar pressures had to have been present in England between the 1400s and 1700s. Figure 9.1 shows which vowels shifted, what they shifted to, and approximately when each shift took place. It is arranged in the approximate shape of a standard vowel chart.

The chart of The Great English Vowel Shift helps us to see how various contemporary English words evolved from their older English forms. The words in Table 9.1, arranged according to where their vowels appear

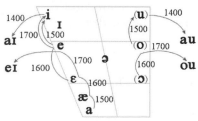

FIGURE 9.1 The Great English Vowel Shift

TABLE 9.1 Examples of The Great English Vowel Shift

PLACE

		front	central	back
H E I G H T	close/high	from mys [mis] to mice [mais]		from mus [mus] to mouse [maus]
	close-mid	from ges [ge:s] to geese [gis]		from gos [go:s] to goose [gus]
	open-mid		from cwen [kwɛn] to queen [kwin] from manig [mænɪg] to many [mɛni]	from rostian [rɔstian] to roast [rost]
	open/low		from name [na:mə] to name [neim]	

on a vowel chart, show how the shift affected specific words. (See Chapter 3 for more about vowel charts.)

Of course, not every word changed in the same way in every dialect of English. For example, the Canadian English pronunciation of *house* is closer to [hus] than to [haus], and the chart does not include the development of the [ɔi] sound that you can hear in some pronunciations of *oil*, nor does it include the development of the New Orleans pronunciation of [bəid] (*bird*). Most recently, linguist Penny Eckert has been studying a new set of vowel changes that adolescent girls are beginning to use in California to set themselves off as "cool" or "trendy." For example, [e] seems to be shifting downward to sound more like [æ] (so that words like *friend* sound more like *frand*), while [æ] is splitting into two different sounds, [iyæ] (before nasals) and [a], so that *stand* sounds more like [stiyænd] and *that* [ðæt] sounds more like *thot* [ðat]). Examples like these, detailed on Eckert's website, and others you can probably think of yourself, serve as reminders that language is constantly changing.

 WEBLINK   To read about the differences between British and American English, and the history of the English language, go to http://anthropology.wadsworth.com/ottenheimer_language.

Language Change and Language Families

If it is clear that English is both different from and related to Old English, is it equally easy to see similar similarities between other languages related to English? Here are some words from English, Dutch, and German:

English	Dutch	German
day	dag	Tag
daughter	dochter	Tochter
fish	vis	Fisch
flesh	vlees	Fleisch
foot	voet	Fuß [fus]
hand	hand	Hand

man	man	Mann
mouse	muis	Maus
needle	naald	Nadel
round	rond	rund
sail	zeil	Segel
ship	schip	Schiff
soft	zacht	sanft
swine	zwijn	Schwein
to eat	eten	essen

Even a casual examination of these words suggests that these are languages that are related to one another through the same kind of slow evolutionary change that we have just been looking at. And just as we can determine regular sound changes between Old and Modern English we can also see regular sound shifts between contemporary English, Dutch, and German. A <t> in German, for example, is a <d> in Dutch and English (as in *Tag* : *dag* : *day*). A <v> in Dutch is an <f> in English and German (as in *vis* : *fish* : *Fisch*). In addition, we can spot some interesting vowel changes that are reminiscent of the Old English to Modern English vowel changes. You can see some of this in the grouping of *mouse* : *muis* : *Maus*, for example.

When we find groups of languages that are related like this, we say that they are members of the same "family" of languages. A **family of languages** is a set of languages thought to have descended (or developed) from a common ancestor. The ancestral language is thought of as a "mother" language, and the descendants are all referred to as "daughter" languages. We also say that languages that belong to the same family are "genetically related" languages. **Genetically related languages** are languages that have descended from the same ancestor language. It's important to note that this is only a statement of historical relationship between languages; it is not a biological statement at all. It is interesting, however, to note that the nineteenth-century research into language families and language evolution was influential in the development of biological theories of evolution that emerged toward the end of that century. Of course, as Boas argued so clearly, there is no one-to-one relationship between biology and language (for a full discussion of Boas's argument see Chapter 1).

Much of the nineteenth-century research on language families and language evolution was fueled by the discovery, by Sir William Jones (1746–1794), of the relationships between Sanskrit (an ancient religious language of India), Greek, and Latin. Sir William was a British judge who lived in India in the 1700s. Fascinated with languages, he took it upon himself to study as many languages as he could. In his (now famous) address to the Royal Asiatic Society in 1786, he noted that resemblances between Sanskrit, Greek, and Latin seemed to be "stronger . . . than could possibly have been provided by accident" (Jones 1786/1799). In addition, Sir William suggested that the three languages must have "sprung from some common source, which, perhaps, no longer exists." Now, this was a really new idea! Prior to this, language scholars had assumed that languages evolved in a unilinear fashion, one from another, from another. In the old model, Sanskrit would have had to have evolved into Greek and Greek into Latin. Sir William's idea, that three languages could have evolved from a single ancestor, opened up the field of language scholarship to proposing and researching all sorts of new language groupings. It also introduced the idea that an ancestral language might no longer exist! This meant that it might be possible to reconstruct an ancestral language using contemporary data rather than relying entirely on written sources.

The language family that Sir William identified has come to be known as Proto-Indo-European. Proto-Indo-European is a fairly large language family that includes languages spoken from northern and western Europe (English, Danish, Irish, Italian, French, German, Spanish, Norwegian, Swedish, Welsh, and more) through central, eastern, and southern Europe (Armenian, Bulgarian, Czech, Greek, Polish, Russian, Ukrainian, and more), and eastward through India (Bengali, Hindi, Punjabi, and Urdu). The many languages included in Proto-Indo-European might be thought of as distant "cousins," and the relationships among the various languages are often shown as a drawing of a "family tree," with branches and subbranches, revealing the degrees of relatedness between languages. Proto-German is shown as one branch, for example, with Proto-West-German and Proto-North-German being shown as subbranches of Proto-German. Most of the eighteenth- and nineteenth-century work on language families and language evolution focused on reconstructing Proto-Indo-European; this was in large part because the language scholars engaged in the research were Europeans themselves. But gradually attention turned to other language families so that now most of the world's language families have been identified and protolanguages have been reconstructed for them.

Reconstructing Protolanguages   So, how do linguists reconstruct these ancient languages? Mostly by comparing sets of words in related languages, by observing and analyzing the sound shifts that appear to have taken place in each related language, and by positing "rules" to describe those sound shifts. Let's take a look at how it works. First of all, you need to be sure that the words you are working with are words that evolved from the ancestor language rather than words that were borrowed into one or another of the contemporary languages after they split apart. You need, in other words, to be sure you are working with cognate words, or "cognates." **Cognates** are sets of words in related languages that can be shown to have descended from a common ancestral language. Cognates have similar meanings, and they show regular sound correspondences, such as the ones we examined a few paragraphs earlier, between English, German, and Dutch. Cognates allow you to see relationships between languages and also to see the ways that each of the different languages in a particular family might have changed over time. It is not always easy to sort out the cognates and differentiate them from borrowed words, but that is an essential step in reconstructing a protolanguage. You want to be sure you are working entirely with cognates in a reconstruction so that you can be sure which sounds belong in the ancestral language and which ones might have been introduced by borrowing. Here are some cognate and borrowed words in French, German, and English to help you see the differences between cognates and borrowings.

English	German	French	
flesh	Fleisch	chair/viande	(*flesh* and *fleisch* are cognates)
beef	Rindfleisch	boeuf	(*beef* is borrowed from French)
calf	Kalbe	veau	(*calf* and *Kalbe* are cognates)
veal	Kalbfleisch	veau	(*veal* is borrowed from French)
swine	Schwein	porc	(*swine* and *Schwein* are cognates)
pork	Schweinefleisch	porc	(*pork* is borrowed from French)

The really fascinating thing is that, if you have a set of cognates, you can use them to reconstruct what the original, ancestral language must have been like. Using the reconstructions, and the similarities and differences among the contemporary cognates, you can also develop descriptions of the specific changes that must have taken place in each language for the cognates to end up sounding as similar, yet different, as they do. The trick is to line up all the cognates and then to examine them for **correspondence sets,** or sets of sounds that appear to correspond to one another in each of the languages. In the English and German words above, the <c> of English (actually it's a velar [k]) corresponds to the <k> of German, and the <s> of English corresponds to the <sch> of German, at least at the beginning of words.

Once you have listed all the possible sound correspondences, the next step is to reconstruct (or guess at) the most likely ancestor sound from which the contemporary sounds could have evolved and to build a hypothetical phonetic chart using those sounds. There are two ways to choose among the sounds of a correspondence set in reconstructing an ancestral sound. The first, the **phonetic plausibility strategy,** is just what it sounds like: The choice must seem plausible given what is known about the ways that languages change and the relationships between the sounds on a reconstructed phonetic chart. Some sound shifts that are thought to be more plausible than others include **palatalization,** or moving the point of articulation closer to the palate (such as moving from an [s] to an [ʃ] or from a [t] to a [tʃ]); **assimilation,** or changing the point of articulation so it is closer to that of a neighboring sound (such as changing an alveolar [n] to a bilabial [m] when it is next to a bilabial [b]); and **voicing,** or changing the manner of articulation to make a sound voiced (such as changing an [s] to a [z]).

In the Dutch, English, and German examples of *vis : fish : Fisch* that we saw before, we have the correspondence set [s] : [ʃ] : [ʃ]; phonetic plausibility causes us to choose the unpalatalized [*s] as the reconstructed Proto-German sound and then to posit that the sound became palatalized to [ʃ] in English and German. (Note that we use asterisks to indicate the sounds that we are reconstructing because we don't really have any examples of the ancestral sounds to check against. Reconstructions really are just that—they are hypothetical models that we have constructed, and as such they are subject to further analysis and change if we find new data.)

The second strategy for choosing between sounds is the **majority rules strategy,** which is that, if there is no phonetically plausible reason to choose a particular sound, then the choice should be based on whichever sound appears most frequently in the correspondence set. Using this strategy, it makes perfect sense to reconstruct an ancestral [*k] for Proto-German from the correspondence set *calf : Kalbe,* where both the <c> and the <K> are pronounced [k].

Here's an example of how reconstruction works, using just one word from four contemporary Polynesian languages.

Maori	*Hawaiian*	*Samoan*	*Fijian*
tapu	kapu	tapu	tabu (English: taboo)

A table of correspondence sets built up out of this one word looks like this:

M	*H*	*S*	*F*
t	k	t	t
a	a	a	a
p	p	p	b
u	u	u	u

A reconstruction of the ancestral (proto)phonemes for these four languages looks like this:

M	*H*	*S*	*F*	*Proto*	*Strategy*
t	k	t	t	*t	majority rules
a	a	a	a	*a	majority rules
p	p	p	b	*p	majority rules and phonetic plausibility (voicing)
u	u	u	u	*u	majority rules

The beginnings of a phonemic chart for these proto-phonemes are shown in Tables 9.2 and 9.3.

TABLE 9.2 Proto-Polynesian consonants		
	PLACE	
	bilabial	alveolar
M A N N E R	stops	*p	*t

TABLE 9.3 Proto-Polynesian vowels			
	PLACE		
	front	central	back
H E I G H T	close/high			*u
	open/low		*a	

Rules to describe the changes can now be written. These rules must show the change from [*t] to [k] in Hawaiian and the voicing of [*p] into [b] in Samoan. The rules should look something like this:

Hawaiian   *Samoan*

[*t] → [k]   [*p] → [b]

                  (or [*p] → [voiced])

Finally, if you want to reconstruct the ancestral word, to see what Proto-Polynesian might have looked and sounded like, the result would most likely be [*tapu].

Reconstruction is mainly composed of a set of educated guesses like this, but of course the more languages you know and can compare, the more deeply you understand how sound systems work, and the longer you have studied the whole process of reconstruction, the more sophisticated your reconstructions can be. The workbook/reader provides some guided practice with reconstructing words in a protolanguage.

Reconstructing Cultures   Reconstructing protolanguages is more than just an interesting exercise in discovering ancestral languages and family relationships among languages. Reconstructed protolanguages can also provide important windows into the culture and environment of the people who might have spoken those languages. This is especially important for archaeologists who are trying to trace ancient cultures through artifacts. Words can help to pinpoint searches and to confirm hypotheses. For example, the reconstruction of Proto-Indo-European reveals it had words for trees such as birch, beech, fir, oak, and willow, but not for fig, grape, or olive. There are words reconstructed for animals such as bear, fox, and wolf, but not for elephant, monkey, or tiger. There are also words for cattle, goats, horses, sheep, and pigs, and for barley, bees, and honey. Water denizens include otter, salmon, and turtles. Evidence from such reconstructions suggests that the speakers of Proto-Indo-European lived in a temperate, forested climate. Some scholars suggest central Europe, others a location a little further east on the coast of the Baltic Sea, and others a location still further to the east on the steppes of Russia or central Asia (possibly in Anatolia and the regions east and south of the Caspian Sea), with the Baltic area serving as a location where the northern and western branches of the language family began to separate from the others. A reconstructed protolanguage can also provide clues about the culture of its original speakers. For example, it is clear that Proto-Indo-European speakers kept domesticated animals, gathered honey, and included barley in their diet. We also can guess that they were patrilocal because it is possible to reconstruct a word for daughter-in-law but not for son-in-law.

Other language families for which similar linguistic and cultural reconstructions have been attempted include Algonkian, a family of Native American languages, and Bantu, a large family of languages in spoken in Africa. Proto-Algonkian words for woodland caribou, harbor seal, and lake trout suggest that the original speakers of Proto-Algonkian most likely lived "between Lake Huron and Georgian Bay and the middle course of the Ottawa River" (Siebert 1967). Proto-Bantu appears to have been originally spoken in the Cameroon region, with an eventual expansion to the east and then another one, later on, to the southeast and southwest. The original population appears to have practiced slash-and-burn agriculture and to have grown West African crops such as calabashes, cowpeas, and yams in a mixed rain-forest/savannah environment. They also engaged in fishing and they kept cattle. New crops such as sorghum and millet and new technologies such as ironworking appear to have been adopted by Bantu speakers as they moved eastward, into the lake area of eastern Africa (Ehret 1982a, 1982b).

Macrofamilies and the Origins of Language   If you can use contemporary languages to reconstruct a protolanguage, can you also use a group of protolanguages to reconstruct even earlier models? Some contemporary scholars are even working on this very idea, reconstructing earlier and earlier versions of protolanguages, attempting to discover the links among all the languages and language families of the world. Such research is controversial but fascinating. It suggests the existence of relationships among distinct language families, grouping them into **macrofamilies,** or **phyla,** sets of language families that appear to have descended from a common ancient language. One such macrofamily that has been proposed is called Nostratic and includes Indo-European, Uralic (which includes Finnish and Hungarian), Altaic (which includes the Turkic languages), Afro-Asiatic (which includes the Semitic languages), Dravidian (the languages of South India), Kartvelian (the languages of the southern Caucasus), and Korean. Nostratic is not completely accepted by historical linguists, some of whom maintain that a different macrofamily, Eurasiatic, is a more likely construction. Eurasiatic includes Indo-European, Uralic, Altaic, Korean-Japanese-Ainu, and several Siberian and American language families such as Gilyak, Chukchi-Kamchatkan, and Eskimo-Aleut, but it does not include Afro-Asiatic, Kartvelian, and Dravidian, all of which are classified as separate language families. The massive amounts of detail involved in these reconstructions, and the fact that reconstructions are, it must be remembered, just models built out of linguistic data, makes it clear that these kinds of reconstructions must be regarded as tentative, even though they are indeed suggestive. Some fascinating recent scholarship has attempted to link these macrofamilies to human biological evolution, but here, too, it is important to remember that such links are just as tentative as the reconstructions of macrofamilies. They certainly are controversial. Again, it is helpful to recall Boas's observation that it is difficult, if not impossible, to demonstrate a perfect one-to-one correspondence among language, culture, and race. This is especially true today and, no doubt, was equally true in ancient times; as people move and encounter speakers of other languages, their languages change, sometimes to the point of adopting the languages of the areas that they move into or adopting the languages of the peoples who move into—should we say invade?—their areas.

Is it possible to reconstruct something called "Proto-World" at this point? Probably not, although attempts have been made recently that are also intriguing. Here, for example, is a list of words that shows the difficulties, as well as the possibilities:

Family	Language	Word	Meaning
Niger-Congo	KiSwahili	mbili	'two'
Nilo-Saharan	Baka	brue	'two'
Afro-Asiatic	Oromo	bira	'two'
Indo-European	Czech	půl	'half'
Indo-European	English	pair	'pair'
Uralic	Samoyed	peele	'half'
Dravidian	Tamil	pal	'part, portion, share'

Indo-Pacific	Ndani	bere	'two'
Australian	Ngiyambaa	bula	'one of a pair'
Austro-Asiatic	Palaung	par	'you two'
Austronesian	Javanese	kembar	'twin'
Amerind	Huave	apool	'snap in two'
Amerind	Quechua	pula	'both'

Bengtson and Ruhlen (1994, 316–17)

Work such as this, at the macrofamily level and beyond, is doubly controversial due to the fact that language families are often proposed through the use of **mass comparison,** a technique in which lists of words from large numbers of languages are compared all at once rather than by the slow, painstaking method of reconstructing protolanguages from languages already known to be related. A good example of the controversy surrounding this approach is the classification of African languages. In the 1950s, linguistic anthropologist Joseph Greenberg (1915–2001), used mass comparison to reclassify the many languages of Africa into just a few large families. Africanist scholars who had been using standard reconstruction techniques, and who had painstakingly developed a rather large list of African language families, resisted Greenberg's new classification. The idea of comparing a great many languages all at once, rather than in pairs, or in small groups of demonstrably related languages, seemed too abrupt. Greenberg's classification turned out to answer many important questions, however, and to facilitate further research into African linguistics. Today, it is the accepted classification system for African languages. Greenberg next turned his mass-comparison technique to working with Native American languages. As with African languages in the 1950s, Native American languages are currently classified into a great many different language families. Greenberg's results, however, suggest that Native American languages can be grouped into just three major language families. Proposed in the 1990s, it is still a controversial classification. Perhaps fifty years from now it, too, will be the accepted classification. Perhaps not. Only time, and further analysis, will resolve the issue.

Language Isolates   Finally, it is important to realize that not every language can be assigned to a specific language family. Despite the best efforts of historical and comparative linguists, some languages remain unclassified. Basque, spoken in northern and western Spain, is one such language. Languages that cannot be classified into any language family are known as **language isolates.** One explanation for these so-called language isolates is that they split off from other languages so long ago that it is not possible (or at least it is too difficult at present) to know which language family they might belong to. As linguists continue to reconstruct ancient language families, and even macrofamilies, it may become possible to discern the placement of these language isolates. For the moment, however, we must continue to consider them as language families in and of themselves.

Timing Language Separation   You might be wondering, since it is possible to develop academic reconstructions of ancient languages, whether it is possible to know when those ancient languages might have been spoken and when the various daughter languages in a particular language family actually separated from each other and from their parent languages. Such a determination would be of great value to archaeologists in tracing population movements and in more accurately identifying the inhabitants of archaeological sites. In the 1950s, linguistic anthropologist Morris Swadesh (1909–1967) suggested that it might indeed be possible to develop a mathematical means of determining degrees of language separation and to translate that information into a measure of time. He called the method **glottochronology,** or **lexicostatistics,** or the science of measuring time change in language. Glottochronology, according to Swadesh, could provide linguistic anthropologists with a reliable way to determine the dates when related languages had separated from one another and perhaps also the times when specific ancient speech communities might have existed.

To measure language separation, Swadesh suggested relying on words that were as "culture-free" as possible. Words carrying specific cultural information, such as words for various animals or plants would, he reasoned, be likely to change as people moved from one place to another. On the other hand, universal—or near-universal—kinds of words, words for items and concepts, such as 'fire' and 'earth,' 'food' and 'water,' 'eating' and 'drinking,' might be less resistant to change over time. Such words would probably be retained no matter where people moved. So Swadesh developed a list of 100 basic (or "culture-free") vocabulary items (he later expanded the list to 200 words). He then tested this list with several languages, comparing old and new forms of each word. Using languages for which there was at least 1,000 years of data, such as Chinese, Greek, and Latin, Swadesh found that the words on his basic lists changed at remarkably stable rates. In the 100-word list, only eighteen to twenty words appeared to change (or get replaced) during 1,000 years. Using this rate as a constant, Swadesh developed a mathematical formula to estimate how many years ago any two related languages might have separated from one another. According to the formula the t (or time) when two languages had separated was equal to the log of the C (or the percentage of cognates) multiplied by two times the log of r (or the constant rate of retention that Swadesh had proposed). All you had to do was to find out how many cognates there were in two 100-word lists from two related languages and plug that number into the formula. The result would give you a number that you could compare with archaeological data or with other linguistic data. The method was fairly easy to apply, and it did yield

Doing Linguistic Anthropology 9.2

OBSERVING LANGUAGE CHANGE

The German noun *Gemütlichkeit* denotes a state of feeling cozy at home with one's family. I asked my friend and informant, H, if the word occurs in Yiddish, a language whose lexicon is 60 percent derived from German. He responded that it may have been introduced in literary Yiddish in the nineteenth century, but it had never caught on in regular speech.

I have been a participant within a secular Jewish community organization in Los Angeles, where Yiddish is more nostalgia than a living language and knowledge of it confers prestige on the speaker. A few weeks after H's pronouncement on the status of *Gemütlichkeit,* I overheard a conversation between H and L. L used the word *gemütlike,* which I recognized as an adoption of the German adjective form of the word in question. When I later asked H why he didn't tell me about *gemütlike,* he responded with the words all too familiar to anthropologists, "That isn't what you asked me."

My friend's view was confirmed by further research. Alexander Harkavy's *Yiddish English Dictionary,* published in 1898, lists these Yiddish words of German origin: *gemith, gemithlikh,* and *gemithlikhkeyt.* The first simply means 'mood, feeling, or spirit,' while the latter two are the adjective and noun in question ('cozy' and 'coziness,' respectively). This reflected the usage of the late-nineteenth-century Yiddish writers, many of whom were intellectuals who knew more German than Yiddish and peppered their writing with German vocabulary. By the time Harkavy's *Yiddish-English-Hebrew Dictionary* was published in 1928, only *gemit* (the <h> was dropped) remained. Nahum Stutchkoff's *Thesaurus of the Yiddish Language,* published in 1950, has only *gemit* as well. *Gemitlekh,* but not *gemitlekhkeyt,* reappears in 1968 in Uriel Weinrech's *Modern English-Yiddish Yiddish-English Dictionary.*

Martin Cohen, *California State University—Northridge and Los Angeles City College*

intriguing results. According to this method, Proto-Indo-European appears to have a time depth of around 5,000 to 6,000 years, for example, which matches nicely with some of the archaeological data. Estimates for Proto-Algonkian range from 2,500 to 4,000 years ago, and estimates for Proto-Bantu range from around 2,000 to 3,000 years ago. Proto-Niger-Congo (the family to which Bantu belongs) may even date back as far as 5,000 years. In spite of these intriguing results, glottochronology is not widely used today. Many of the assumptions underlying the method make the results somewhat controversial. For example, a controversial recent estimate based on glottochronology suggests a time depth of 9,000 years (instead of 5,000–6,000 years) for Proto-Indo-European. Some linguists limit lexicostatistics to measuring no more than the "genetic" separation between languages, relying instead on archaeology to estimate time depth. Recently, this approach has been used particularly effectively in Bantu linguistics.

✻ LANGUAGES IN CONTACT

When we reconstruct languages and determine family relationships among languages, we are working with languages that we already know to be related in some way. We understand the processes of language change, especially internal language change, and how those processes contribute to the development of sets of related languages from common ancestral languages. Now let's explore external change in more detail.

Mixed Languages: Pidgins and Creoles

There are some languages that do not follow the model of slow internal change at all. Instead, they seem to spring—almost fully developed—from specific situations of population contact. Most of the time these are situations in which traders (or occupying colonists) speaking one language encounter a population speaking a completely different language. Instead of one group of speakers learning the language of the other, they combine elements of their two languages to create a third one.

This new language could be described as something like a hybrid between the two contributing languages. Often times, the new language combines the vocabulary of one of the two languages (generally the language of the visitors or colonists) with the grammar of the other one of the two languages (generally the language of the hosting or colonized group). A language that has developed through contact, out of two unrelated languages, is called a **pidgin.** The word *pidgin* is thought to derive from a particular pidgin spoken in China, in which the English word *business* was repronounced as *pidgin.*

Because pidgin languages are primarily trade languages, they are generally short-lived. They don't often last more than a generation or two. People tend to use them as second languages only. They are never really used as first languages. Generally they are too "restricted" to be of much more use than that. Their vocabulary is limited to the needs of the situation, and their grammar is usually highly simplified. Complex noun inflections or verb tenses tend to disappear in pidgin languages. So do adjective agreement patterns. Still, the African pidgins that developed during the years of European colonialism in Africa appear to have been particularly useful as a medium of communication among slaves who were taken from Africa and brought to the New World. Although it was sometimes possible for slaves from a single speech community to end up in the same plantation or farm in the New World, the more common pattern was for slaves on a single plantation, especially a large one, to be brought from many different parts of the African continent. As long as they could use one or another variety of African pidgin, they had access to a contact language that they could use for bare-bones communication with one another.

As short-lived as pidgins may be, they sometimes do serve as the base material for the development of full-blown languages. This is thought to happen in situations where a pidgin is the only language that people have in common, such as on many of the plantations in the New World. When African slaves used pidgin as a contact language among themselves and to communicate with their owners, we assume that they used it as a second language. Slave children, born on plantations, however, might very well have heard more pidgin spoken around them than any single African language. What else did plantation children hear around them? Perhaps a little of the language of the slave owners as well. And so, building on what they heard around them, plantation children developed more complete languages, something they could use to play games, talk to each other and their parents, and do everything else that you need to do with a language. We call this more complete variety of language, which was developed on plantations and in long-term colonial situations, a "creole." A **creole**, then, is a complete language that has emerged out of a pidgin. A creole can serve as someone's first language because it is complete enough to convey anything that that person needs or wants to say.

The word *creole* was originally used by French colonists to designate a person of French descent, born in the New World. In time it came to designate other things that were particularly characteristic of the New World, such as foods, house types, and even languages. Creoles of color, for example, meant individuals of mixed African and French descent born in the Americas. Creole tomatoes were the variety of tomatoes grown in Louisiana. And the word *creole*, applied to language, meant the varieties of language spoken by the slaves of French people in the Americas. Nowadays, we use the word "creole" to refer to any language that developed out of a pidgin, not just French creole. Interestingly, as each creole developed, it added more and more words from the dominant language into its vocabulary. This makes sense as that is the most common language around for people to listen to and to borrow words from. We use the term **lexifier language** to designate the language that contributes the majority of words to a pidgin or a creole. As with pidgins, the lexifier languages of creoles are generally the dominant language. This means that the longer a creole exists, the more it begins to sound like the dominant (or lexifier) language around it. So, for example, creoles spoken in English-dominant communities begin to sound more and more like English, and creoles spoken in French-dominant communities begin to sound more and more like French. The various creoles retain their original grammars, however, and as a result they frequently end up being judged to be "bad French" or "bad English." In other words, English speakers hear English creoles as having plenty of English words, but as having somewhat unfamiliar grammar. They attribute the unfamiliar grammar to mistaken understandings of what they consider to be "proper" grammar rather than to accurate renditions of African grammar. Compared to "proper" French, for example, Haitian Kreol, a French-lexified creole spoken in Haiti, is thought of as "bad French" rather than as a language with an African-derived grammar and a French-derived vocabulary. Compared to "proper" English, African American Vernacular English, an English-lexified creole derived from plantation creole and still widely spoken in the United States, is thought of as "bad English" rather than as a language with an African-derived grammar and an English-derived vocabulary. It is important to remember, however, that mixed languages such as pidgins and creoles, often derive their heritage from two (or more) language families and should not be judged to be bad examples of either of their parent languages. They are new languages, and as such they are fascinating examples of how languages changed and develop.

Classifying Pidgin and Creole Languages How do you classify a pidgin or creole language? Does it belong to the language family that contributed the words? Or does it belong to the language family that contributed the grammar? Is it a member of the language family of the conquerors (traders, explorers, intruders, or colonists) or is it a member of the language family of the conquered (indigenous) folks? In general, we tend to classify pidgins and creoles with the languages whose grammars they most closely resemble. This is because it is more difficult to borrow grammar than words, so if two languages have similar grammatical structures, they are thought to be related to one another. Words are easily borrowed. Take the examples of English that we talked about earlier. Even though English has borrowed lots of words from French, and from other languages as well, it is still classified as a Germanic language because its grammatical patterns most closely resemble other languages in that language family (German, Dutch, Frisian, and so on). Likewise, those pidgin languages that developed on the west coast of Africa, for example, during the years of European colonialism and slavery, are best thought of (at least linguistically) as members of Niger-Congo, a large African language family with members in west, central, and eastern Africa. African pidgin languages reflected diverse vocabularies, depending on which European colonial power was present in a particular area. They sounded more French, or more English, or more Portuguese, depending on which of those languages had contributed most of the vocabulary items to the mix. Parts of Africa colonized by French speakers, for example, developed French-sounding pidgins; parts of Africa colonized by English speakers developed English-sounding pidgins. Still, the grammars of all of these African pidgins were fairly similar to one another, as well as to the underlying grammar of Niger-Congo languages.

One intriguing idea about pidgins and creoles is that they do not belong to any language family at all. Instead, they represent a return to a level of language that is more universally encoded in the human brain. This kind of argument is made primarily by theoretical linguists, such as Derek Bickerton, who believe they see strong grammatical similarities among the world's pidgins and creoles. These linguists argue that the similarities are caused by the fact that pidgins are formed by stripping away everything that is different between two languages in contact: Complexities of tense, adjective agreement, inflections for plural or for case, detailed differentiation of pronouns, and so on all disappear when a pidgin is created. Getting down to the simplest, most fundamental elements of the two languages results in getting down to the most fundamental characteristics of language in general, which also results in all pidgins being similar to one another grammatically. To explain the emergence of creoles from pidgins, these theoretical linguists rely on the idea of a **bioprogram,** or an innate grammar, that guides children as they create full-blown creole languages out of the limited pidgins that they have as primary input (see Chapter 8 for more about the idea of bioprogram). This is an intriguing argument and, if true, it would mean that pidgins and creoles provide an important window into questions of language origins. The problem remains that pidgins and creoles *do* exhibit elements of grammar that appear to derive from specific donor languages. Here, for example, is the set of pronouns used in Cape York Creole, an English-lexified creole spoken in northern Australia, across from Papua New Guinea:

Cape York Creole	*English Equivalent*
ai, mi	'I, me' (first person singular)
yu	'you' (second person singular)
i, im	'he/she/it, him/her' (third person singular)
yumi, yumtu	'me and you' (first person dual, includes listener)
mitu	'me and him/her' (first person dual, excludes listener)
mipela, wi	'me and you all' (first person plural, includes several listeners)
mitupela, wi	'me and them all' (first person plural, excludes listener, includes others)
yutupela	'you two' (second person dual)
yupela	'you all' (second person plural)
tupela	'them two' (third person dual)
ol, dempela	'them all' (third person plural)

(Crowley and Rigsby 1979, 174–75)

It would be difficult to argue that this level of pronoun complexity was a feature of the bioprogram. It would be much easier to argue that it was a feature of the original indigenous Australian language from which this creole first derived its grammar. Clearly, it is not a feature of English grammar.

Here is another example of how creole languages may have retained specific grammatical patterns from their parent language families. This time let's look at two African languages and two African-derived creoles. The African languages are from two different geographical extremes of the Niger-Congo language family: Isoko (spoken in Nigeria) and Shin-zwani (spoken in the Comoro Islands). The African-derived creoles are from two different islands in the Caribbean: Carriacou (spoken in the Grenadines) and Haitian Kreol. Note how the English grammar has the verb change its form (*say, says, said, saying*), while the African and Caribbean grammars maintain the form of the verb but add particles (or prefixes, in the case of Shinzwani) in front of the verb. As with the Cape York Creole example, it seems clear that the presence of these verb particles in the Caribbean creoles is a feature that is shared with (and probably derives from) the original African languages from which the Caribbean creoles derived their grammar.

Isoko	*Shinzwani*	*Carriacou*	*Haitian Kreol*	*English*
ta	-rongoa	se	di	say
o ta	a-rongoa	shi se	li di	she says/has said
o te ta	a-tso-rongoa	shi go se	li va di	she will say
o be ta	a-ku-rongoa	shi da-se	li ap-di	she is saying
o ta-no	a-ka-rongoa	she di se	li te di	she (had) said

Isoko, Carriacou, and Haitian provided by Ron Kephart (personal communication, January 2004)

There are also other theories about pidgins and creoles. For example, some historical linguists have suggested that whatever similarities exist among pidgins and creoles could possibly be attributed to an early European common trade language known as Sabir. Also called the lingua franca, Sabir was a tenth-century (and perhaps even older) southern French dialect that was widely used by sailors and traders throughout the Mediterranean. It included elements of French, Spanish, Italian, Arabic, Greek, and Turkish, and it may itself have been a pidgin. The idea is that as Europeans spread out and colonized various parts of the world in the sixteenth through nineteenth centuries they brought Sabir with them, and it became the basis of all subsequent contemporary pidgins and creoles.

Social and Cultural Issues   It should be clear from the Oakland school board discussion that Ebonics (see Cross-Language Miscommunication 9.2: Ebonics in Oakland) stands in a somewhat disadvantaged position relative to the "standard" English. It is often the case that when a creole

---

Cross-Language Miscommunication 9.2

EBONICS IN OAKLAND

In 1996, the Oakland, California, school board passed a resolution recognizing Ebonics as the "primary language" of the district's African American students. Ebonics (a variety of African American English), they argued, was historically "different" from English. It was, they stated, "genetically based, and not a dialect of English." By this, they meant that Ebonics had descended from African languages, not European ones. It was a creole, in other words, that could trace its ancestry—and especially its grammatical structures—to the Niger-Congo family of languages. Even though it had borrowed a great many words from English, it was not grammatically related to English. Most important, it was not "bad" English, it was just a different language from English. Because Ebonics was so different from English, perhaps a bilingual approach might be helpful in teaching English to speakers of Ebonics.

Public outcry against the Oakland school board's proposal was swift and strong. Some people argued Ebonics really was just "bad" English and that a bilingual approach would just pamper students and encourage them not to learn "good" English. Others argued that letting students use Ebonics in the classroom would slow their progress toward learning proper English. Still others pointed out that not all African American children were "native" speakers of Ebonics, that Ebonics might just be a particular version of African American English typical of inner-city "street toughs." Many, however, misunderstood the school board's use of the words "genetically based," thinking it was a racist comment! If only they had understood something of the ways that linguists have been classifying languages into families and tracing their "genetic" relationships and patterns of separation and descent, they might not have reacted so strongly to the school board's proclamation. The important part of the phrase that the school board used was "not a dialect of English." It was this phrase that was intended to be the starting point for an experiment in bilingual education that might just have helped students who came to school using primarily Ebonics to become more fluent in both their own language and the dominant one.

HJO

---

coexists with another language the creole is considered as substandard in some way, while the dominant language is considered to be a standard, to which all members of the larger speech community should aspire. This is, in fact, a common situation whenever there are two or more varieties of language spoken in a single community. As we said earlier in this chapter, when discussing related dialects that split from a common parent language, there is no way to judge the superiority or inferiority of any particular way of speaking purely on linguistic grounds. Different varieties of languages are just different. This is also true for different languages. A creole is different from its lexifier language simply by virtue of having evolved from a different set of ancestral languages. This doesn't make it any better or any worse than its lexifier language, just different.

So how do different languages and language varieties get their reputations as "bad" or "good" or "standard" or "slangy"? They get their reputations through the social status of their speakers. A friend of mine once called this "stigma transfer," meaning that if the speaker of a language is looked down on in some way, then the variety of language that that person speaks will also be looked down on. In other words, the fact that the ancestors of African Americans were once slaves puts them into a lower status relative to European Americans, and this value judgment transfers to Ebonics, a language that many African Americans speak today.

One interesting observation is that when speakers of two or more different language varieties live in the same community the speakers of the less highly valued variety generally become bilingual, learning the language of the dominant group, while the speakers of the dominant language remain monolingual. It's an economic kind of decision. It makes sense for you to know the language of your potential employers and of the folks who are "in power" in your community. This is also true for most immigrants, who need to learn enough of the language of their new country in order to hold jobs and raise children. On the other hand, there's no special need for those in power to learn the language of those they employ.

Stable and Transitional Bilingualism

Bilingualism, or the ability to speak two languages, is more common than most Americans realize. And bilingual, even multilingual, communities exist in many parts of the world, as well as in parts of the United States. The fact that English is becoming an international language of commerce and communication means that English speakers are both advantaged and disadvantaged: advantaged because it is becoming easier and easier to find English speakers just about anywhere you might travel, so English speakers can travel widely without having to learn another language; and disadvantaged because being limited to knowing only one language means you can only speak with people who also know that language.

As we mentioned, many immigrants and many individuals who speak languages that are devalued in some way choose to become bilingual in their communities. Most of these individuals speak one of their languages (usually the dominant one) in the workplace, in schools, and in other public settings and speak the other language (usually the subordinated one) at home, with friends, and in various informal settings. In many cases, the children and grandchildren of these bilingual individuals abandon their home language over time. This process is referred to as **transitional bilingualism,** in which individuals gradually abandon their bilingualism in favor of speaking a more dominant language. The history of the United States is replete with examples of transitional bilingualism. Generally, the process is complete within three generations, so that the first generation in an immigrant family speaks primarily the home language, with just enough of the new country's language to be able to get by; the second generation (their children) generally grows up speaking both languages fluently; and the third generation (the grandchildren of the immigrants) often speaks only the language of the host country. Some of this is due to external pressures from the dominant society (the Americanizing idea of the "melting pot" for example), and some of it is due to internal pressures (such as the fact that there really are fewer and fewer places in which the home language can be used). It takes a special effort to convince children to continue to use a language that they only hear at home. I am familiar, for example, with Shinzwani-speaking immigrants in France who send their children "home" to the Comoros each summer so that they will continue to speak Shinzwani and to value the speaking of Shinzwani.

 Stable bilingualism, in contrast, is a situation in which individuals and communities maintain their bilingualism on a long-term basis. Stable bilingualism may continue for many generations, with individuals growing up speaking one language at home, another at school, and in some cases still another in business or other public settings (in which case, it is stable multilingualism). In most cases, one or more of the languages in question is considered as an **official language,** or a language designated as official by government policy. Official languages, the ones used in government offices and legal documents, tend also to be adopted by many speakers for other public uses, such as higher education or commerce. Sometimes, the reverse is true—a language that is widely spoken in public settings becomes the de facto official language. It isn't officially designated as such, but everyone uses it as if it were official. In any case, whenever there are several languages spoken in a single country, there is a good chance that a situation of stable bilingualism may develop.

 Canada is an example of a country with two languages that have been spoken side by side for generations. With French spoken primarily in Quebec and the eastern parts of the country and English spoken in the central and western parts of the country, not everyone in Canada is bilingual. Still, the country considers itself to be officially bilingual and has an official language policy that guarantees that citizens should be able to receive federal services in the "official language of their choice" (Secretariat, Official Languages Branch, Treasury Board of Canada 2003). Switzerland is another country where more than one language is official.

Switzerland recognizes the right of its citizens to speak French, German, Italian, and Romansh (a language descended from Latin). India is even more complexly multilingual. India has eighteen officially recognized languages. Hindi is the most widely spoken of the eighteen, and it is designated as a national language, as well as the official language of several states. Each of the others is official in at least one state of India. English is also widely used, in addition to the eighteen other languages, and it is accepted as "official" in the sense that it can be used for official communication between two states when one of the official state languages is not Hindi. This means that a child might learn and use a local language at home, a regional one at primary school, a nationally recognized one (such as Hindi) at college or university, and either Hindi or English for business and public affairs. In other words, many citizens of India become trilingual or quadrilingual or more. I found this sort of multilingualism in the Comoro Islands, as well, where young adults were competent speakers of Shinzwani, Arabic, Malagasy, French, and sometimes even English.

Stable bilingualism is characteristic of communities in which speakers of the various languages feel strongly about maintaining their various languages. Most of the time, this is because individuals in those communities feel that their languages are linked to their sense of ethnic or national identity—to give up your language may feel like giving up some piece of your identity. At the same time, the language that has achieved "official" status, the language that is used in business, or education, or government, is clearly a "language of power." To speak the language of power means to have access to that power. Language thus becomes a commodity. It has "value" for its speakers. The value of your home language might be that it encapsulates and represents your sense of heritage. The value of the official language might be that it provides access to education and jobs. The situation is, of course, more complicated than this, but you can see how becoming bilingual, or even multilingual, can mean acquiring access to a variety of speech communities and to the opportunities provided by each. It can also mean having to choose how and when to use your different languages or dialects. This can sometimes be a daunting task, especially when some varieties are less highly valued than others by the speech community in which you live.

A similar situation exists when the varieties of language that coexist are different versions of the same language rather than different languages. Linguistic anthropologists call such a situation **diglossia**, or a situation in which two (or more) varieties of the *same* language are used by speakers in different kinds of settings. In other words, the two varieties are compartmentalized so that each variety is judged appropriate for use in very specific conditions. Diglossia was first defined by Charles A. Ferguson (1921–1998) in the 1950s, and he used the term to describe the uses of Classical Arabic (in formal situations) and colloquial Arabic (in everyday situations) in several different Arabic-speaking countries. Designating the formal variety of the language as the H (or high) variety, and the everyday variety as the L (or low) variety, Ferguson pointed out several other regions where diglossic situations existed. In Switzerland, for example, standard German is considered H and Swiss German is L. In Greece, standard Greek is regarded as H and colloquial Greek as L. Although all speakers in a diglossic situation know both the high and the low varieties, they tend to judge the H variety to be "purer" or "more correct" and to use it in formal situations, such as religious sermons, university lectures, public speeches, and so on. They switch to the L variety for folk tales, jokes, television shows, and just chatting with friends.

Over time, the term diglossia has been extended to refer to almost any situation in which H and L varieties of language coexist and are used in this way, including situations of stable bilingualism in which the two varieties in question are different languages, not just different dialects. Questions of differential access to power and prestige, or intimacy and authenticity, then, are important whether we are talking about bilingualism or diglossia. The important thing is the way that people use the language varieties around them; how they manipulate them, consciously or unconsciously; how they "read" such uses; and how they make their own choices about language use on a daily basis. In every case, your language reveals much about you, and the ways in which this works has become the focus of much contemporary linguistic anthropology.

Codeswitching

Of course, if you speak more than one language variety you need to know when and where to use each one. In situations of stable bilingualism, this is something you learn as a member of your speech community. You know which language people tend to use for public ceremonies and special occasions and which ones to use at home or in your neighborhood bar. You know, or you learn from others around you, when and how to use the linguistic resources at your disposal. You learn the subtle and not-so-subtle implications of using one or another of your languages. You understand how your choice of language variety signals membership, even loyalty, to a particular social class, ethnic group, or national entity. My choice between using my New York [ɹ], for example, or leaving it behind depends on whether I want to sound like I still "fit in" in New York or I want to sound "more educated" or more like "a Kansan." Most of the time, we are not consciously aware of making these choices, but we definitely make them.

Codeswitching is the term we use to describe using more than one variety of language. Often codeswitching refers to using more than one variety of language in a single situation (often within a single sentence or even word), but it can also mean using different varieties of language in different situations. Shinzwani-speaking Comorians might use Shinzwani at home, for example, Shingazidja when they travel to the neighboring island of Grande Comore, French when they are speaking with a school teacher, or Arabic when praying in the mosque or giving a highly formalized public speech, for instance at a wedding ceremony. Studies of codeswitching tend to focus more on language-switching within sentences, however, and most of these studies indicate that most of the time the switches take place at grammatically significant boundaries in one or both languages. A good example of codeswitching at a grammatically significant boundary is a phrase that I heard a Shinzwani friend of mine use one day. We were choosing our seats in a movie theater when my friend said *nitso- sit here!* Now, *nitso-* in Shinzwani is the beginning part of a verb and it means 'I will,' it should be followed by a verb stem to form a complete Shinzwani word, as in *nitsokentsi* 'I will sit.' But the fact that it can be followed by a wide range of verb stems (e.g., *nitsoenda* 'I will go,' *nitsopiha* 'I will cook,' *nitsosoma* 'I will read') indicates that it precedes a grammatical boundary, marking off the subject (*ni-*) and tense (*-tso-*) from the rest of the verb in Shinzwani and making this a grammatically logical location for switching from Shinzwani into English.

Codeswitching works best when all individuals present know all of the languages or dialects that are being used. The fact that my friend and I both knew Shinzwani and English made it possible for her to switch between the two languages and for both of us to understand what she had said. I used to marvel at how young adults in the Comoros would switch among four and five languages, so long as everyone in the conversation knew all the languages. If someone joined a conversation who didn't know one of the languages, then that language would be dropped from the conversation!

LANGUAGE AND IDENTITY, LANGUAGE AND POWER

The idea that having an official language in a country will unify that country is a powerful one, but the idea that your language is your heritage is even more powerful. In recent years, the language-as-heritage idea has been gaining strength among many of the world's people. Although language is always changing, most people are not very aware of those changes. Instead, they focus on maintaining the language that they grew up with or that they still hear older folks speaking in their communities. This has not always been the case. In the 1800s and 1900s in the United States, for example, immigrants, Native Americans, and former slaves were encouraged to abandon their ancestral languages in favor of "becoming American." Children were encouraged to learn English as the language of the nation, and many learned to be embarrassed by their parents' and grandparents' ways of speaking. In some states, English was designated the official language and it became illegal to teach or worship or publish in any other language. In 1919, for example, the Nebraska legislature passed a bill that not only made English the official language of the state but expressly forbade the teaching of foreign languages (in this case, they had German in mind) until the ninth grade. Although parts of the bill were found to be unconstitutional a few years later, the net result was that many individuals who trace their ancestry to the German-speaking communities of Nebraska are today largely monolingual speakers of English. In some cases, the pressure was not as formalized, but the results were similar. Children growing up in places where their language was discouraged, or devalued, chose to abandon their language in favor of the more highly valued language. Sometimes teachers would call immigrant parents in to school or make home visits to explain to the parents that they should attempt to speak only English at home in order to hasten their children's adjustment to their new country. These kinds of pressures explain much about how America came to be such a monolingual country. Such monolingualism is, in fact, quite rare elsewhere in the world.

The fear that it is language that drives groups apart or that lies at the base of "nation-building" is actually falsely placed. Switzerland, Canada, and India are just a few examples of countries where the existence of multiple languages has not led to the breakup of the countries. The similarities between Urdu, the language of Pakistan, and Hindi, the most widely spoken language of India, are so strong that it would be a mistake to think that India and Pakistan were divided from one another because of language; it was religious and cultural differences that lay at the heart of the India-Pakistan separation. Likewise, the differences between Czech and Slovak are so miniscule that, even as an outsider who speaks neither language, it is easy enough for me to read the directions on a packet of instant soup in either of the two languages. The separation of Czechoslovakia into the Czech Republic and Slovakia was for cultural reasons, not for linguistic ones.

Examples of stable bilingualism and diglossia make it clear, however, that it is not necessary to give up one language in order to use another. Many people, in many situations, find it possible, indeed perhaps even natural, to maintain a variety of languages and dialects, switching among them as the occasion requires, choosing to use whichever ones seem most appropriate for the situations they find themselves in. As they make these choices, they influence the direction of change in each of the languages they speak. Change and choice are inextricably linked together, and the sooner we understand this fact, the sooner we can move away from forcing people into making choices they may later regret.

SUMMARY

All languages change over time. Language change is categorized into internal and external change. External change refers to the kinds of change caused by language contact and borrowing. Internal change refers to the kinds of changes caused by the ways that speakers gradually modify their language over time. External change is more rapid than internal change. Both kinds of change can affect any part of a language including phonology, morphology, syntax, spelling, and more.

Words are the most easily borrowed items between languages. Some languages are more resistant to borrowing than others. Words that are borrowed from one language to another tend to be repronounced according to the sound system of the borrowing language. Over time, due to changes in pronunciation, it may become difficult to trace a word to its language of origin. Borrowed words may take on new meanings in their new languages as well. Or they may be disassembled into parts and the parts combined with existing words in the language to form new words.

Internal change, in addition to being slower than external change, is more predictable. This is because internal change generally takes advantage of the structural possibilities that already exist in a language. Social pressures also affect the rate and direction of language change. If certain sounds come to be associated with particular social or cultural groups, then this will also affect the ways that such changes are adopted and spread throughout a language.

There are many factors that influence the rate at which language changes. Attitudes toward change, exposure to speakers of other languages, and the presence or absence of a writing system are just a few factors. As languages change, new varieties of those languages can develop. When two or more different varieties develop from a single language, at first they are considered to be dialects of that language. At the point at which they become different enough from each other that speakers can no longer understand one another, the varieties are said to be distinct languages. Language varieties that develop from a single language in this way are said to be genetically related. The language they developed from is called a mother language and the new languages are called daughter languages. Related languages are said to belong to the same family of languages. The difference between a language and a dialect is a matter of where in the process of change a particular variety may be, as well as of the attitudes that speakers may have toward the way that they speak and toward the way that their way of speaking identifies them as a unique group. Attitudes toward languages and dialects are complexly intertwined with attitudes toward the speakers of those languages and/or dialects.

Research into language families took off in the nineteenth century. Language families such as Indo-European were identified and techniques were developed for reconstructing the original protolanguages from which each family of languages might have evolved. Attempts have been made to use the vocabularies of reconstructed protolanguages to determine how ancient peoples lived, as well as where they may have lived. In some cases, it is possible to determine when two or more languages split apart. The technique is called glottochronology (or lexicostatistics), and some of the results correlate well with archaeological data.

Understanding situations of language contact helps us to understand the processes of language change. Pidgins are languages that result from specific kinds of language contact. Used almost exclusively in trading situations, pidgins are usually short-lived and incomplete. If a complete language evolves from a pidgin, it is called a creole. A creole can be the primary language of a population of speakers. Creoles are generally classified with the language families from which their grammars are derived, even though they "sound" more like the languages from which most of their words have been borrowed. This can result in confusion about the heritage of a creole language, as well as prejudice about the linguistic abilities of the speakers of that language. Pidgins and creoles provide important insights into how languages change. Some scholars also think that pidgins and creoles provide a window into the origins of human language, arguing that pidgins reveal whatever grammar is innately shared by all humans.

Another result of language contact is the development of bilingualism, or the ability to speak two languages. In the contemporary world, many individuals are bilingual or even multilingual. Much depends on attitudes about speaking more than one language and attitudes about the specific language varieties that are spoken. In situations where one of the languages spoken is devalued, bilingualism will be transitional because individuals will gradually abandon the language that is more poorly regarded. Where the different languages spoken are more equally valued, or are associated with ethnic or national identities, bilingualism is more likely to remain stable, and people learn to switch between their various languages as needed.

Diglossia refers to a situation in which more than one variety of the same language is used in one speech community. Generally, each variety is used in a specific kind of setting, such as a formal setting as opposed to a more casual one. Codeswitching is the term used to describe the way that people switch between different varieties of a language or between different languages. In general, choosing how and when to use any specific language variety is a way of signaling membership in a particular social class, ethnic group, or national identity. Language, and ideas about language, can be used to drive groups apart or hold them together. But it is important to remember that as languages change, so do attitudes toward languages, and, as attitudes change, so do the choices that people make about what they will speak, and with whom, and when.

KEY TERMS

assimilation
bilingualism
bioprogram
codeswitching
cognates
correspondence sets
creole
diglossia
external change
family of languages
genetically related languages
glottochronology
internal change
language isolates
lexicostatistics
lexifier language
macrofamilies
majority rules strategy
mass comparison
official language
palatalization
phonetic plausibility strategy
phyla
pidgin
reanalysis
related dialects
related languages
stable bilingualism
transitional bilingualism
voicing

FURTHER READING

About Language Change and Reconstructing Languages

Arlotto, Anthony. 1972. *Introduction to historical linguistics*. Amsterdam: John Benjamins. This is an excellent presentation of the methods of historical-comparative reconstruction.

Campbell, Lyle 1999. *Historical linguistics.* Cambridge, MA: MIT Press. This is a more recent treatment than Arlotto's and also highly recommended.

About Language Families and Language Evolution

Lyovin, Anatole V. 1997. *An introduction to the languages of the world.* Oxford: Oxford University Press. This is a great introduction to the variety of languages in the world, explaining genetic, typological, and sociological classification systems. It also includes a chapter on pidgins and creoles.

Ruhlen, Merritt. 1994. *The origin of language: Tracing the evolution of the mother tongue.* New York: John Wiley & Sons. This is a good introduction to the mass-comparison method.

About Pidgins, Creoles, and the Ebonics Controversy

Baugh, John. 2000. *Beyond Ebonics: Linguistic pride and racial prejudice.* New York: Oxford University Press. This book includes the origins of the term and insights into the linguistic and political issues surrounding the controversy.

Monaghan, Leila, Leanne Hinton, and Ron Kephart. 1997. Can't teach a dog to be a cat? The dialogue on Ebonics. *Anthropology Newsletter* 38(3): 1, 8, 9. Linguistic anthropologists weigh in on the Ebonics controversy.

Morgan, Marcyliena, ed. 1994. *Language and the social construction of identity in creole situations.* Special publication #10. Los Angeles: Center for Afro-American Studies, UCLA. This is a feisty collection of essays exploring creoles in the Caribbean, Hawai'i, Papua New Guinea, and the United States; it provides important insights into diaspora, ethnicity, nationalism, identity, and language loyalty.

Thomason, Sarah G. 2001. *Language contact: An introduction.* Washington, DC: Georgetown University Press. This is a detailed study of what happens when languages come into contact, ranging from borrowing to pidginization and covering bilingual situations, as well. It is technical but readable.

About Language, Power, and Identity

Jaffe, Alexandra. 1999. *Ideologies in action: Language politics on Corsica.* New York: Mouton de Gruyter. This is a prize-winning study of local resistance to language shift and language dominance on the French island of Corsica.

Smitherman, Geneva. 2000. *Talkin that talk: Language, culture, and education in African America.* New York: Routledge. This is a collection of

Smitherman's essays on Ebonics, language, and power and an introduction to the perspective of critical linguistics.

Zentella, Ana Celia. 1997. *Growing up bilingual: Children in El Barrio.* New York: Basil Blackwell. This is an excellent study of bilingualism.

 STUDENT ACTIVITIES

Readings

The workbook/reader for this book has readings that can help you to further explore and understand the issues introduced in this chapter. The readings provide insights into issues of classification, choice, and change in language.

Exercises

A set of writing exercises in the workbook/reader will assist you in understanding the issues introduced in this chapter and in practicing some of the techniques introduced in the chapter.

Web Exercises

The companion website for this book has a series of links designed to help you explore the issues introduced in this chapter in greater depth and to better understand them. The companion website also contains study questions that will help you to review important concepts.

Guided Projects

If you are creating a language, you may want to take some time to borrow a few words from another language-creating group in your class and to assess the impact those borrowed words have on your language. Or you may want to consider entering into a bilingual arrangement with another group in your class and to assess the impact that situation has on identity, choice, and language retention for both groups. If you are working with a conversation partner, your instructor may assign a writing project to identify the language families that your two languages belong to and to explore and compare some of the attributes of each language family. Your instructor will be your guide.

CHAPTER 10

Doing Linguistic Anthropology

"So you can't define harassment?" said the professor from education.

We were gathered together, at the request of the university provost, to write a university policy prohibiting racial and ethnic harassment. We had already broadened the charge to include harassment based on gender, national origin, religious preference, and sexual orientation. The question we had to deal with, however, was whether we could even define *harassment*. As a diverse group of faculty and staff, we all agreed that we "knew" harassment when we saw it, but we were having difficulty with the definition.

"If you *feel* harassed then you *are* harassed," said my colleague from sociology. "It's like if I *feel* that you are harassing me then you *are*."

"But what if I don't *mean* to harass you?" said my colleague from education. "Doesn't there need to be intent?"

"Well," I jumped in, "if someone feels harassed, then something *has* to have happened. The point is to find out *what*. That way, if you wanted to, you could avoid harassing that person again."

"But, if each case of harassment is completely individual and up to the person who feels harassed, then we can't define *harassment*, except on a case-by-case basis. It means no one can ever say anything to anyone else for fear of harassing them."

"Yes, I understand the difficulty," I said, "but, if we are going to write a policy, then we need to be able to write a definition. Maybe linguistic anthropology can help us," I continued. "There's lots of recent research into how the context of a situation can affect the meanings that words take on."

"Yes, we'll need to find a way to take context into account if we're going to be able to frame a definition of *harassment*," my colleagues agreed. "You're definitely going to be on the subcommittee assigned to come up with a definition!"

So there I was, "doing linguistic anthropology" again.

HJO

As you probably realize by now, "doing linguistic anthropology" can cover a wide range of activities. It can involve everything from collecting word lists and analyzing grammatical systems to translating across cultural and linguistic boundaries. It can range from reconstructing ancient languages or exploring language origins to helping revive a dying language. While some linguistic anthropologists are testing the reaches of linguistic relativity, others may be searching for universal grammatical patterns. While some linguistic anthropologists work with speakers of little-studied languages to construct dictionaries and grammars, others describe the politics and economics of codeswitching in contemporary speech communities. As a part of the broader field of anthropology, linguistic anthropology is concerned with all aspects of language, from technical to social and cultural.

The range of things that we linguistic anthropologists do is so broad that it is impossible to cover all of it in this chapter, let alone in this book. Some of us get involved in language planning, helping government officials to understand the complexities of establishing official languages for example. Some of us get involved in accent evaluation, helping people to change their accents, develop special ones for theater presentations, or understand how different accents convey different things about race, place, and identity (often unintentionally) to listeners. Some of us are interested in working with educators and helping to develop bilingual programs (transitional or continuing), to establish language training programs, or to explore the way children learn to read in one or more languages. Some of us get involved in translation and interpretation, bringing an understanding of the cultural contexts to the translations we produce. Some of us are called on to testify as expert witnesses in courtrooms, whether the issue is identifying a speaker through the analysis of taped examples of speech, or interpreting intent by analyzing paralinguistic cues, or helping a jury to understand issues of dialect discrimination. There are so many different ways that linguistic anthropology can be used and so many careers that make use of linguistic anthropology skills that it is almost impossible to list them all here. In this chapter, we present a sampling—but just a sampling—of the kinds of things that linguistic anthropologists are doing today. The companion website for this book maintains a section on doing linguistic anthropology today, where there is information on careers in linguistic anthropology, current issues in linguistic anthropology, and ideas and suggestions for ways that you can apply the linguistic anthropology skills that you have gained from this book.

 WEBLINK   To read about careers using linguistic anthropology, go to http://anthropology.wadsworth.com/ottenheimer_language.

I find occasions to use my linguistic anthropology almost every day. I once used ethnosemantics to analyze a complex collegewide curriculum change proposal, building tree diagrams to elucidate how the new sets of requirements categorized courses differently from the old ones. The old requirements had categorized symbolic logic courses as philosophy, since they were taught in the Philosophy Department. The new requirements suggested counting symbolic logic courses as part of a broader quantitative and symbolic reasoning requirement. People were amazed at the clarity that the diagrams brought to the discussion, but it was a simple process of taking the words we were using (*humanities, social sciences, quantitative and symbolic reasoning,* and so on) as indications of nodes and branches in a semantic tree. My students once did the same thing on a more spatial-visual basis, analyzing the various food-service sections of the campus cafeteria to explore how sections that had more choices (indicating cultural emphasis) could be broken down into multiple sections, thus improving the flow of traffic and making lines shorter.

Recently, an actor in a local community theater group asked me to help him develop a Greek "accent" for the character he was portraying. I looked up a phonetic chart for Greek and, just like I ask my students to do comparative phonetic analyses with their conversation partners, I compared the chart for Greek with a chart for American English. I made a list of possible shifts that my actor friend might make and we spent an afternoon going through the script together, trying the different pronunciations to see what would work and what would sound overly stereotyped. We especially wanted to avoid creating any negative stereotypes. We also didn't want to develop an overly strong accent. We really only wanted to achieve a hint of an accent, so audiences would imagine the character to be a recent immigrant, which was what the role called for. Even though the accent we developed was very subtle, we got a lot of comments from audience members on how "authentic" the character seemed. We had fun, and it was another way for me to apply my own linguistic anthropology skills to something very different.

Understanding, and even helping out, in situations where people misunderstand one another due to different speech practices is another way to "do linguistic anthropology." In classrooms and committee meetings, at conferences or at weddings, wherever people of different backgrounds gather, there is always going to be some degree of misunderstanding based on language use. Interceding and explaining can go a long way toward smoothing over those misunderstandings and toward helping people to understand some of the different expectations associated with language use. One of my former students just wrote the following to me about his wedding in New York: "Our wedding was a huge success. We managed to get most of my family from western Kansas to the Bronx for the ritual. I remember [your] linguistic comparison between New Yorkers and Midwesterners and was delighted to watch [your] predictions play out in relation to the different . . . linguistic styles. I was especially impressed with the sheer volume and speed with which the New Yorkers

Doing Linguistic Anthropology 10.1

LANGUAGE REVITALIZATION IN OKLAHOMA

The Apache Tribe of Oklahoma has only three elderly members who still speak their language, Ná'ishą. In the 1990s, the tribe established projects to document and revitalize their language. I began working with them on these endeavors, assisting with the recording, transcribing, and archiving of language materials. Younger members of the tribe, most of whom had heard Ná'ishą while growing up, also came to the language sessions and also worked to record and use the language.

The results of having the younger members at the language sessions and their dedication to the task of learning this language have shown that perseverance can lead to positive outcomes. Between 1996 and the present, the language sessions have led to one younger man becoming partially fluent in the language—he can understand what is said in Ná'ishą to a great extent and can speak in simple sentences, with a few pauses and gaps here and there—and four others gaining the ability to understand spoken Ná'ishą. The members who now understand Ná'ishą are working on their speaking skills, in hopes of reaching some level of fluency.

Recording and documenting the language also are key to providing resources for those interested in learning the language at a later date. Tapes and transcripts also make it possible for the session attendees to review what they heard and learned at each session. We are working on creating introductory and advanced language materials in Ná'ishą based on the data present in the recordings. With any luck, at least a few younger speakers of Ná'ishą will result from the concerted work of the dedicated tribal members.

Pamela J. Innes, *University of Wyoming*

spoke to each other" (Wygal, personal communication, 2004). Opportunities to apply linguistic anthropology are just about everywhere. Now that you have made it through a class on linguistic anthropology, you will probably be much more aware of many of these opportunities.

WORKING WITH ENDANGERED LANGUAGES

Language revitalization is one example of the important work that linguistic anthropologists are doing today. Language extinction is different from language change. As we saw in the chapter on change and choice, languages are constantly changing and individuals often choose to speak one language or another based on the social, economic, and political "values" that different languages provide. But, if you give up the language of your childhood in order to speak a language that gives you access to a good job, that is different from learning to switch between those two languages, and, if enough people give up their childhood languages, those languages are threatened by extinction. If enough Comorians in Paris give up their Comorian and speak only French, then Comorian will die out in that community. "But Comorian is such a *little* language," said a Comorian-French teenager recently, much to his parents' dismay. "Why continue to speak it?" A brief lecture from the visiting Comorian-speaking linguistic anthropologist on the benefits of bilingualism and the role of language in maintaining cultural worldview was enough to convince him to maintain his Comorian, as well as to add English to his repertoire of languages!

Language extinction occurs when there are no more speakers of a particular language. This may occur gradually, as when fewer and fewer people speak a language, or it may occur all at once, as when all the speakers of a language are wiped out due to disease or colonialism or warfare. Recent research suggests that in the last 500 years the world has lost nearly half of its languages. Contemporary estimates suggest that the rate at which languages are now dying has increased dramatically. Although population size is not a perfect indicator, languages with few speakers are probably at greater risk than languages with millions of speakers. Of the 6,300 languages listed in the *International Encyclopedia of Linguistics,* nearly 500 have less than 100 speakers, approximately 1,500 have fewer than 1,000 speakers, and around 3,300 have fewer than 10,000 speakers! Many linguists consider 20,000 speakers to be essential if a language is to be considered out of danger; this means that nearly 4,000 of the world's languages are currently in some sort of danger. Thus, the world is in danger of losing two-thirds of its languages in the near future.

Language revitalization is the attempt to assist people in maintaining endangered languages. Linguistic anthropologist Akira Yamamoto (1998, 114) lists nine factors that can help to "maintain and promote" small languages: a dominant culture that favors linguistic diversity, a strong sense of ethnic identity among the speakers of the endangered language, educational programs about the endangered language and its culture, bilingual and bicultural programs in schools, training native speakers as language teachers, involving the speech community itself, creating easy-to-use language materials, developing a literature (from traditional as well as new sources), and maintaining environments in which the language is used. Of course, the perceived prestige and power of the community is also important, as is the degree to which speakers are encouraged to maintain their ability to codeswitch. As more and more speakers of small and endangered languages have begun to assert their language rights, linguistic anthropologists have begun committing themselves in increasing numbers to assisting these communities to revive and revitalize their languages. In some cases, it has been possible to revive languages no longer spoken, using the materials collected by linguistic anthropologists over 100 years ago. Working with communities in this way is one very important way to be "doing linguistic anthropology" today.

 WEBLINK To read about language endangerment and revitalization, go to http://anthropology.wadsworth.com/ottenheimer_language.

REVEALING RACIST AND SEXIST LANGUAGE

Recognizing and uncovering bias in language is another area in which linguistic anthropologists have been making significant contributions recently. You would think that racist or sexist language is easy to spot, especially since all the consciousness-raising the United States has gone through since the 1960s. But racist and sexist language is more subtly hidden than many of us realize. Some of it is hidden in grammar—in grammatical assumptions that we make when we construct sentences or choose forms of words. Some of it is hidden in words—in the ways that we name and describe things around us. And some of it is hidden in discourse—in the ways that we talk to each other, in the jokes that we tell, and in the metaphors that we use.

Bias in Grammar

When we use words like *waitress, actress, hostess,* and *bachelorette* or phrases like *light beer, women's basketball,* and *Black history,* we are revealing a hidden bias in the grammar of English. In each of these cases, there is a basic form (*waiter, actor, host, bachelor, beer, basketball, history*) and a special form (*waitress, actress, hostess,* and so on). The grammar therefore pushes us to treat the basic forms as basic, or neutral, or the "norm," and it implies that the special forms are different, special, not normal, not ordinary. In linguistics, this phenomenon is called **marking,** or indicating linguistically a nonneutral form of a word. We have to be careful here because we know that a word like *waiter* is not really neutral. But the language treats it as if it is neutral, and that is what is important for this discussion.

When we talk about the phenomenon of marking, we say that there are "marked" and "unmarked" forms. The **unmarked forms** are the ones that the language treats as neutral or base forms; the **marked forms** are the ones that are derived from the base forms. In the pair *waiter/waitress,* *waiter* is the unmarked (neutral, base, default) form, *waitress* is the marked form, and the morpheme {*-ess*} is the marker that derives the marked from the unmarked form. In the pair *history/Black history, history* is the unmarked form, *Black history* is the marked form, and the word *Black* serves as the marker to indicate that it is a special kind of history that is being described. In most cases like this, the unmarked forms are the ones that designate men, men's activities, and even (as in our *history* example) White men. The marked forms are generally those that designate women, women's activities, and non-White activities and subject matter. So English grammar carries a hidden bias, and English speakers are rarely aware of it.

Lots of languages do this kind of marking. In Spanish, the unmarked form *professor* is marked for femininity by the addition of an {-*a*} ending. As a result, if I go to a Spanish-speaking country, I expect to be called *professora*. In Czech, the feminine form is *profesorka*. In addition, Czech women have the suffix {-*ová*} added to their names to designate 'femaleness.' This means that while I was teaching in Prague I was known as *Profesorka Ottenheimerová*. It took a bit of getting used to. Languages that mark gender in this way may be encoding attitudes about gender. This is why, in the 1960s, feminists in the United States began to argue that marked forms should be done away with, in the hope that a change of language would promote a change in attitude. Today most actresses call themselves *actors,* hostesses have become *hosts,* and waitresses have become *waiters* or *servers.* (I especially enjoyed the waiter in New Orleans who introduced herself as a *waitroid!*)

Bias in Words

If the last sentence caused you to stop and reread, that's because I used the word *waiter* to refer to a woman. In spite of over forty years of change, the word *waiter*—at least on the printed page and with no other clues—still seems to imply a man and not a woman. The fact is that there are plenty of words like this in English that, even though they are intended to cover individuals of any gender, seem to imply primarily men. Words such as *he* and *man* are supposed to mean both men and women, but they really don't. If they did, then a sentence like *Anyone in Oklahoma can ask for an abortion if he wants one* would make good sense. But the sentence doesn't really work, and it's because the bottom line is that the word *he* really does bring to mind a man and not a woman. The interesting thing about switching to neutral terms like *waiter* and *actor* is that in a language like English, with its hidden grammatical bias, these neutral terms end up denoting men more than women, and the women are at risk of disappearing linguistically. Other words that suggest hidden bias in English are *flesh-toned* for bandages that match the skin tones of European-Americans and *qualified* when referring to a minority or female applicant.

Bias in Discourse

Some of the most fascinating current research into hidden bias in language is the work of linguistic anthropologist Jane Hill, whose studies of "pejorative" or "mock" Spanish reveal how racism can be unconsciously carried along in a language for a long time. Mock Spanish is a form of language play that occurs primarily among Anglos. It includes jokey expressions such as *no problemo* or *hasta la pasta* or *numero two-oh,* as well as more aggressively negative expressions as *hasta la vista, baby* (as heard, for example, in the *Terminator* movies). Hill's study reveals that these kinds of expressions seem funny or aggressive primarily because, for their Anglo speakers, they access hidden negative stereotypes of Spanish speakers and, in particular, of Mexicans and Mexican Americans. There are probably other examples of such stereotyping of less powerful ethnic or racial groups through language play, and they deserve to be studied as well. The mock African American dialects that are attributed to the fun-loving characters in Hollywood cartoons (think, for example, of the crab character in *The Little Mermaid* or the crows in *Dumbo*) are probably good examples of the same sort of hidden linguistic racism. So is the mock Western dialect of the poacher character in *The Rescuers* ("purty feather, boy"). Becoming aware of these kinds of hidden bias ought to help us to understand much more about the very subtle ways that our language can influence our thinking. As Hill (1995) says, "linguistic anthropologists are especially well-qualified, by the power and subtlety of the analytical tools that are available to us today, to make progress in these matters that are so important to the health of our society."

 WEBLINK   To read about Mock Spanish online article, go to http://anthropology.wadsworth.com/ottenheimer_language.

✳ LINGUISTIC ANTHROPOLOGY TODAY

The field of linguistic anthropology has grown and changed in its 100-plus years of existence. In the earliest days of the field, the emphasis was on collecting and cataloging languages. Working to move beyond racist theories of language evolution, linguistic anthropologists stressed the differences among language, race, and culture. In the United States, especially, linguistic anthropologists strove to document many of the Native American languages that appeared—in many cases due to U.S. government policies—to be in danger of dying out. Texts and word lists were collected, phonological and syntactic systems were analyzed, and dictionaries and grammars were published. Although it was clear that language and culture could be separate entities, linguistic anthropologists also recognized the complex relationships between the two. Of special interest was learning how grammatical systems might influence ways of thinking about the world and how semantic systems might reflect particular cultural foci.

Over time, linguistic anthropologists have turned their attention even more intently to the social and cultural contexts in which language is

Doing Linguistic Anthropology 10.2

LANGUAGE AND IDENTITY IN CORSICA

Fieldwork—Four scenes:

1. I am in my neighbor Marie's kitchen, and a conversation is going on around me in Corsican. I understand most of it and make verbal and visual signs that I do. Marie's husband, however, does not acknowledge my comprehension and addresses me systematically in French.
2. My husband is in another neighbor's kitchen, surrounded by elderly ladies who begin by speaking French in order to include him but end up speaking Corsican, even though he does not understand anything they say in this language.
3. It is early evening, and I am sitting outside with friends from the village where I live. A car pulls up; relatives or friends step out for a moment to say hello and to shake a few hands. I am introduced as the "American who speaks Corsican just like us."
4. I am in a literary gathering, and there is a question and answer period at the end. An acquaintance of mine, also an author, is sitting next to me. He keeps prompting me in whispers to ask a question in Corsican. I decline. He finally raises his own hand, identifies me as an American who speaks Corsican and therefore shows that it can be learned, and says I want to ask a question.

In all of these situations, we see Corsicans involved in constructing and defining the social meaning(s) of outsiders' linguistic competence in the minority language. In the first context, Marie's husband could not "hear" my competence over the noise of my status as a for-

used, studying the complex ways that words (and speech acts in general) derive meanings from the situations in which they are uttered. Questions of identity, power, and access have become the focus of much research. The act of speaking has come under increased scrutiny as linguistic anthropologists work to understand how language is learned and used in different speech communities. To whom are we speaking? When and where? Using which variety of language? With what goals in mind? With what effect? Linguistic anthropologists have worked to uncover many of the subtle and unconscious ways in which language, both spoken and signed, is learned and used in different cultures and in different social situations.

Renewed attention to the origins of language; to the potential role of language in the evolution of humans; and to historical, genetic, and ty-

eigner. Corsican for him was an intimate code linked with Corsican identity; I was not Corsican so I could not possibly speak it. My husband's experience, on the other hand, shows how the attribution of intimacy can override knowledge of linguistic "incompetence." For the ladies he was sitting with, my husband was not "stranger" enough to keep their habitual language of interaction—Corsican—at bay. In the third scenario, a scene replayed over and over again for me, my intimates systematically exaggerated my Corsican competence in recognition of my effort to speak and in recognition of my status as "their" American. Language competence, in this instance, was available as a discourse of inclusion, a discourse of identity. Even though I was always slightly embarrassed by these remarks, and the inevitable request to perform in Corsican that followed them, I recognized them as inclusive and benevolent.

From this perspective, the fourth scenario was rather different as an experience for me because the setting was no longer an intimate one and, therefore, the meaning of my forced performance was not about my social inclusion. Rather, it was an element in a moral and political discourse directed at Corsicans by other Corsicans. The message was: There is no excuse for not speaking the language of identity; this language is accessible to you if you make an effort. While it was, of course, perfectly true that francophone Corsicans could take the same classes and read the same books as I had to learn Corsican, the implications of that process of apprenticeship was very different for them than it was for me. This is because of the strength of the ideological link between being and speaking Corsican. Being Corsican and being a novice speaker was a source of identity dissonance and social ambiguity. It was only later that I found the words to express this in these kinds of situations.

Alexandra Jaffe, California State University—Long Beach

pological relationships among languages has brought important new insights into the ways that language changes over time and space. In turn, these new understandings of language origins and change has brought increased clarity to understanding how the possession of a writing system, and the ability to read and write, can affect the chances that any particular language has to survive and spread, as well as to the choices that people make about language loyalty and identity. Understanding the implications of these decisions has become as important to linguistic anthropology as describing and analyzing the actual words that people use when they speak.

There are a great many ways to "do linguistic anthropology" and this book has introduced you to a representative sampling of them. As the field of linguistic anthropology continues to evolve, additional applications will certainly emerge. Language is all around us, and in some sense each of us is doing linguistic anthropology all of the time. The workbook/reader associated with this book can give you practice with some of the more technical aspects of the field; it also provides some recent and classic readings that can help to expand your understanding of the issues. The companion website can point you to additional readings, as well as to examples of new and exciting research discoveries and applications of linguistic anthropology. The more you understand the field, the more empowered you will be in applying what you have learned.

Today, language is understood to be a cultural resource with economic, historical, and political value and speaking is understood to be a cultural practice, learned and used in specific speech communities and in specific situations. Because it is the branch of anthropology that focuses its lens on language, linguistic anthropology addresses *all* these issues. It is, in the deepest sense, an anthropology of language.

 WEBLINK To get more information about the Society for Linguistic Anthropology, go to http://anthropology.wadsworth.com/ottenheimer_language.

SUMMARY

Doing linguistic anthropology covers a wide range of activities. Indeed, the field of linguistic anthropology covers many different areas of inquiry. This is, in part, because of the four-field nature of anthropology itself and the complex ways in which linguistic anthropology is a part of anthropology and intersects with the other parts of anthropology. Linguistic anthropology is concerned with all aspects of language, including the technical, the social, and the cultural.

Opportunities to use your linguistic anthropology are just about everywhere. Wherever and whenever you encounter a social situation in which language is being used, you can begin to practice your new skills. This book has provided you with a set of tools and an understanding of how to use them. From learning new languages to helping bridge cross-language misunderstandings, your new linguistic anthropology skills are there for you.

You may also want to read more, or become involved in, some of the contemporary work that linguistic anthropologists are doing. Language revitalization is an important example of this kind of current work. With languages dying out at an alarmingly rapid rate, many small communities of speakers have begun to take action to protect and rejuvenate their endangered languages. Another important area of research and action is learning to recognize and uncover the hidden biases in your own language. Understanding how language conceals and perpetuates stereotypes can help you to take greater control of your own speech acts, as well as to understand the issues of power and identity that often surround language.

Linguistic anthropology has grown and changed during its evolution as a field of study. Consistently in tune with the four-field approach of anthropology, especially in the United States, linguistic anthropology has maintained a sharp focus on understanding both the structure of language and the social and cultural contexts in which language is used. It connects research about language origins and signed languages with research about language learning and development. It connects research about language contact and language change with research about culture, power, identity, and linguistic choice. Seeking connections is one of the strong points of linguistic anthropology. Linguistic anthropology draws on all four subfields of anthropology, as well as on other fields of study, in order to understand language as a human phenomenon.

KEY TERMS

language extinction
language revitalization
marked forms
marking
unmarked forms

FURTHER READING

About Endangered Languages and Language Revitalization

Crystal, David. 2000. *Language death.* Cambridge: Cambridge University Press. This is a small book with a big message. It reviews the reasons why language death is such an important topic and what is being done about it.

Hinton, Leanne. 1994. *Flutes of fire: Essays on California Indian languages.* Berkeley, CA: Heyday Books. This is a collection of essays on California Indian languages, what clues they provide to ancient migrations and contemporary cultures, and what different groups are doing to revive their languages and pass them along to the next generation.

Hinton, Leanne, and Kenneth Hale. 2001. *The green book of language revitalization in practice: Toward a sustainable world.* San Diego, CA: Academic Press. This is a collection of articles describing a variety of successful revitalization projects.

Hinton, Leanne, Matt Vera, and Nancy Steele. 2002. *How to keep your language alive: A commonsense approach to one-on-one language learning.*

Berkeley, CA: Heyday Books. This manual, with exercises, will be of use to speakers and learners of any endangered language.

Nettle, Daniel, and Suzanne Romaine. 2000. *Vanishing voices: The extinction of the world's languages.* New York: Oxford University Press. This is an excellent overview of endangered languages, arguing that language death is part of the larger question of environmental destruction—a passionate call to arms.

About Racism and Sexism in Language

Lakoff, Robin. 2001. *The language war.* Berkeley: University of California Press. This is a superb discussion of language and power, showing how control of language affects access to power, with examples from recent news events.

Lippi-Green, Rosina. 1997. *English with an accent: Language, ideology, and discrimination in the United States.* London: Routledge. This is a great discussion of how the media and entertainment industries in the United States promote linguistic stereotyping and how discrimination based on accent supports and perpetuates unequal power relations.

Van Dijk, Teun. 1987. *Communicating racism: Ethnic prejudices in thought and talk.* Newbury Park, CA: Sage. This is a readable study of the ways that racism is hidden in everyday communication.

About Linguistic Anthropology Today

Duranti, Alessandro. 1997. *Linguistic anthropology.* Cambridge: Cambridge University Press. This is an advanced-level discussion of the field today emphasizing its focus on language as a cultural resource and on speaking as a cultural practice. It includes a good short summary of the history of linguistic anthropology.

 STUDENT ACTIVITIES

Readings

The workbook/reader for this book has readings that can help you to further explore and understand the issues introduced in this chapter.

Exercises

A set of writing exercises in the workbook/reader will assist you in understanding the issues introduced in this chapter.

Web Exercises

The companion website for this book has a series of links designed to help you explore the issues introduced in this chapter in greater depth and to better understand them. The companion website also contains study questions that will help you to review important concepts.

Guided Projects

If you are creating a language, now is the time to prepare a skit for your classmates using your language and to give your group's project book to your instructor for final grading. If you are working with a conversation partner, now is the time to begin making your goodbyes and to make arrangements to stay in touch if you have become good friends. Your instructor will be your guide.

GLOSSARY

acoustic phonetics   the branch of phonetics that studies the physical properties of sounds and the nature of the sound waves that they produce

acquire language   map the details of a specific language onto an innate universal grammar

act sequence   the actual sequence of events in a speech act

adaptor   a gesture that facilitates the release of body tension

affect display   a gesture that conveys emotion

affix   a morpheme that attaches to a base (to form new words)

affricate   the combination of a stop followed by a fricative

allokine   a variant form of a kineme

allomorph   a variant form of a morpheme

allophones   variant forms of phonemes; members of a group of sounds that together form a single phoneme

alphabetic writing   a system in which graphic signs represent individual consonants and vowels

alveolar   a sound modified with the tip of the tongue and the alveolar (gum) ridge

alveopalatal   a sound modified with the tip of the tongue behind the alveolar (gum) ridge

American Usage System   a set of phonetic symbols that can easily be typed; developed by Kenneth Pike and used by many American linguistic anthropologists

anthropology   the study of humans in all times and places; a holistic, comparative, and fieldwork-based discipline, anthropology seeks to understand differences and to discover similarities in human behavior

approximant   a sound in which there is only a small amount of obstruction in the air flow

arbitrariness a design feature of language referring to the fact that there is no necessary or causal connection between a signal and its meaning

articulated for sounds, characterized by being modified in the vocal tract

articulatory phonetics the branch of phonetics that studies how speech sounds are produced

assimilation the phonetic process in which the point (or manner) of articulation of a sound changes so it is closer to that of a neighboring sound

auditory phonetics the branch of phonetics that studies how sounds are perceived

awareness in rich point analysis, the recognition that different expectations have caused a rich point to occur

base a morpheme to which an affix can be attached; a base can be either a root or a stem, and it serves as a foundation for building other words

behaviorist theories applied to language learning, theories that children need to hear language from others around them (stimulus) and to receive praise (positive feedback) from parents and/or caretakers in order to develop their linguistic abilities

bilabial a sound modified with two lips

bilingualism the ability to speak two languages

bioprogram an innate grammar, thought by some to guide children in constructing creole languages from pidgins

blending mixing two signals to form a new one

bound morpheme a morpheme that must be attached to another morpheme

broadcast transmission and directional reception a design feature of language referring to the sending out of sounds in all directions and the perception of the direction from which sounds are coming

Broca's area the area in the frontal region of the left cerebral hemisphere named for Paul Broca, who first located it and proposed its connection with language

case   a way of marking how a noun functions in a sentence (for example, as the subject or object of the sentence)

categorization system   the way a language categorizes items

cerebral hemispheres   the two halves of the human brain

circumfix   a morpheme that attaches simultaneously to the beginning and the end of a base form (part of the circumfix attaches at the beginning and part of it at the end)

clicks   voiceless stops in which the air is released inward rather than outward

codeswitching   using more than one variety of language in a single situation or sometimes in different situations

cognates   sets of words in related languages that can be shown to have descended from a common ancestral language; cognates have similar meanings, and they show regular sound correspondences

cognitive anthropology   an anthropological approach in which vocabulary is analyzed to learn about systems of meaning and perception (same as ethnoscience, ethnosemantics)

cognitivist theories   applied to language learning, theories that suggest that children develop language simultaneously with their mental abilities

communication   the sending of signals *or* the sending and receiving of signals *or* the sending and receiving of signals and the evoking of a response

communicative competence   the ability to speak a language well; the ability to use a language correctly in a variety of social situations

community of practice   a group of individuals who interact regularly, developing unique ways of doing things together

comparative   in anthropology, characterized by gathering and comparing information from many cultures, times, and places, often in an effort to discover possible underlying similarities and differences

complementary distribution   a pattern in which different variants (or allophones) of a phoneme are distributed between complementary (differing) word environments (same as conditioned variation)

complete writing system   a system that can record any and all thoughts and words

complex alternative sign language a gestural system used instead of a spoken language in situations where speech is not possible

componential analysis a method for revealing the culturally important features by which speakers of a language distinguish different words in a semantic domain (same as feature analysis, contrast analysis)

conditioned variation a pattern in which the different variants (or allophones) of a phoneme are thought of as conditioned (affected) by the sounds around them (same as complementary distribution)

consonants sounds with audible constriction in the air flow

context the larger cultural and social situation in which speech acts take place

contrast analysis *see* componential analysis

corpus callosum the membrane that connects the cells of the two cerebral hemispheres

correspondence sets in linguistic reconstruction, sets of sounds that appear to correspond to one another

cortex the convoluted surface of the brain

creole a complete language that has emerged out of a pidgin

cultural emphasis an important aspect of a culture, often reflected in the vocabulary

cultural relativity the idea that differences exist among cultural systems, that different cultural systems can make as much sense as your own, and that it is possible to learn to understand different cultural systems

cupped hand a sign language prime in which the hand is shaped like a cup

deep structure in a generative grammar, the underlying grammar, produced by phrase structure rules, that allows you to produce sentences

derivation the process of creating new words (for example, *catty* from *cat*)

descriptive grammar a grammar that is designed to describe the structure and patterning of a language on its own terms

descriptive phonetics *see* articulatory phonetics

design features of language a set of features proposed by Charles Hockett by which human language can be identified and distinguished from other forms of animal communication

determinative a sign added to another sign to clarify meaning or create new words

diacritics a special set of phonetic symbols used to indicate additional modification of sounds, such as tilde for nasalization or colon for lengthening

dialects of a language specific varieties or subdivisions of a language; ways of speaking that are characteristic of a particular group of people; the varieties are mutually intelligible

diglossia the situation where two (or more) varieties of the *same* language are used by speakers in different settings

discreteness a design feature of language referring to the fact that the units used for communication can be separated into distinct units that cannot be mistaken for one another

displacement a design feature of language referring to the fact that you can talk about things that are not present

duality of patterning a design feature of language referring to the fact that discrete units of language at one level (such as the level of sounds) can be combined to create different kinds of units at a different level (such as words)

emblem a gesture with a direct verbal translation

emics the level of cultural analysis that focuses on subjectively relevant, internally verifiable units of culture

ends the reasons for which a speech event is taking place; the goals that people have for speaking in a particular situation

ethnocentrism not understanding different systems on their own terms, using your own cultural system to interpret other cultural systems, and believing that your own cultural system makes more sense than any other

ethnography an anthropological study of a culture

ethnography of communication an ethnography that focuses on describing and analyzing the ways that people use language in real situations (same as ethnography of speaking)

ethnography of speaking   *see* ethnography of communication

ethnoscience   *see* cognitive anthropology

ethnoscientific model   the image that speakers are said to have of the world; can be built by analyzing vocabulary (same as mental map)

ethnosemantics   *see* cognitive anthropology

etics   the level of cultural analysis that focuses on objectively identifiable, externally observable units of culture

external change   a linguistic change that occurs due to language contact and borrowing between speakers of different languages

family of languages   a set of languages thought to have descended from a common ancestor

feature analysis   *see* componential analysis

fieldwork   in cultural and linguistic anthropology, gathering information by living in another culture and learning the language from its speakers, adapting and adjusting your frames of reference so that you can understand another culture and language as an "insider"

fist hand   a sign language prime in which the hand is shaped like a fist

flat hand   a sign language prime in which the hand is held flat

four-field tradition   in anthropology, training in the four traditional fields of study archaeology (or historical anthropology), physical (or biological) anthropology, cultural anthropology, and linguistic anthropology

frames of reference   the ways that we see, interpret, and understand the world around us

free morpheme   a morpheme that can stand alone

fricative   a sound made with friction in the air stream

generative grammar   a grammar that is designed to provide rules that can generate (or create) all of the possible sentences of a language

genetically related languages   languages that have descended from the same ancestor language

genres   different kinds of speech acts or events

glottal a sound modified in the glottis (the space between the vocal cords)

glottis the space between the vocal cords

glottochronology the science of measuring time change in language (same as lexicostatistics)

grammatical gender a category into which words (usually nouns) are classified in a language

grapheme the smallest segment of speech that is represented in a writing system

hierarchy in word building, the specific order in which affixes can be attached to bases

holistic characterized by seeing the whole picture, with getting the broadest view possible; in anthropology, refers to the four-field tradition

illustrator a gesture that depicts or illustrates what is said verbally

implosives voiced stops in which the air is released inward rather than outward

index hand a sign language prime in which the index finger is extended outward

indirection making a request without asking directly

infix a morpheme that is inserted into the middle of a base form

inflection the process of modifying existing words (for example, *cats* from *cat*)

innatist theories applied to language acquisition, theories that suggest that language is already hard-wired into the human brain at birth

instrumentalities the channels that are used (speaking, writing, signaling with flags, etc.) as well as the varieties of language that speakers use (language, dialect, and register)

interchangeability a design feature of language referring to the fact that speakers can send and receive identical signals

interdental a sound modified with the tip of the tongue between the teeth

internal change a change that occurs due to the way speakers of a language gradually modify their language over time

International Phonetic Alphabet (IPA) a system of phonetic transcription

interweaving a process in which a morpheme is interspersed throughout a base form

key the mood or spirit in which communication takes place

kineme a minimal unit of visual expression; now also a meaningful unit of visual expression

kinemorph meaningful unit of visual expression (older term)

kinesics the study of body movements, facial expressions, and gestures

labiodental a sound modified with the lower lip against the upper teeth

language acquisition device in innatist theories, the part of the brain that compares specific languages with the core grammar and helps children to make the necessary adjustments as they acquire specific languages

language extinction the situation in which there are no more speakers of a particular language

language isolates languages that cannot be classified into any language family

language revitalization the attempt to assist people in maintaining endangered languages

larynx location of the vocal cords, which modify the air, creating sound waves

learn language discover the details of a specific language by interacting with the individuals who speak it

lengthening in phonetics, holding a sound for a longer period of time

lexeme a unit of writing that is surrounded by white space on a page

lexicostatistics *see* glottochronology

lexifier language language that has contributed the majority of the words in a pidgin or a creole

linguistic anthropology the study of language from an anthropological perspective

linguistic community   a group of people who share a single language variety and focus their identity around it (see speech community)

linguistic competence   a speaker's underlying ability to produce (and recognize) grammatically correct expressions in a language

linguistic determinism   the idea that your language affects, even determines, your ability to perceive and think about things, as well as to talk about them

linguistic relativity   the idea that languages are different, that they are arbitrary systems, and that knowing one language does not allow you to predict how another language will categorize and name the world

logographic writing   a system in which graphic signs represent words or the ideas associated with words

logosyllabic writing   a system in which signs can carry both semantic and phonetic information

lungs   source of air for most speech production

macrofamilies   sets of language families that appear to have descended from a common ancient language (same as phyla)

majority rules strategy   in historical reconstruction, the assumption that, if there is no phonetically plausible reason to choose a particular sound for a reconstruction, then the choice should be based on whichever sound appears most frequently in the correspondence set

manner   how air is modified in speech

M-A-R   in rich point analysis, mistake, awareness, and repair

marked forms   linguistic forms that are considered to be nonneutral in a language and that are derived from neutral or base forms

marking   the linguistic phenomonon of deriving a nonneutral form from a neutral form in a language; the phenomenon of linguistically tagging a word as nonneutral

mass comparison   a technique in which lists of words from large numbers of languages are compared all at once to determine that languages are related rather than using the slow, painstaking reconstruction of protolanguages from languages already known to be related

mental map   *see* ethnoscientific model

minimal pair   a pair of words in which a difference in sound makes a difference in meaning

mistake   in rich point analysis, the recognition that a rich point has occurred

morpheme   the smallest unit of meaning in a language

morphological analysis   the analysis of word structure; it has two parts identifying and describing morphemes, and analyzing the way morphemes are arranged into words

morphology   the analysis of words and how they are structured

mutually intelligible   characterized by speakers of different speech varieties being able to understand one another; if two speech varieties are mutually intelligible, it is assumed they are dialects of the same language

mutually unintelligible   characterized by speakers of different speech varieties not being able to understand one another; if two speech varieties are mutually unintelligible, it is assumed they are separate languages

nasal   a sound in which air resonates and escapes through the nasal cavity

nasalization   in phonetics, letting a sound travel through the nasal cavity instead of the mouth

neocortex   in the brain, the younger and larger part of the cortex

new ethnography   a linguistic-based field method for analyzing the categorization systems of a language

nonverbal communication   the process of transmitting messages without spoken words

norms   the expectations that speakers have about the appropriateness of speech use

obligatory category   a grammatical category that must be expressed when speaking (for example, singular and plural in English and case in Czech)

official language   a language designated as official by government policy

palatal   a sound modified with the middle of the tongue and the hard palate (roof of the mouth)

palatalization   the phonetic process in which the point of articulation of a sound is moved closer to the palate

paralanguage   the sounds that accompany speech but are not directly part of language

partial writing system   a system that is limited in what it can convey

participants   individuals who can or should be involved in various speech events or conversations; also refers to the levels of participation expected of individuals in a speech event

pharyngeal   a sound modified in the pharynx (the area above the vocal cords)

pharynx   the area above the vocal cords in which air resonates on its way to the mouth and nose

phonemes   sounds that function to distinguish one word from another in a language

phonemic chart   a chart that shows just the distinctive sounds (phonemes) of a language

phonemics   the analysis of the way sounds are arranged in languages

phones   the sounds on a phonetic chart

phonetic chart   a chart that shows all of the sounds of a language

phonetic determinatives   in a writing system, signs that help to distinguish words that are pronounced differently by providing phonetic clues

phonetic plausibility strategy   in historical reconstruction, the assumption that the choice among alternative reconstructions should be based on what seems plausible given what is known about the ways that languages change and the relationships between the sounds on a reconstructed phonetic chart

phonetic sign   in a writing system, a graphic mark that represents one or more of the sounds of a language

phonetics   the identification and description of language sounds

phonological rules   in a generative grammar, the rules that assign specific sounds to a surface-level sentence so that it is pronounceable

phonology   the study of language sounds

phrase structure rules   in a generative grammar, the rules that produce sentences at the level of deep structure

phyla   *see* macrofamilies

pictographic "writing"   a system that uses pictures or images to represent things (a partial writing system)

pidgin   a language that has developed, through contact, from two unrelated languages

pitch   the relative height of a sound on a scale of "notes" from low to high

place   where air is modified in speech

plosive   *see* stop

portmanteau   a process in which morphemes blend into one another to form a new word

prefix   a bound morpheme that attaches at the beginning of a base form or stem

prescriptive grammar   a grammar that is designed to serve as a model of "proper" speech

primes   in sign languages, elements of signs corresponding to the phonological elements of a spoken language; they are categorized by hand shape, hand placement, and hand movement

principle of linguistic relativity   the idea, articulated by Whorf, that speakers of different languages have different views of the world

productivity   a design feature of language that allows you to produce and comprehend entirely new utterances that you've never spoken or heard before

proxemics   the study of how people perceive and use space

rapid fading   a design feature of language referring to the fact that spoken language sounds don't last long

reanalysis   the process by which speakers analyze unfamiliar words into familiar-looking components and assign familiar meanings to those components

rebus writing   a writing system that uses a single picture to represent two or more words that sound the same

reduplication   a process that creates an affix from part of an existing base form and then attaches that affix to the base form (as a prefix, suffix, or infix)

registers varieties of a language that are considered appropriate to specific situations (e.g., formal or informal situations)

regulator a gesture that controls or coordinates interaction

related dialects dialects that have developed from a single parent language

related languages languages that have developed from a single ancestral language

repair in rich point analysis, the developing of new sets of expectations to use for communicating

retroflex a sound modified with the tip of the tongue and the hard palate (roof of the mouth)

rich point the kind of moment in which things "go wrong" in a speech situation

root a word, or a morpheme, that serves as the underlying foundation for other words

rounded a vowel produced with lips in round shape

Sapir-Whorf Hypothesis see linguistic determinism (same as Whorf-Sapir Hypothesis, Whorfian Hypothesis)

segments the basic consonants and vowels of a language

semantic determinatives in a writing system, signs that help to distinguish words that are pronounced similarly by providing semantic clues

semantic domain an area of meaning in a language (e.g., plants, or animals)

semantic sign in a writing system, a graphic mark that represents a specific idea or meaning

semanticity a design feature of language referring to the fact that specific sound signals can be directly linked to specific meanings

setting/situation the location in which a conversation or speech event is taking place, as well as the overall psychological feeling of that place

sign language language performed in three-dimensional space; not modeled on any spoken language

S-P-E-A-K-I-N-G   in the ethnography of communication, setting/situation, participants, ends, act sequence, key, instrumentalities, norms, and genres

specialization   a design feature of language referring to the fact that the primary function of language sounds is for linguistic communication

speech acts   the specific utterances that people make during a speech event

speech community   a group of people who share one or more varieties of language and the rules for using those varieties in everyday communication (see linguistic community)

speech event   one or more speech acts involving one or more participants

speech situation   the entire setting or situation in which people speak

speech substitutes   systems of communication in which sound signals substitute for spoken words or parts of words

stable bilingualism   a situation in which individuals and communities maintain their bilingualism on a long-term basis

stem   a word, or a collection of morphemes, that is derived from a root and to which additional affixes can be attached

stop   a sound in which the air is stopped momentarily (same as plosive)

Strong Whorf   a form of linguistic determinism that suggests that language forces you to think and perceive only in certain ways (language is a prison)

substitution frame   grammatical frame into which you can place related words; useful for discovering relationships among groups of words or identifying categories of words in a language

suffix   a bound morpheme that attaches at the end of a base form or stem

supralaryngeal vocal tract   the area above the vocal cords where sound waves take on distinctive shapes and become recognizable speech sounds

suprasegmentals   additional modifications (e.g., nasalization, lengthening, and alteration of pitch) that can be applied to basic consonants and vowels (segments) of a language

surface structure   in a generative grammar, the actual sentences that are produced in a language

syllabic writing   a writing system in which graphic signs represent individual syllables

syntax   the analysis and description of the ways that words are arranged in phrases and sentences

tap   a sound made with one quick tap of the tongue

taxonomy   a chart showing how words in a specific semantic domain are related to one another

the theory theory   applied to language learning, the theory that children observe and interact with the world around them and form theories about language from their experiences

theoretical linguistics   the study of language from a structural point of view, without much attention (if any) to cultural contexts of language use

total feedback   a design feature of language referring to the fact that speakers can hear themselves talk

traditional transmission   a design feature of language referring to the fact that language is learned in social groups

transformational rules   in a generative grammar, the rules that transform deep structure sentences into different formats (for example, from a statement to a question)

transitional bilingualism   a situation in which individuals gradually abandon their bilingualism in favor of speaking a more dominant language

trill   a sound made with many fast taps of the tongue

unmarked forms   linguistic forms that are considered to be neutral or base forms in a language

uvula   the small soft bit of flesh hanging down at the back of the mouth

uvular   a sound modified with the back of the tongue and the uvula

velar   a sound modified with the back of the tongue and the velum

velum   the area between the hard palate (roof of mouth) and the uvula

vocal auditory channel   a design feature of language referring to the fact that speaking and hearing are key aspects of human language

vocal cords   a set of muscles inside the larynx that can be opened (loose and relaxed) or closed (tense and vibrating) to modify the air stream on its way out of the lungs (same as vocal folds)

vocal folds   *see* vocal cords

voiced   for sounds, produced with vocal cords close together and vibrating

voiceless   for sounds, produced with vocal cords open and relaxed

voicing   the phonetic process in which the manner of pronunciation is changed to make a sound voiced

vowels   sounds with minimal constriction in the air flow

Weaker Whorf   a form of linguistic determinism that suggests that language subtly influences the ways that you think and perceive (language is a room)

Wernicke's area   the area in the temporal lobe of the left cerebral hemisphere named for Carl Wernicke, who first located it and proposed its connection with language

Whorfian Hypothesis   *see* Sapir-Whorf Hypothesis

Whorf-Sapir Hypothesis   *see* Sapir-Whorf Hypothesis

writing   the graphic representation of language

BIBLIOGRAPHY

Agar, Michael H. 1986. *Independents declared: The dilemmas of independent trucking*. Washington, DC: Smithsonian Institute Press.

———. 1994. *Language shock: Understanding the culture of conversation*. New York: William Morrow and Company.

Akiyama, Jun. 1997–2003. Japanese syllabary. *Aikiweb*. Available at: http://www.aikiweb.com/language/syllabary.html. Accessed May 13, 2004.

Arlotto, Anthony. 1972. *Introduction to historical linguistics*. Amsterdam: John Benjamins.

Axtell, Roger E. 1997. *Gestures: The do's and taboos of body language around the world*. New York: John Wiley & Sons.

Basso, Keith. 1972. "To give up on words": Silence in Western Apache culture. In *Language and social context*, ed. P. P. Giglioli, 67–86. Harmondsworth, UK: Penguin Books.

———. 1979. *Portraits of the whiteman*. Cambridge: Cambridge University Press.

Baugh, John. 2000. *Beyond Ebonics: Linguistic pride and racial prejudice*. New York: Oxford University Press.

Bender, Margaret. 2002. *Signs of Cherokee culture: Sequoyah's syllabary in Eastern Cherokee life*. Chapel Hill: University of North Carolina Press.

Bengtson, John D., and Merritt Ruhlen. 1994. Global etymologies. In *On the origin of languages: Studies in linguistic taxonomy*, ed. Merritt Ruhlen, 277–336. Stanford, CA: Stanford University Press.

Berlin, Brent, and Paul Kay. 1969. *Basic color terms: Their universality and evolution*. Berkeley: University of California Press.

Birdwhistell, Ray. 1952. *An introduction to kinesics*. Louisville, KY: University of Louisville Press.

Bloomfield, Leonard. 1933. *Language*. New York: Holt, Rinehart & Winston.

Boas, Franz. 1911. Introduction to *Handbook of American Indian languages*. Bureau of American Ethnology, bulletin 40, pt. 1, 1–83. Washington, DC: Smithsonian Institution.

Bohannan, Laura. 1966. Shakespeare in the bush. *Natural History* 75 (August/September): 28–33.

Bourdieu, Pierre. 1977. *Outline of a theory of practice*. Cambridge: Cambridge University Press.

———. 1991. *Language and symbolic power*. Cambridge, MA: Harvard University Press.

Boyarin, Jonathan, ed. 1992. *The ethnography of reading*. Berkeley: University of California Press.

Brenneis, Donald. 1984. Grog and gossip in Bhatgaon: Style and substance in Fiji Indian conversation. *American Ethnologist* 11: 3.

Brenneis, Donald, and Ronald K. S. Macaulay, eds. 1996. *The matrix of language: Contemporary linguistic anthropology*. Boulder, CO: Westview Press.

Bright, William, ed. 1992. *The international encyclopedia of linguistics*. New York: Oxford University Press.

Burling, Robbins. 1964. Cognition and componential analysis: God's truth or hocus-pocus? *American Anthropologist* 66: 20–28.

Campbell, Lyle. 1999. *Historical linguistics*. Cambridge, MA: MIT Press.

Carroll, John B., ed. 1956. *Language, thought and reality: Selected writings of Benjamin Lee Whorf*. New York: Wiley; and Cambridge, MA: MIT Press.

Chomsky, Noam. 1957. *Syntactic structures*. The Hague: Mouton.

———. 1965. *Aspects of the theory of syntax*. Cambridge, MA: MIT Press.

Coe, Michael D. 1992. *Breaking the Maya code*. New York: Thames and Hudson.

Comrie, Bernard. 1989. *Language universals and linguistic typology: Syntax and morphology*. 2nd ed. Chicago: University of Chicago Press.

Condon, John. 1985. *Good neighbors: Communicating with the Mexicans*. Yarmouth, ME: Intercultural Press.

Conklin, Harold C. 1955. Hanunóo color categories. *Southwestern Journal of Anthropology* 11: 339–44.

Corballis, Michael. 2003. *From hand to mouth: The origins of language*. Princeton, NJ: Princeton University Press.

Coulmas, Florian. 2003. *Writing systems: An introduction to their linguistic analysis*. Cambridge: Cambridge University Press.

Crowley, Terry, and Bruce Rigsby. 1979. Cape York Creole. In *Languages and their status*, ed. Timothy Shopen, 153–207. Philadelphia: University of Pennsylvania Press.

Crystal, David. 2000. *Language death*. Cambridge: Cambridge University Press.

Damasio, Antonio R., and Hanna Damasio. 1992. Brain and language. *Scientific American* 267(3): 88–95.

Daniels, Peter T., and William Bright, eds. 1996. *The world's writing systems*. New York: Oxford University Press.

Deacon, Terrence. 1998. *The symbolic species: The co-evolution of language and the brain*. New York: Norton.

DeFrancis, John. 1989: *Visible speech: The diverse oneness of writing systems*. Honolulu: University of Hawaii Press.

Duranti, Alessandro. 1997. *Linguistic anthropology*. Cambridge: Cambridge University Press.

———. 2001a. Linguistic anthropology: History, ideas, and issues. In *Linguistic anthropology: A reader*, ed. Alessandro Duranti, 1–38. Malden, MA: Blackwell.

———, ed. 2001b. *Linguistic anthropology: A reader*. Malden, MA: Blackwell.

Efron, David. 1941. *Gesture and environment: A tentative study of some of the spatio-temporal and "linguistic" aspects of the gestural behavior of eastern Jews and southern Italians in New York City, living under similar as well as different environmental conditions*. New York: King's Crown Press.

Ehret, Christopher. 1982a. The first spread of food production to southern Africa. In *The archaeological and linguistic reconstruction of African history*, ed. Christopher Ehret and Merrick Posnansky, 158–81. Berkeley: University of California Press.

———. 1982b. Linguistic inferences about early Bantu history. In *The archaeological and linguistic reconstruction of African history*, ed. Christopher Ehret and Merrick Posnansky, 57–65. Berkeley: University of California Press.

Ekman, Paul, and Wallace V. Friesen. 1969. The repertoire of nonverbal behavior: Categories, origins, usage, and coding. *Semiotica* 1: 49–98.

Falk, Dean. 1983. Cerebral cortices of East African early hominids. *Science* 221: 1072–74.

Farnell, Brenda. 1995. *Do you see what I mean? Plains Indian Sign Talk and the embodiment of action*. Austin: University of Texas Press.

Fishbach, Gerald D. 1992. Mind and brain. *Scientific American* 267(3): 48–49.

Gazzaniga, Michael S. 1970. *The bisected brain*. New York: Appleton-Century-Crofts.

Gentner, Dedre, and Susan Goldin-Meadow, eds. 2003. *Language in mind: Advances in the study of language and thought*. Cambridge, MA: MIT Press.

Geertz, Clifford. 1960. *The religion of Java*. New York: The Free Press.

Givens, David. 2002. The nonverbal dictionary. Available at: http://members.aol.com/nonverbal2/nvcom.htm/. Accessed May 1, 2004.

Gleason, Henry A. 1955. *Workbook in descriptive linguistics*. New York: Holt, Rinehart & Winston.

Goodall, Jane. 1986. *The chimpanzees of Gombe: Patterns of behavior*. Cambridge, MA: Belknap.

Goodenough, Ward. 1957. Cultural anthropology and linguistics. In *Report of the Seventh Annual Round Table Meeting on Linguistics and Language Study*, ed. Paul L. Garvin, 167–73. Monograph Series on Languages and Linguistics, no. 9. Washington, DC: Georgetown University Press.

Goody, Jack. 2000. *The power of the written tradition*. Washington, DC: Smithsonian Institution Press.

Gopnik, Alison. 2001. Theories, language, and culture: Whorf without wincing. In *Language acquisition and conceptual development*, ed. Melissa Bowerman and Stephen C. Levinson, 45–69. Cambridge: Cambridge University Press.

Gopnik, Alison, and S. Choi. 1990. Do linguistic differences lead to cognitive differences? A cross-linguistic study of semantic and cognitive development. *First Language* 10: 199–215.

———. 1995. Names, relational words, and cognitive development in English and Korean speakers: Nouns are not always learned before verbs. In *Beyond names for things: Young children's acquisition of verbs*, ed. Michael Tomasello and William E. Merriman, 63–80. Hillsdale, NJ: Lawrence Erlbaum.

Greenberg, Joseph H. 1977. *A new introduction to linguistics*. New York: Anchor Books.

Gumperz, John J., and Dell H. Hymes. 1972. *Directions in sociolinguistics: The ethnography of communication*. New York: Holt, Rinehart and Winston.

Hall, Edward T. 1966. *The hidden dimension: Man's use of space in public and private*. London: Bodley Head Ltd.

Harris, Randy Allen. 1995. *The linguistics wars*. New York: Oxford University Press.

Haviland, William A. 2002. *Cultural anthropology*. 10th ed. Fort Worth, TX: Harcourt College Publishers.

Headland, Thomas N., Kenneth L. Pike, and Marvin Harris, eds. 1990. *Emics and etics: The insider/outsider debate*. Newbury Park, CA: Sage Publications.

Hickey, Joseph V., and William E. Thompson. 1988. Personal space: The hidden element of cowboy demeanor. *Midwest Quarterly* 29: 264–72.

Hill, Jane. 1993. Hasta la vista, baby; Anglo Spanish in the U.S. Southwest. *Critique of Anthropology* 13: 145–76.

———. 1995. *Mock Spanish: A site for the indexical reproduction of racism in American English*. http://www.language-culture.org/colloquia/symposia/hill-jane.

Hinton, Leanne. 1994. *Flutes of fire: Essays on California Indian languages*. Berkeley, CA: Heyday Books.

Hinton, Leanne, and Kenneth Hale, eds. 2001. *The green book of language revitalization in practice: Toward a sustainable world*. San Diego, CA: Academic Press.

Hinton, Leanne, Matt Vera, and Nancy Steele. 2002. *How to keep your language alive*: *A commonsense approach to one-on-one language learning*. Berkeley, CA: Heyday Books.

Hockett, Charles F. 1958. *A course in modern linguistics*. New York: Macmillan.

———. 1960. The origin of speech. *Scientific American* 203(3): 88–96.

Hombert, Jean-Marie, and Larry M. Hyman, eds. 1999. *Bantu historical linguistics: Theoretical and empirical perspectives*. Stanford, CA: CSLI Publications.

Hymes, Dell. 1972a. Introduction. In *Functions of language in the classroom*, ed. Courtney Cazden, Vera P. John, and Dell Hymes, xi–lvii. New York: Teachers College Press.

———. 1972b. On Communicative competence. In *Sociolinguistics: Selected readings*, ed. J. B. Pride and Janet Holmes, 269–93. Harmondsworth, UK: Penguin Books.

———. 1974. *Foundations in sociolinguistics: An ethnographic approach*. Philadelphia: University of Pennsylvania Press.

International Phonetic Association. 1999. *Handbook of the International Phonetic Association: A guide to the use of the International Phonetic Alphabet*. Cambridge: Cambridge University Press.

Irvine, Judith T. 1974. Strategies of status manipulation in Wolof greeting. In *Explorations in the ethnography of speaking*, ed. Richard Bauman and Joel Sherzer, 167–91. Cambridge: Cambridge University Press.

Jaffe, Alexandra. 1999. *Ideologies in action: Language politics on Corsica*. New York: Mouton de Gruyter.

Jones, Sir William. 1786/1799. The third anniversary discourse, On the Hindus. Delivered 2 February, 1786, to the Asiatick Society of Bengal. In *The works of Sir William Jones*, vol. 1, 19–34. London: Robinson and Evans. (Reprinted in W. P. Lehmann, ed. 1967. *A reader in nineteenth century historical Indo-European linguistics*, 7–20. Bloomington, IN: Indiana University Press.)

Joseph, Pleasant, and Harriet J. Ottenheimer. 1987. *Cousin Joe: Blues from New Orleans*. Chicago: University of Chicago Press.

Keenan (Ochs), Eleanor. 1974/1989. Norm-makers, Norm-breakers: Uses of speech by men and women in a Malagasy community. In *Explorations in the ethnography of speaking: Studies in the social and cultural foundations of language*, 2nd ed., ed. Richard Bauman and Joel Sherzer, 125–43. Cambridge: Cambridge University Press.

Kendon, Adam. 1981. *Nonverbal communication, interaction and gesture*. The Hague: Mouton.

———. 1997. Gesture. *Annual Review of Anthropology* 26: 109–28.

Key, Mary Ritchie. 1975. *Paralanguage and kinesics: Nonverbal communication*. Metuchen, NJ: Scarecrow Press.

Klima, Edward S., and Ursula Bellugi. 1979. *The signs of language*. Cambridge, MA: Harvard University Press.

Ladefoged, Peter. 2001a. *A course in phonetics*. 4th ed. Fort Worth, TX: Harcourt College Publishers.

———. 2001b. *Vowels and consonants: An introduction to the sounds of languages*. Malden, MA: Blackwell.

Laitman, Jeffrey T., Joy S. Reidenberg, Samuel Marquez, and Patrick J. Gannon.

1996. What the nose knows: New understandings of Neanderthal upper respiratory tract specializations. *Proceedings of the National Academy of Science, U.S.A.* 93: 10543–45.

Lakoff, George, and Mark Johnson. 1980. *Metaphors we live by*. Chicago: University of Chicago Press.

Lakoff, Robin. 1990. *Talking power: The politics of language*. New York: Basic Books.

———. 2001. *The language war*. Berkeley: University of California Press.

Landweer, M. Lynn. 1998. Indicators of ethnolinguistic vitality: Case study of two languages—Labu and Vanimo. In *Endangered languages: What role for the specialist?* ed. Nicolas Ostler, 64–72. Bath, UK: Foundation for Endangered Languages.

Lave, Jean, and Etienne Wenger. 1991. *Situated learning: Legitimate peripheral participation*. Cambridge: Cambridge University Press.

Lee, Richard. 1969. Eating Christmas in the Kalahari. *Natural History* 78 (December): 14, 16, 18, 21–2, 60–3.

Lieberman, Philip. 1977. *Speech physiology and acoustic phonetics*. New York: Macmillan.

———. 1984. *The biology and evolution of language*. Cambridge, MA: Harvard University Press.

———. 1994. The origins and evolution of language. In *Companion encyclopedia of anthropology: Humanity, culture and social life*, ed. Tim Ingold, 108–32. London: Routledge.

Lieberman, Philip, and E. S. Crelin. 1971. On the speech of Neanderthal man. *Linguistic Inquiry* 2: 203–22.

Lippi-Green, Rosina. 1997. *English with an accent: Language, ideology, and discrimination in the United States*. London: Routledge.

Lucas, Ceil, Robert Bayley, and Clayton Valli. 2003. *What's your sign for pizza? An introduction to variation in American Sign Language*. Washington, DC: Gallaudet University Press.

Lucy, John A. 1992a. *Grammatical categories and cognition: A case study of the linguistic relativity hypothesis*. Cambridge: Cambridge University Press.

———. 1992b. *Language diversity and cognitive development: A reformulation of the linguistic relativity hypothesis*. Cambridge: Cambridge University Press.

Lyovin, Anatole V. 1997. *An introduction to the languages of the world*. New York: Oxford University Press.

Malinowski, Bronislaw. 1935/1978. An ethnographic theory of language and some practical corollaries. Supplement to *Coral gardens and their magic*. New York: Dover.

Matthews, Peter H. 1974. *Morphology*. Cambridge: Cambridge University Press.

Meissner, Martin, and Stuart B. Philpott. 1975. The sign language of sawmill workers in British Columbia. *Sign Language Studies* 9: 291–308.

Mitchell, William E. 1988. A goy in the ghetto: Gentile-Jewish communication in fieldwork research. In *Between two worlds: Ethnographic essays on American Jewry*, ed. Jack Kugelmass, 225–39. New York: Cornell University Press.

Moerman, Michael. 1988. *Talking culture: Ethnography and conversational analysis*. Philadelphia: University of Pennsylvania Press.

Monaghan, Leila, Leanne Hinton, and Ron Kephart. 1997. Can't teach a dog to be a cat? The dialogue on Ebonics. *Anthropology Newsletter* 38(3): 1, 8, 9.

Monaghan, Leila, Karen Nakamura, Constanze Schmaling, and Graham H. Turner. 2003. *Many ways to be deaf*. Washington, DC: Gallaudet University Press.

Morgan, Marcyliena, ed. 1994. *Language and the social construction of identity in creole situations*. Special publication #10. Los Angeles: Center for Afro-American Studies, UCLA.

Morrison, Terri, Wayne A. Conaway, George A. Borden, and Hans Koehler. 1995. *Kiss, bow or shake hands: How to do business in sixty countries*. Holbrook, MA: Adams Media Corporation.

Nettle, Daniel, and Suzanne Romaine. 2000. *Vanishing voices: The extinction of the world's languages*. New York: Oxford University Press.

Ochs, Elinor, and Bambi B. Schieffelin. 1982. *Language acquisition and socialization: Three developmental stories and their implications*. Working Papers in Sociolinguistics, no. 105. Austin, TX: Southwest Educational Development Laboratory.

Padden, Carol A., and Tom Humphries. 1988. *Deaf in America: Voices from a culture*. Cambridge, MA: Harvard University Press.

Pike, Evelyn. 1949. Controlled infant intonation. *Language Learning* 2: 21–24.

Pike, Kenneth L. 1954–1960. *Language in relation to a unified theory of the structure of human behavior*. 3 vols. Glendale, CA: Summer Institute of Linguistics. (Part 1: 1954; Part 2: 1955; Part 3: 1960; published as one volume in 1967, The Hague: Mouton.)

———. 1998. A linguistic pilgrimage. In *First person singular III: Autobiographies by North American scholars in the language sciences,* ed. E. F. K. Koerner, 143–58. Studies in the History of the Language Sciences 88. Amsterdam: John Benjamins. Available at: SIL International, http://www.sil.org/klp/index.htm. Accessed May 4, 2004.

Pine, Judith M. S. 2000. Lahu writing/writing Lahu: Literacy and the possession of writing. In *Globalization and the East Asian economic crisis: Indigenous responses, coping strategies, and governance reform in Southeast Asia,* ed. Geoffrey B. Hainsworth, 175–86. Vancouver, Canada: Centre for Southeast Asia Research, Institute of Asian Research, University of British Columbia.

Pinker, Steven. 1994. *The language instinct: How the mind creates language*. New York: Harper-Collins.

Poizner, Howard, Edward S. Klima, and Ursula Bellugi. 1987. *What the hands reveal about the brain*. Cambridge, MA: MIT Press.

Pullum, Geoffrey, and William A. Ladusaw. 1996. *Phonetic symbol guide*. 2nd ed. Chicago: University of Chicago Press.

Rubin, D. L. 1992. Nonlanguage factors affecting undergraduates' judgments of nonnative English-speaking teaching assistants. *Research in Higher Education* 33: 511–31.

Ruhlen, Merritt. 1994. *The origin of language: Tracing the evolution of the mother tongue*. New York: John Wiley & Sons.

Sagan, Carl, Linda Salzman Sagan, and Frank Drake. 1972. A message from Earth, *Science* 175: 881.

Sapir, Edward. 1912. Language and environment. *American Anthropologist*, n.s. 14: 226–42.

———. 1929. The status of linguistics as a science. *Language* 5: 207–14

———. 1931. Conceptual categories in primitive languages. *Science* 74: 578.

Savage-Rumbaugh, Sue, Stuart Shanker, and Talbot J. Taylor. 1998. *Apes, language, and the human mind*. New York: Oxford University Press.

Saville-Troike, M. 1989. *The ethnography of communication: An introduction*. Oxford: Basil Blackwell.

Scollon, Ron, and Suzanne Wong Scollon. 1981. *Narrative, literacy and face in interethnic communication*. Norwood, NJ: Ablex.

Schieffelin, Bambi. 1990. *The give and take of everyday life: Language socialization of Kaluli children*. New York: Cambridge University Press.

Secretariat, Official Languages Branch, Treasury Board of Canada. 2003. President of the Treasury Board of Canada introduces new directions for official languages. Available at: http://www.tbs-sct.gc.ca/media/nr-cp/2003/1118_e .asp. Accessed November 20, 2003.

Siebert, Frank S. 1967. *The original home of the proto-Algonkian people*. Anthropological series bulletin no. 214. Ottawa, Canada: National Museum of Canada.

Smitherman, Geneva. 2000. *Talkin that talk: Language, culture, and education in African America*. London: Routledge.

Spradley, James P., and Brenda J. Mann. 1975. *The cocktail waitress: Woman's work in a man's world*. New York: McGraw Hill.

Swadesh, Morris. 1959. Linguistics as an instrument of prehistory. *Southwestern Journal of Anthropology* 15: 20–35.

Tannen, Deborah. 1984. *Conversational style*. Norwood, NJ: Ablex.

———. 1990. Who's interrupting? Issues of dominance and control. In *You just don't understand: Men and women in conversation*, 188–215. New York: William Morrow.

Tecumseh Fitch, W. 2000. The phonetic potential of nonhuman vocal tracts: Comparative cineradiographic observations of vocalizing animals. *Phonetica* 57: 205–18.

Thomason, Sarah G. 2001. *Language contact: An introduction*. Washington, DC: Georgetown University Press.

Tobias, Phillip V. 1987. The brain of *Homo habilis*: A new level of organization in cerebral evolution. *Journal of Human Evolution* 16: 741–61.

Tomlin, Russell S. 1986. *Basic word order: Functional principles*. London: Croom Helm.

Trager, George L. 1958. Paralinguistics: A first approximation. *Studies in Linguistics* 13: 1–12.

Trask, R. L. 1995. *Language: The basics*. London: Routledge.

Van Dijk, Teun. 1987. *Communicating racism: Ethnic prejudices in thought and talk*. Newbury Park, CA: Sage.

Webster, Donald H., and Wilfried Zibell. 1970. Iñupiaq online dictionary. Available at: http://www.alaskool.org/language/dictionaries/inupiaq/. Accessed May 4, 2004.

Whorf, Benjamin Lee. 1940/1956. Linguistics as an exact science. In *Language, thought and reality: Selected writings of Benjamin Lee Whorf*, ed. John B. Carroll, 220–32. New York: Wiley, and Cambridge, MA: MIT Press.

———. 1941/1956a. A linguistic consideration of thinking in primitive communities. In *Language, thought and reality: Selected writings of Benjamin Lee Whorf*, ed. John B. Carroll, 65–86. New York: Wiley, and Cambridge, MA: MIT Press.

————. 1941/1956b. The relation of habitual thought and behavior to language. In *Language, thought and reality: Selected writings of Benjamin Lee Whorf,* ed. John B. Carroll, 134–59. New York: Wiley, and Cambridge, MA: MIT Press.

Wilkins, Wendy K., and Jennie Wakefield. 1995. Brain evolution and neurolinguistic preconditions. *Behavioral and Brain Sciences* 18(1): 161–226.

Yamada, Haru. 1997. *Different games, different rules.* New York: Oxford University Press.

Yamamoto, Akira Y. 1997. A survey of endangered languages and related resources. *Newsletter of the Foundation for Endangered Languages* 5: 8–14.

————. 1998. Retrospect and prospect on new emerging language communities. In *Endangered languages: What role for the specialist?* ed. Nicolas Ostler, 113–20. Bath, UK: Foundation for Endangered Languages.

Zentella, Ana Celia. 1997. *Growing up bilingual: Children in El Barrio.* New York: Basil Blackwell.

CREDITS

This page constitutes an extension of the copyright page. We have made every effort to trace the ownership of all copyrighted material and to secure permission from copyright holders. In the event of any question arising as to the use of any material, we will be pleased to make the necessary corrections in future printings. Thanks are due to the following authors, publishers, and agents for permission to use the material indicated.

Chapter 1. 9: Pamela J. Innes, University of Wyoming. Used with permission.

Chapter 3. 37: Alan Joseph, used by permission **53:** From "A Linguistic Pilgrimage." in E.F.K. Koerner, (ed) First Person Singular III: Autobiographies by North American Scholars in the language sciences, 1998, pp.143-158. Used with kind permission by John Benjamins Publishing Company, Amsterdam/Philadelphia. www.benjamins.com

Chapter 6. 132: top © Arnd Wiegmann/Reuters/CORBIS **131:** Lelah Dushkin, Kansas State University. Used with permission. **139**: Photo courtesy of Leila Monaghan. **138-139:** Leila Monaghan, Indiana University. Used with permission.

Chapter 7. 155: Copyright © 1963 The University of Chicago. All rights reserved. Reproduced by permission. **155:** Copyright © 1989 University of Hawaii Press. Reproduced by permission. **158:** Copyright © 2003 www.aikiweb.com Reproduced by permission. **159**: Copyright © 2003 www.aikiweb.com Reproduced by permission.

Chapter 8. 189: Source: Kenneth L. Pike: "A Linguistic Pilgrimage" in First Person Singular III: Autobiographies by North American Scholars in the Language Sciences, edited by E.F.K Koerner, 1998, John Benjamins Publishing Co., Amsterdam/Philadelphia. pp 154-155. With kind permission of John Benjamins Publishing Company. **194:** Alan Joseph, 2004. Used by permission. **195**: Alan Joseph, 2004. Used by permission.

Chapter 9. 213: Laura Bathurst, University of California, Berkeley. Used with permission. **219:** Courtesy of www.peak.org **230:** Martin Cohen, California State University, Northridge and Los Angeles City College. Used with permission.

Chapter 10. 251: Pamela J. Innes, University of Wyoming. Used with permission. **257:** Alexandra Jaffe, University of California, Long Beach. Used with permission. **250-251:** Wygal, personal communication, 2004. Used with permission.

INDEX

Page numbers in boldface refer to figures and tables.